POLITICAL ELITES
AND
SOCIAL CHANGE

ISℓL

INTERNATIONAL YEARBOOK FOR STUDIES OF LEADERS AND LEADERSHIP

A Northern Illinois University Series

General Editors
Moshe M. Czudnowski
Northern Illinois University

Heinz Eulau
Stanford University

POLITICAL
ELITES
AND
SOCIAL
CHANGE

Studies of Elite Roles and Attitudes

Edited by
Moshe M. Czudnowski

Northern Illinois University Press

Library of Congress Cataloging in Publication Data

Main entry under title:

Political elites and social change.

    (International yearbook for studies of leaders and
leadership)
    Includes bibliographies.
    1. Power (Social sciences)—Addresses, essays,
lectures.   2. Elite (Social sciences)—Addresses,
essays, lectures.   3. Politicians—Addresses, essays,
lectures.   4. Political parties—Addresses, essays,
lectures.   I. Czudnowski, Moshe M., 1924–
II. Series.
JC330.P638   1983   305.5'24   83–2461
ISBN 0-87580-093-9 (v. 2)
ISBN 0-87580-530-2 (pbk.: v. 2)

CONTENTS

CONTRIBUTORS

Volumes 1 and 2

Juan J. Baldrich is assistant professor of sociology at the University of Puerto Rico, where he has taught since 1978. From 1973 to 1977, he was a predoctoral fellow in the Yale University Comparative Sociology Training Program, doing research for a period in Jamaica. In 1981 he received his Ph.D. degree from Yale. He is the author of *Class and State: The Origins of Populism in Puerto Rico, 1934–1952*.

Wendell Bell has been professor of sociology at Yale University since 1963, serving as chairman of the department during 1965–1969 and directing the Comparative Sociology Training Program during 1969–1977. He has also served on the faculties of UCLA, Northwestern University, and Stanford University, after receiving his Ph.D. degree in 1952 from UCLA. His publications include *Social Area Analysis* (1965), *Public Leadership* (1961), *Jamaican Leaders* (1964), *Decisions of Nationhood* (1964), *The Democratic Revolution in the West Indies* (1967), *The Sociology of the Future* (1971), and *Ethnicity and Nation-Building* (1974). He is continuing his research in the Commonwealth Caribbean and his comparative studies of England and the United States, focusing primarily on inequality and social justice, race and class, and social change and futuristics.

Roland Cayrol is a member of the Fondation Nationale des Sciences Politiques, where his work focuses on the study of political elites and political personnel and also on the mass media in politics. He is professor at the Institut d'Etudes Politiques of Paris and serves as an advisor to the polling organization Louis Harris France. He is the author of the book *François Mitterrand 1945–1967* (Presses de la FNSP, 1967) and the coauthor (with Jean-Luc Parodi and Colette Ysmal) of *Le Député Français* (A. Colin, 1973). He has published many articles about French militants, mostly in *Revue Française de Science Politique* and *Projet*. He directs, with Karlheinz Reif, a cross-national survey of party congress delegates among 50 parties in Western Europe.

Harold D. Clarke is professor of political science and department head, Virginia Polytechnic Institute and State University. He is coauthor of *Political Choice in Canada, Citizen Politicians—Canada*, and *Representative Democracy in the Canadian Provinces*, and coeditor of *Parliament, Policy and Representation* and *Political Support in Canada: The*

Crisis Years. His articles have appeared in journals such as the *American Journal of Political Science*, the *British Journal of Political Science*, the *Canadian Journal of Political Science*, *Comparative Politics*, and *Comparative Political Studies*.

Maurizio Cotta is associate professor of political science at the University of Siena. He has studied political science at the University of Florence with Giovanni Sartori and has recently spent a year as visiting fellow at Yale University. His major research interests have been in the field of legislative institutions and parliamentary elites. On these subjects he is author of the book *Classe politica e parlamento in Italia, 1946–1976*. He is currently engaged in comparative research on party system change in postauthoritarian democracies.

Moshe M. Czudnowski received his doctoral degree from the Sorbonne, Paris. Between 1959 and 1971, he was a member of the political science department at the Hebrew University in Jerusalem and held various visiting appointments in the United States, England, and West Germany. Since 1971 he has been professor of political science at Northern Illinois University. His works include books, book chapters, and journal articles on political recruitment, the social psychology of elites, and the methodology of comparative political analysis. He is cosponsor and managing editor of the International Yearbook for Studies of Leaders and Leadership.

Hans Daalder has been professor of political science at Leiden University since 1963. He received his doctorate from the University of Amsterdam in 1960, which was later published as *Cabinet Reform in Britain, 1914–1963* (Stanford University Press, 1963). From 1976 to 1979, he was head of the department of political and social sciences of the European University Institute, Florence, Italy. His major research interests are comparative European politics, elite analysis, legislative behavior, and party systems. At present he is one of the directors of a comparative study of changes in European party systems since 1945, sponsored by the European Consortium for Political Research. He is a founding member of this organization and served as its chairman from 1976 to 1979.

Salustiano del Campo is professor of sociology and head of the department of social structure at the University of Madrid. His books include *El ciclo vital de la familia española* (1980), *La cuestión regional española* (with Manuel Navarro y José Félix Tezanos) (1977), *Análisis de la población de España* (second edition, 1975) and *Cambios sociales y formas de vida* (second edition, 1973). He has edited *La Sociedad* (published in 1972 and currently out of print) and *Diccionario de Ciencias Sociales* in two volumes, sponsored by UNESCO and published in 1975–1976.

Samuel J. Eldersveld has been professor at the University of Michigan since 1946, specializing in American and comparative political parties, and elites and mass behavior. In 1964 he published *Political Parties: A Behavioral Analysis*, and more recently he has published *Citizens and Politics: Mass Political Behavior in India* (1978) (with Bashir Ahmed), and *Elite Images of Dutch Politics: Accommodation and Conflict* (1981) (with Jan Kooiman and Theo van der Tak).

Heinz Eulau is William Bennet Munro Professor and chair of the department of political science at Stanford University. A former president of the American Political Science Association, he now chairs the Board of Overseers, National Election Studies, Center for Political Studies at the University of Michigan; and he serves as an associate director of the Inter-University Consortium for Political and Social Research. A member of the American Academy of Arts and Sciences, he is the author or coauthor of many books and articles, including *The Legislative System* (1962), *The Behavioral Persuasion in Politics* (1963), *Micro-Macro Political Analysis* (1969), *Labyrinths of Democracy* (1973), *Technology and Civility* (1977), and *The Politics of Representation* (1978). Since 1980 he has been editor of the journal *Political Behavior*.

Bohdan Harasymiw, associate professor of political science at the University of Calgary, has published a number of articles on leadership and recruitment in the USSR. Among these have been his seminal explorations of the unique Soviet political patronage system, the *nomenklatura*, which appeared in the *Canadian Journal of Political Science* (1969) and *Osteuropa* (1977). He is a former secretary-treasurer and president of the Canadian Association of Slavists.

Suzanne Keller is professor of sociology at Princeton University. She received her Ph.D. degree from Columbia University in 1955. Dr. Keller has worked as a survey analyst and translator in Paris, Munich, Vienna, and Athens. She has received both a Fulbright and a Guggenheim award. Her interests include the planning of new communities, futurism, and the study of social hierarchies and elites. Her many publications include a 1981 study, *Building for Women*, for which she was the editor; a forthcoming publication, "Social Differentiation and Social Stratification: The Special Case of Gender"; and the pioneering study of elites, *Beyond the Ruling Class* (Random House, 1963). Dr. Keller was the first woman to be awarded tenure at Princeton University.

Michael Keren has been a lecturer at Tel Aviv University since 1975, at which time he received his Ph.D. in political science from the University of Minnesota. His major field of interest is "knowledge and power" in the context of societal policy making. Recent articles in this field have been published in *Policy Sciences, Behavioral Science,* and

Knowledge. Between 1978 and 1980, Keren was a research fellow at the Ben Gurion Research Institute and Archives at Sde Boker, Israel, where he was granted first access to Ben Gurion's private papers. His book, *Ben Gurion and the Intellectuals: Power, Knowledge, and Charisma* is forthcoming from Northern Illinois University Press.

Chong Lim Kim is professor of political science and associate director of the Comparative Legislative Research Center of the University of Iowa. His recent publications include *Legislative Connection: The Politics of Representation in Kenya, Korea, and Turkey* (Duke University Press, forthcoming); *Legislative Systems in Developing Countries* (Duke University Press, 1975); and *Political Participation in Korea* (ABC-Clio Press, 1980). He has also published articles in *American Political Science Review, American Journal of Political Science, American Politics Quarterly, Comparative Political Studies, Comparative Politics,* and *Legislative Studies Quarterly.*

Allan Kornberg is professor of political science at Duke University. He is author of *Canadian Legislative Behavior, Influence in Parliament: Canada* (with William Mishler), and *Citizen Politicians—Canada* (with Joel Smith and Harold Clarke). He also is coauthor and editor of *Legislatures in Developmental Perspective, Legislatures in Comparative Perspective,* and *Political Support in Canada: The Crisis Years.* He has contributed numerous articles to journals such as the *American Political Science Review,* the *British Journal of Political Science, Canadian Journal of Political Science,* and *The Journal of Politics.*

J. A. Laponce is professor of political science at the University of British Columbia, Vancouver, Canada. His main interests are the study of political perceptions, ethnic conflicts, and experimentation on small groups. His main works include *The Protection of Minorities* (1961), *The Government of France under the Fifth Republic* (1962), *People vs. Politics* (1970), and *Left and Right: The Topology of Political Perceptions* (1981).

Keith Legg (Ph.D., University of California, Berkeley) is professor of political science at the University of Florida. He has written extensively on Greek politics, including *Politics in Modern Greece* (Stanford University Press, 1969) and on political clientelism.

Peter McDonough is senior study director at the center for political studies, Institute for Social Research, University of Michigan. He is author of *Power and Ideology in Brazil, The Politics of Population in Brazil,* and of articles on Spain, Portugal, India, and Pakistan.

Dwaine Marvick is professor of political science at the University of California, Los Angeles. He is the author of *Career Perspectives in a*

Bureaucratic Setting, Competitive Pressure and Democratic Consent (with Morris Janowitz), and editor of *Political Decision Makers: Recruitment and Performance* and *Harold D. Lasswell on Political Sociology.* His writings on political recruitment and party activists have appeared in a wide range of journals and symposia. He is secretary of the Research Committee on Political Elites of the International Political Science Association.

Samuel C. Patterson, professor of political science at the University of Iowa, has been interested primarily in legislative elites. His books include: *The Legislative Process in the United States* (3rd ed., 1977, with M. E. Jewell); *Comparative Legislative Behavior: Frontiers of Research* (1972, coedited with J. C. Wahlke); *Representatives and Represented* (1975, with R. D. Hedlund and G. R. Boynton); and *Comparing Legislatures* (1979, with G. Loewenberg). His current work focuses on comparative analysis of legislator selection, focusing on state legislative elections in the United States. He has served as editor of the *American Journal of Political Science* and currently serves as coeditor of the *Legislative Studies Quarterly.* In 1980–1981, he was president of the Midwest Political Science Association.

Pascal Perrineau is doing research at the Centre d'Etude de la Vie Politique Française contemporaine (Fondation Nationale des Sciences Politiques, Paris) and is Maître de Conférence at the Institut d'Etudes Politiques de Paris. His main interests are the French Socialist party and voting behavior. He received his Doctorat d'Etat de Science Politique for a study of the electoral consequences of urban change in France under the Fifth Republic. He has contributed to several joint works devoted to democratic socialism, the most recent, *Eurocommunism and Transition in Western Europe: A Comparative Analysis,* published in London in 1982.

Thomas Rochon is an assistant professor in the department of politics at Princeton University. He is the author of articles on Dutch and Japanese political behavior and a forthcoming book on political activists in the Netherlands. He is currently working on a study of governmental response to citizens' movements in Western Europe.

Walter Santin is assistant professor of sociology at the University of Madrid and is working on his Ph.D. dissertation.

John R. Schmidhauser received his Ph.D. degree from the University of Virginia in 1954. He taught constitutional law and judicial process, as well as American government, at the University of Iowa from 1954 to 1973. He was a senior fellow in law and behavioral sciences at the University of Chicago Law School in the academic year 1959–1960.

Since 1973, he has been professor of political science (chairman of the department in 1973–1975 and 1977–1980) at the University of Southern California. Schmidhauser served as a member of the U.S. House of Representatives representing the 1st District of Iowa in 1965–1967 (89th Congress). His publications include *Constitutional Law in the Political Process* (Rand McNally, 1963), *Judges and Justices: The Federal Appellate Judiciary* (Little, Brown and Company, 1979), and numerous articles in political science and legal journals.

Edward Shils is Distinguished Service Professor in the Committee on Social Thought and in the department of sociology at the University of Chicago and Honorary Fellow of Peterhouse, Cambridge, England. His most recent major works include a collection of his selected papers: *Intellectuals and the Powers* (vol. 1, 1972), *Center and Periphery* (vol. 2, 1975), and *The Calling of Sociology* (vol. 3, 1980); *Tradition* (1981); and *The Constitution of Society* (1982).

José Félix Tezanos is associate professor of sociology at the University of Madrid. His words include *Estructura de classes y conflictos de poder en la España postfranquista* (Madrid, 1978) and *Alienacion, dialectica y libertad* (1977).

Joop Th. J. van den Berg has been director of the Dr. Wiardi Beckman-stichting, the Research Office of the Dutch Labour party, since 1981. He was appointed in 1971 to a teaching and research post in the field of parliamentary history at Leiden University. He is the joint author of a critical study of Dutch politics, *Crisis in de Nederlandse Politiek* (1974) and of a study of the working of the Dutch Parliament. He has recently completed a doctoral dissertation at Leiden University on the social background of members of the Dutch Lower House from 1848 to 1967.

Klaus von Beyme studied political science, sociology, and history at the universities of Heidelberg, Munich, Paris, and Moscow. He has been professor of political science at the University of Heidelberg since 1974. From 1973–1975 he served as president of the German Political Science Association. His major publications include *Challenge to Power: Trade Unions and Industrial Relations in Capitalist Countries* (Sage, 1977) and *Political Parties in Western Democracies* (St. Martin's Press, forthcoming). He is also editor of *German Political Studies* (published by Sage). He has published numerous articles in such journals as *German Studies Review*, *Government and Opposition*, *International Political Science Review*, and the *Journal of Politics*. Von Beyme is currently the president of the International Political Science Association.

POLITICAL ELITES
AND
SOCIAL CHANGE

Celebrities as a National Elite

Suzanne Keller

"In the future," Andy Warhol once announced, "everybody will be famous for fifteen minutes." This is a trenchant way of saying that ours is the century of the celebrity as a central social form. Celebrities have been defined as those who are "well-known for being well-known" (Monaco, 1978:7). Magazines have been created to advance this knowledge yet more—*People* magazine, for example, now has a circulation of nearly 2 million and a "Notes on People" column now appears even in the *New York Times*. In this connection I recall a telling incident of a few years ago. I was standing in line in a coffee shop at breakfast time during the Annual Sociology Congress, when a friend stopped by and said something mildly appreciative about a panel discussion I had been on the day before. She had barely moved on when the man in front of me turned around excitedly, his eyes alight with expectation: "Are you somebody?" he cried.

In an orgy of classy hucksterism, celebrities are used to sell everything, from cars to bed linens. Most notorious currently are the designer jeans hawked by pubescent youngsters in TV commercials. Celebrities are also used in fund raising, public service, and lobbying activities. Thus, Brooke Shields, the sixteen-year-old actress, is seen both in Calvins and before a congressional committee testifying on why it is cool not to smoke (25 June 1981). It is a time when Walter Cronkite is at the top of the dream list of the American lecture circuit (outdistancing by far another celebrity, Henry Kissinger) and when in a strange reversal of rank, a prominent political leader such as Fidel Castro is all excited at the prospect of being interviewed by "Barbara" (who would herself later pursue, with equal vigor, an interview with the virtually uninterviewable Willie Nelson, whose political—but not popular—clout ended with the Carter administration).

Furthermore, celebrities are not only important in themselves; they are increasingly used to certify the importance of powerful others.

Thus the very film and stage stars who were once shunned in respectable society are today hobnobbing with the rich and powerful
at election rallies, charity galas, sports tournaments, and White House
dinners. Celebrities lend their names and their prestige to such events
to help assure their success.

The election of an actor-turned-president is perhaps the most dramatic symptom of the convergence between celebrity status and political and economic power, but the phenomenon is everywhere in
evidence for as yet unexplained reasons. Thus, given their prominence and the prominent use made of them, celebrities are worthy
of study not only as glamorous and desirable individuals but as an
increasingly powerful and significant national elite.

For those of us who define elites narrowly as part of the key decision-making structure of society, elite celebrities would not at first
seem to fit the traditional image of elites. But this changes when one
considers the vast audiences for films, newspapers, and above all,
television, that they attract. Take the "Tonight Show" and its phe-
nomenal host, Johnny Carson. Now seen by more than 17 million
viewers, Carson reigns over an empire that is larger than many a
nation. If we add to this the audiences of the other talk shows and
national spell binders such as "Dallas," we must acknowledge that
the Carsons, Griffins, Donahues, and J. R. Ewings are powerful by
some criterion and cannot be neglected in a study of elites.

In this paper, therefore, I would like to explore the nature and
functions of the contemporary celebrity elite. I will pay particular
attention to the role of the media in the growth of this elite and its
emerging ideological impact. Throughout, the problem of definitions
is apparent. It is briefly discussed on page 8.

Who Are the Celebrities?

C. Wright Mills was among the first to include celebrities among
the elites he studied. As early as the 1950s, he drew attention to the
social significance of the easy and frequent interaction between politicians, industrialists, and entertainers. Imagine, he wrote, that a
man can gain social access to the president of the United States
mainly by knocking a small white ball into a series of holes better
than anyone else (Mills, 1956:74). Indeed, Mills concluded that celebrities "have stolen the show" from the upper class, who have
partly relinquished that show and who have also partly been pushed
aside. Serious public figures, he said, must henceforth compete with
celebrities for national attention. "Those who would now claim
prestige in America must join the world of the celebrity or fade from
the national scene" (p. 77).

And Orrin Klapp, who was likewise impressed with the celebrity
phenomenon early on, saw the stars of stage, screen, and television

as central figures in "a great modern institution"—the "cult of celebrities," built around the personalities of people who have been glorified by "image-making and fame-building processes" (Klapp, 1964:13).

In my own early work, I also called attention to the significance of celebrities as strategic elites, representing certain values to their publics who looked up to them for identification and guidance (Keller, 1979:160).

All three writers insisted that celebrities must be seen not only as glamorous and prominent individuals but as part of a collective phenomenon that warrants systematic research. This research would address the social origins and characteristics of celebrities, the reasons for their current prominence, and their relative importance across nations.

The Role of the Mass Media

Mills believed that celebrities have been created by the mass media. It is via national means of mass communications that entertainers and athletes "come fully and continuously into national view," and they are celebrities because of what they do on and to these media (Mills, pp. 71, 74).

This has long been the case. Take the rise of popular biography before World War I. The circulation of books by Emil Ludwig, André Maurois, Lytton Strachey, and Stefan Zweig reached into the millions; and they became international best-sellers (Lowenthal, 1961:109).

Then there was Hollywood. The silent movies created such stars as Chaplin, Gish, and Pickford. In the 1920s and 1930s, radio, magazines, newspapers, and the talkies accentuated this process (Monaco, p. 87), and screen idols became modern divinities. It is said that at the death of screen lover Rudolf Valentino, millions of women mourned him; and the suicide of Marilyn Monroe reverberated around the world, headlined along with national and international political news. And when James Bond first alighted on the screen in the 1960s department stores were quick to display thousands of copies of Bond raincoats, shoes, hats, and other insignia of the hero. This communal appropriation of symbols rather than substance was not unlike the commensal rituals of preliterate societies in the hope for a magical sharing of charismatic power.

With the advent of television, the celebrity phenomenon escalated to its current scale. "In the sixties, it became perfectly clear once and for all that the main life of the nation was inextricably cross-woven with media" (Monaco, p. 7). There was the emergence of the talk show—"true home of the celebrity" (p. 7)—and quite ordinary unknowns could become celebrities by being featured on television.

Videoculture also created a special readiness for public drama. "It encouraged the emergence of true life high dramas—in hijackings and kidnappings; in terrorism; in all events that rivet attention" (Monaco, p. 7).

Television gave rise to new patterns of communication between audience and performer. In essence, their exchange is nonreciprocal and under the control of the performer; yet there is strong involvement and even intimacy between them. This curious phenomenon was labelled "para-social interaction" by Horton and Wohl some twenty-five years ago (Horton and Wohl, 1956:217). They showed how television, more than any other medium, gives an illusion of personal or face-to-face relationships between audience and celebrity (Hadden and Swann, 1981:65). This intimacy is achieved by the familarity of the setting, the frequent use of first names, and by what Dave Garroway once called the "subjective camera" that can follow the performer off the set into homes or dressing rooms (Horton and Wohl, p. 217).

The ability of television to create celebrity status has forced traditional elites to make use of this medium as well. They do so on talk shows, on interview programs, and in political debates. Thus it is increasingly true that the "people who make the media make history" (Monaco, p. 6).

Here again we see the fusion of celebrity power with political power. Todd Gitlin in his study of the radical movements of the 1960s has shown how the media made the radical leaders into celebrities, thereby hurting these movements. The damage came when the media selected quotable and vivid, even exhibitionistic personalities who were good performers and who "became addicted to stardom," in the process altering the nature of radical leadership (Gitlin, 1980:153). Thus the media create celebrity not only by the extent of their reach but also by whom they select for media prominence. And while the radical movement elevated many leaders, the media chose only those who most closely matched prefabricated images of what an opposition leader should look and sound like: "articulate, theatrical, bombastic . . ." (Gitlin, p. 154). The spotlight became a resource (p. 162) and created envy and spite within the movement by separating the celebrity leaders from the other leaders, who lacked the needed television presence. In thus subverting the direction of radical leadership by magnifying the individual's stakes in success, the media played a decisive, if unacknowledged, role in national politics.

A quite different example, but one which yet attests to a similarly powerful—and conservative—impact of television concerns the increasing tendency for TV celebrities to make public pronouncements on contemporary social issues ranging from government policies and national elections to family life and sexual mores. My own informal observational study of four major talk shows over a two-year period—those of Johnny Carson, Merv Griffin, Mike Douglas, and Joe Franklin—has led me to note a trend away from celebrity as glamorous and distant idol toward celebrity as living-room pundit and philosopher.

One example should serve to illustrate this. It concerns a major star of a popular weekly TV series. As always, he was asked to talk about his personal life, which he did without hesitation, revealing that he had been married for thirteen years, that he lived in a dream house, and that he took seriously his parental obligations to four children. All that was done with considerable pride but no gross immodesty. It was his proffered value judgments that are relevant here, however. First he announced that his marriage would last because he and his wife "tried hard to make their marriage work" and because he did not believe in divorce. He then added that divorce is not only bad for children but is proof of some moral defect. And on it went. In effect, his audience became privy to a whole series of moral platitudes stated in the smug and self-satisfied tone of one who felt in control of his life and was surprised that everyone else was not.

This commonplace event would be of no concern were it not for the fact that barely a year later, on a similar talk show, this same man was made to admit that his surefire recipe had not worked after all; and he was now confronting a divorce he was at a loss to explain. What had happened to the open communication between him and his wife and to the tight family unity they had shown off as badges of their moral fiber? No comment. Interestingly, then, while moral shibboleths were presented to the public when things went well, no attempt at interpretation or analysis occurred when they did not. This has the latent function, I suggest, of shoring up the traditional moral order and reinforcing feelings of guilt and moral inadequacy among those who fail to live up to its demands.

I find this example intriguing in yet another sense. In the past, artistic elites, movie stars, and members of café society were expected to be nonconformists, bent on pleasure rather than duty. By contrast, these living-room celebrities do not display or indulge their star status in the same way. As they enter into the homes of their audiences, they become bound to them in some mysterious way. Perhaps because television stardom is less impersonal than literary or movie stardom, the way in which it plays up to the audience and its values is intensified. This is evident in the opinions these stars express on social and personal issues. To give just one example, I suggest the advice on marriage and family life that George Burns— an octogenarian whose image since his merry widowerhood began (with the 1964 death of Gracie Allen) has been quite as far from the family as from any childrearing he and Allen may have done in the early years of their long—and long ago—marriage: "It's important to

be happily married. . . . Raising children should be the most reward-
ing experience in a person's life. . . . Raising kids is an experience
I'd recommend to almost anyone who wants to better his or her life"
(George Burns, as quoted in *Star*, 2 June 1981, p. 11).

Such celebrity moralizing is unlike official preachings and pronouncements in that it is unobtrusively offered to the public. The
very techniques that sustain the illusion of intimacy also help conceal the opinion-molding function of celebrity pronouncements. Thus
one can say of television fare what was said of sixteenth century
court dramas: "They were not entertainments. . . . They were expres-
sions of the age's most profound assumptions about the monarchy"
(Orgel, 1975:8).

From Idols of Production to Idols of Consensus

In his famous study of popular biographies, Leo Lowenthal presented a classification of the heroes prevalent in magazine fiction in
the first four decades of the twentieth century (Lowenthal, 1961:111).
In the early decades, these heroes were active in industry, science,
and business, hence Lowenthal's description of them as "idols of
production," who served as exemplars of opportunity and success.
In the later decades, however, new heroes were featured. Labelled
"idols of consumption," they came predominantly from entertainment and the sphere of leisure-time pursuits (p. 115). Lowenthal
thought that these two types of heroes spoke to very different reader
needs. The first type embodied the themes of ambition, mobility, and
success; whereas the second seems "to lead to a dream world of the
masses" and "is no longer concerned with important social issues"
(p. 117). Moreover, while it was once "rather contemptible" to give
much room to the private affairs and habits of public figures, "this is
now their chief interest" (p. 120). These new heroes "represent a
craving for having and taking things for granted. They seem primarily to seek to satisfy personal, sexual, and recreational needs"
(p. 120). Moreover, these idols of consumption, like modern celebrities, but unlike classical heroes, "need not do anything. Their function is not to act but to be" (Monaco, p. 5). This is why virtually "any
kind of person can be a celebrity . . ." (p. 6). As Jerry Rubin put it,
"People respect famous people. They are automatically interested in
what I have to say. Nobody knows exactly what I have done, but they
know I'm famous" (Rubin, 1976:93).

There are three major categories of celebrity: [1] "Heroes—the individuals who defy danger and triumph over evil," [2] Stars, who
are unlike actors in that they play themselves rather than roles, and
[3] Quasars—who present an image" [Monaco, p. 12]. Of the three, it
is the latter who have proliferated.

Thus, celebrities are part of the *symbolic elite*. They differ from the practical elites who do something concrete for their publics in that they exert their impact on the audience rather than on history. Symbolic leaders "work towards giving some kind of reassurance" to audiences (Klapp, 1964:43). The dramatic hero does this by triumphing over great obstacles; the villain by being punished; the clown by making the audience look superior; and the victim by saying it happened to me, not to you (Klapp, p. 51). All of these give psychic relief from anxiety. "People escape the burdens of their anxieties by retreating into the magic shows of the National Celebrity Theater" (Lapham, 1981:38).

Symbolic leaders move people through the images they present and the styles of life they typify. Celebrities, as symbolic leaders, thus belong to what I have elsewhere called *expressive elites*, whose primary responsibility is to interpret an ever-changing reality in the light of certain collective ideals. Thus, like all elites, the celebrity elite both shapes public consensus and reflects it. Celebrities as "models and mirrors of the ambitions, hopes, and strivings of the masses of men" (Keller, p. 157), become akin to collective projections.

Given their powerful symbolic role as admirable images, the individual members of this elite must ever strive to rise to the demands of their publics and not disappoint them. A preoccupation with image is thus quite unavoidable; indeed, it is so powerful that it has led to a new kind of ailment, "hero's neurosis," in returning war heroes fearful that the image they projected may be better than they are. This induces in them feelings of guilt or embarrassment for not living up to people's expectations. Image trouble has been called an "obscure symbolic problem." In time, celebrities come to be viewed as public property and as proof that "the public has adopted the celebrity as an image of a certain kind" and expects them to live up to that image (Klapp, p. 101).

The celebrity elite thus consists of image-conscious performers playing their parts in what Orrin Klapp has called "The Public Drama," a living spectacle of a changing social reality for "transitory and boundless audiences" (p. 252). This public drama consists of improvisations that lift "people out of their families, jobs, institutions, classes" (p. 253). The major stars of this drama are the celebrities to whom the public turns for guidance in facing the challenges and crises of life. Public drama flourishes when "process rather than structure predominates" and when outcomes are unpredictable (p. 256).

In this view, emergent symbolic leaders embody the longings and needs of a public confronting crisis and change. The public drama transcends normal, and therefore predictable, routines and social roles. And the reign of the leaders selected for this drama is likely to be more unstable than is usually the case, as unforeseen and bizarre events multiply to create a pervasive atmosphere of national suspense. In 1981 national suspense focused for some time on the air controllers' strike, a perfect example of a public drama and of highly visible, if temporary, stars. In a sense, this focus permitted all of us to be present at the creation of the reality that was to be wrought out of the crisis.

Celebrities thus provide "models of what to do and how to live" for their audiences (Klapp, p. 260), acting as guides for coping with unprecedented problems and possibilities. And the current interest in celebrities represents an "anxious groping for certainty by people who live in times of rapid change" (Lowenthal, p. 114). Hence the ideological commentaries of the famous logically play a more important role now than in past, apparently less anxious, times.

This may be why, as has often been observed, the public drama and its leading characters tend to become larger and more compelling than life. The vicarious then becomes the real and "public figures act out our lives for us in movies, television, radio, newspapers, books, and magazines. The fictions they perform "increasingly become more valid than our own unpublicized existence." All of this blurs the line between fact and fiction. "Everyone is more or less fictional, made up, constructed." The absolute line between real and imaginary, false and true, has been erased. Hence such concepts as "factoid" emerge, referring to something artificial that is nonetheless like the real thing (Monaco, p. 9).

In recording a public order of existence, celebrities come to take over our "personal universes formerly occupied by family and friends" (Monaco, p. 10). It would be instructive to ascertain how often people refer to characters in the public domain when trying to discuss some contemporary personal issues. This is when soap operas—real or imagined events their content—become more real than so-called real life.

Media Celebrities as Opinion Leaders

I would now like to turn to consider the kinds of images current media celebrities represent by comparison with earlier times. Traditionally, classic heroes were venerated as morally superior to ordinary mortals, who worshipped them from afar. This was true even for the morally ambiguous idols of early Hollywood, whom their chroniclers depict as larger than life in their pleasures, pains, tastes, and excesses. Their images, featured in fan magazines, stressed self-indulgence, undreamed-of luxury, unbridled passions, and the devotion of millions who followed their lives and careers with zeal.

What a contrast they present to the superstars of television, who turn out to be rather conventional and circumspect in demeanor and conduct. Even when they are not expected to lead exemplary lives as models for youth, we still find their attitudes toward life, family, sex, and success to depart little from the conventional wisdom. This is something of a paradox, given their prominence and high economic and social status. It is as if their key efforts were devoted to being as average as their viewers. "They demonstrate, taken as a group, not the exception but the typical cross section of the socio-psychological condition of modern society" (Lowenthal, p. 129). Moreover, not only do these contemporary idols lack the visible trappings of superstars, but they are not presented as particularly unusual individuals requiring any special honors.

The reasons for this contrast between early and later celebrities are not entirely clear. Some attribute it to the tastes and preferences of sponsors. "The stars of television are very circumspect because the people who sponsor them won't put up with any nonsense. So you have in the mass entertainment medium people who are not particularly colorful, not particularly maverick" (Cockburn, p. 215). Others make the mass audience responsible for the nature of their idols. The average person takes comfort from seeing a hero who "takes a drink, plays golf, and worries about his looks." This person, thereby, gets confirmed in his or her own pleasures and aversions (Lowenthal, pp. 135–36). Thus the values of the media celebrities reflect those of their audiences rather than of themselves. This is evident in interviews as well as on game shows where participants may be "praised for having children. . . . [for a] youthful appearance . . . and . . . likely to be honored the more—with applause from the studio audience—the longer [they have] been 'successfully' married" (Horton and Wohl, p. 223).

The effort to give the appearance of being paragons of middle-class virtues means that celebrities must maintain a special facade by "concealing discrepancies between the public image and the private life" (Horton and Wohl, p. 226). This leads to contrivance, of both the public image and the private life behind it. And it means a collusion between audience and celebrities; for "if the media succeed with their spectacles and grand simplifications, it is because their audiences define happiness as the state of being well and artfully deceived. . . . By telling people what they assume they already know, the media reflect what society wants to think of itself" (Lapham, p. 37).

In all of this, the values stressed are those of social order, social harmony, and social conformity; and the effect is to affirm the basic assumptions of social life (Horton and Wohl, p. 223). "By impressing on the reading masses the idols of our civilization," Lowenthal observed in regard to the popular biographies he studied, "any criticism or even reasoning about the validity of such standards is suppressed" (Lowenthal, p. 127). A similar pattern can be noted with regard to media celebrities.

Unlike yesterday's stars and heroes, then, television celebrities are not permitted to depart too sharply in their opinions and outlook from the publics they depend on. Their need for approbation compels them to cultivate impression management to an extreme degree. This tailoring of the person to public expectations creates a sense of moral discomfort for many. It is not a new experience. "My craving for good repute among men," confessed T. E. Lawrence, "made me profoundly suspect my truthfulness to myself . . . and I began to wonder if all established reputations were founded, like mine, on fraud" (Cockburn, p. 562).

Conclusion

The prominence of the celebrity elite may be traced to both a technical and a social condition. Technically, the mass media of communication, especially television, play a decisive role. And socially, the rapid rates of change in our society have fostered the emergency of the public drama to give expression to the uncertainties and confusions of the times. This is how symbolic leaders become linked to matters of politics and ideology.

Celebrities in their roles of admired models are stepping into the current fluid social and moral scene as symbols of success and personal achievement whose opinions matter because they confirm the traditional value system. And while we tend to focus on the individual personalities of the celebrity elite, this elite is "above all a social phenomenon," one that, according to Gitlin, "the cultural system has routinely needed and produced" for the past two centuries (p. 147).

Nonetheless, it is a phenomenon we insist on considering primarily in its individual manifestations. This may have to do, in Gore Vidal's words, with our reluctance to "examine the sort of society we live in." Instead, we prefer to focus on personalities, rating them "according to their weight, color of eyes, sexual proclivities, and so forth. It avoids having to face, let us say, unemployment—which is a very embarrassing thing to have to talk about. Anything substantive is out" (Cockburn, p. 220).

The media "thus [reflect] what the society wants to think of itself." And the celebrity elite play the "part of the courtier, reassuring their patrons that the world conforms to the wish of the presiding majority" (Lapham, p. 37).

All of this is much more organized than it seems at first glance. The machinery for creating the public drama is big business, and the personality market to supply the individuals who will star in it is not left to chance.

Celebrities are a mainstay of United States society today. There is much that we do not know about their influence on both the wider public and on other elites. The evidence from national polls, content analyses of preferred programs, and program monitoring suggests their impact to be pervasive and growing. By helping to create a public consensus on morals and manners in a rapidly changing world, they are part of the collective representations of our time.

I hope I have made a case for the necessity to include the study of the celebrity elites among other studies of elites. On the basis of my own reflections and preliminary explorations, I would argue that the celebrity elite has an enormous impact not only on the wider public but also on decision makers in politics, business, and science who experience the popular culture through them.

The next main question is how to go about the systematic study of the celebrity elite and its impact. As yet, we have no working definition of the celebrity elite. Following the procedure in the study of other elites, one needs first to delineate the pool of eligibles, both by field and candidates. By field, I would think that film stars, athletes, television stars, pop music stars, and well-known names of the jet set should be included. Within these areas, we will need to follow whatever institutional rating systems these have developed. For example, yearly Oscar winners and box office standings provide indices for the movies. Television would be similar, with Emmy award winners, stars of the most popular programs, and well-known guests on talk shows the indicators. In sports, the highest ranking players and those doing the greatest number of commercials and appearing on the prominent talk shows would provide the pool. For pop music stars, gold records and disc jockey rankings are meaningful indicators, as are mentions in gossip columns and on guest lists of famous charity balls and fund raisers for jet setters. As is true for all elite studies, one needs to grapple with the problem of classifications, cutting points, and criteria for selection.

Having solved these knotty problems, we then turn to impact assessment, which strikes me as even more difficult. Here, too, a key need is to gather the most essential and basic information from scratch. One possible model for this might be the Katz-Lazarsfeld book on *Personal Influence* (1955), but it would have to be placed in the context of a national setting.

There is a whole series of fascinating questions to be explored here. I hope this paper will stimulate responses, views, and suggestions on how best to proceed.

References

Burns, George (1981), as quoted in *Star*, June 2, p. 11.

Cockburn, Alexander (1978) "Why People Are Talking about Gossip." In *Celebrity*, edited by James Monaco. New York: Dell, 1978.

Gitlin, Todd (1980) *The Whole World Is Watching*. Berkeley: University of California Press.

Hadden, Jeffrey K., and Charles E. Swann (1981) *Prime Time Preachers.* New York: Addison-Wesley.

Horton, Donald, and R. Richard Wohl (1956) "Communication and Para-Social Interaction." *Psychiatry* 19:215–31.

Katz, Elihu, and Paul F. Lazarsfeld (1955) *Personal Influence: The Part Played by People in the Flow of Mass Communications.* New York: Free Press.

Keller, Suzanne (1979) *Beyond the Ruling Class.* Reprint. New York: Arno Press.

Klapp, Orrin E. (1964) *Symbolic Leaders: Public Dramas and Public Men.* Chicago: Aldine.

Lapham, Lewis H. (1964) "Gilding the News." *Harper's,* July.

Lawrence, T. E. (1933) *Seven Pillars of Wisdom.* Garden City, N.Y.: Garden City Publishing.

Lowenthal, Leo (1961) *Literature, Popular Culture and Society.* Palo Alto, Calif.: Pacific Books.

Mills, C. Wright (1956) *The Power Elite.* New York: Oxford University Press.

Monaco, James (ed.) (1978) *Celebrity.* New York: Dell Publishing.

Orgel, Stephan (1975) *The Illusion of Power.* Berkeley: University of California Press.

Rubin, Jerry (1976) *Growing (Up) at 37.* New York: M. Evans.

Higher Education and Liberalism among Political Elites

Moshe M. Czudnowski

One of the structural changes in contemporary society that we have been able to monitor as participant observers was the "revolution" which resulted in a mass-system of higher education. It has brought about changes in the nature and scope of higher education; it has increased the distinction between large campuses and smaller colleges; and, above all, between 1940 and 1975 it has tripled the population of those 25 years of age and over (in the U.S.) who have completed college. The number of students enrolled in higher education has multiplied sevenfold, and almost one-third of the adult population has received at least some college education. The 1980 Census should indicate what impact the demographic decline in the high school—and college—age population has had, and will have, on these figures. On the occupational side of this structural change the share of "professional and technical white collar workers" in the labor force has doubled, from 7.5 percent to approximately 15 percent. Managers and administrators now constitute 10.5 percent, and the number of clerical workers has tripled, rising from 6.7 percent to 18 percent. At the other end of the occupational spectrum the percentage of "blue-collar laborers" has decreased from 9.4 to approximately 5.0 and that of farmers from 17.4 to 3.5. Finally, more than 90 percent of the labor force are salaried and working in "organizations."

These changes were part of a technological revolution in communication and transportation, accompanied by a shift toward a service economy and a greater acceptance of a "welfare state" philosophy of government. The history of the last three decades is evidence of changing life-styles, value priorities, and public policies. Some scholars, journalists, and opinion leaders believe that we have witnessed the emergence of a "new class": a liberal and sometimes radical intelligentsia of "knowledge workers" or "manipulators of symbols" which has been held responsible—especially by the so-called neoconservatives—for both the cultural "liberation" from traditional institutional constraints and the political and economic expansion of government. Whether they constitute a class, in the Marxian sense of the term, is probably debatable (see, e.g., Daniel Bell, 1979); but Robert Brym (1980) would argue that this need not prevent them from having class attachments (does this position make Karl Mannheim an ideologue or a utopian?). Be that as it may, the presence of new cultural networks of the liberal intelligentsia and the neoconservatives cannot be denied; they have both influenced public policy and deserve to be seriously studied.

This paper is not an attempt to study this broader question. It addresses a narrower subject by asking whether the mass-system of higher education has had an impact on political elites and their recruitment, and if so, with what consequences? Even within this more narrowly defined subject, this paper raises more questions than it answers; at best, it suggests hypotheses for further investigation. For the purpose of this report, the "political elite" has been defined as the membership of the U.S. House of Representatives and the U.S. Senate (1968–1972 and 1976–1980). Needless to say, the fact that the 1980 election has produced a more conservative House and Senate merely militates for a continuation of the analysis as soon as the relevant data for the current Congress become available.

Thirty Years of Social Change: Congress in 1950 and 1980

The expectation that changing levels and distributions of education in the adult population are likely to be reflected in the periodically elected membership of the national legislature is almost a platitude—but *only* almost. Members of legislatures in western democracies have never been a more or less truthful mirror image of the educational and occupational characteristics of society. They have generally been more highly educated and have overrepresented certain occupations and underrepresented others, with large differences between countries and different periods of time. It may be a good or a bad omen for François Mitterand's presidency that one-third of the 1981 French National Assembly consists of "these somewhat forgotten professors" who are reappearing in strength at all levels of the French political class. The American people have never had, and are not likely to have, an abundance of professors in politics, especially in elective positions. Academic tenure ceases to be a deterrent only for appointments at the level of those offered to a Moynihan, a Kissinger, or a Brzezinski.

Instead, the United States has had an overabundance of lawyers in Congress—and a vast literature trying to explain this phenomenon. In 1950, the percentage of lawyers in the U.S. Congress was

58.5 in the House and 64.5 in the Senate (figures compiled from the January 1950 *Congressional Directory*). Has the preponderance of lawyers in Congress been affected by the mass-system of higher education?

Table 1 presents the educational distribution of the Members of Congress in 1950 and 1980. In the table "no college" merely means that no mention of a college education was found in the *Congressional Directory* for 1950 and the *Almanac of American Politics* for 1980. Looking at the lawyers first (categories 7 and 8), we find a relative decrease of 21.2 percent (an absolute decrease of 12.4 percent) in the number of lawyers in the House in 1980 compared to their numbers in 1950. *In the Senate, there is no change at all.* J.D.s are now almost one-half of all lawyers in the House, as opposed to slightly over 10 percent in 1950, but this is not a difference in educational level in most cases. In the Senate, the increase in the num-

TABLE 1.
Educational Distribution of Members of Congress,
1950–1980 (Percentages)

	1950	1980
U.S. House of Representatives		
1. No college	10.1	4.1
2. Some college	13.0	11.0
3. B.A./B.S.	9.1	18.4
4. B.A. +	3.1	4.1
3 + 4	12.2	22.5
5. M.A./M.S.	2.6	10.3
6. M.A. +	1.2	1.2
5 + 6	3.8	11.5
7. LL.B.	52.3	24.1
8. J.D.	6.2	22.0
7 + 8	58.5	46.1
9. Ph.D., M.D.	2.1	4.6
U.S. Senate		
1. No college	10.4	—
2. Some college	7.3	9.0
3. B.A/B.S.	9.3	11.0
4. B.A. +	2.1	2.0
3 + 4	11.4	13.0
5. M.A./M.S.	3.1	7.0
6. M.A. +	—	2.0
5 + 6	3.1	9.0
7. LL.B.	52.0	47.0
8. J.D.	12.5	17.0
7 + 8	64.5	64.0
9. Ph.D., M.D.	3.1	5.0

ber of J.D.s is comparatively modest (on the possible meaning of differences between LL.B.s and J.D.s, see below). Similar differences in frequencies between the House and the Senate appear in the B.A./ B.S./B.A. + category (3 + 4): in the House their number almost doubled; in the Senate there is a small increase, from 11.4 percent to 13.0 percent. The number of Ph.D.s and other nonlaw doctoral degrees has more than doubled in the House and almost doubled in the Senate.

The decrease in House Members—and the disappearance of Senators—with no college education is not surprising. The relatively high percentage of Members of Congress with only "some college education" is probably not a disappearing phenomenon, given the *increase* in their numbers in the Senate. Senators have been shown to come predominantly from small-town or rural sociodemographic environments (Hacker, 1961), and this fact may explain the survival—after three decades of mass higher education—of a "some college" category among U.S. Senators. While the above changes, or lack thereof, may be of some interest, the relatively largest educational transformation of Congress is the appearance of an approximately 10 percent strong cohort of Members with master's degrees— M.A., M.S., M.B.A., M.P.A., M.S.W., M.Ed., or any other variety thereof. Adding those who have master's degrees and some additional college work, one finds this category to account for 11.5 percent of the House membership and 9 percent of the Senate's. On what dimension should we expect any difference between these highly educated Congressmen and their colleagues with lower levels of education?

Higher Education, Liberalism, and Congressional Ratings: What Are We Measuring?

Conventional wisdom, NORC, Gallup, and Yankelovich polls, as well as academic studies of recent years, tend to indicate that even if we account for differences between the liberal arts, and especially the social sciences on the one hand, and natural science and "the applied sciences" on the other, the number of years of college education is highly correlated with liberal attitudes. Everett Ladd (1979), basing his observations on 1972–1977 survey data, found that variables indicating liberalism, including economic and sociocultural but not national-defense issue-dimensions, were associated with levels of education. One should note, however, that when questions on reduced defense spending are linked to questions on the possible socioeconomic consequences of such reductions (e.g., "even if this means unemployment?"), the percentage of respondents who approve defense cuts drops from 75 percent among college graduates to 66 percent among those with more than a bachelor's degree.

In trying to assess how higher levels of education are associated with the attitudinal spectrum of Congressmen, one ought to bear in mind that while for the general population it is reasonable to hypothesize that level of education and field of study (or subsequent occupation) are causally related to degrees of liberalism, it is far less likely that such a direct relationship should obtain in the population of national legislators. Party affiliation and regional culture, as well as specific constituencies, will act as powerful intervening variables between education and attitudes on the liberalism/conservatism dimension. However, if despite partisan and regional differences, Congressmen with different levels of education display consistent and statistically significant differences on this dimension, one might infer that there is some association between these variables. In examining this problem, three issues require some preliminary clarification.

1. Identifying Levels of Education

In an examination of the relationship between education and any other variable it is useful to identify educational categories as clearly as possible. In the published literature on opinion surveys of the general population, based on national samples, educational categories usually lump together under the same heading all respondents with an education beyond a baccalaureate, irrespective of whether they have earned one, or possibly two, additional degrees or none. Clearly, in a national population sample the number of respondents with one of such higher degrees is insufficient to constitute a statistically significant cell in a distributional matrix. This may not be an important constraint in the analysis of a national population survey. In Congress, however, we find 16.1 percent of the Members of the House in 1980 with a non-law degree beyond the baccalaureate and another 4.1 percent with some college education beyond the bachelor's degree, i.e., a total of 20.25 percent; the corresponding figures for the Senate are 14 percent and 2 percent, i.e., a total of 16 percent. These are not negligible segments of the highest national legislative elite, and they deserve closer scrutiny. One of the intriguing questions that suggested themselves upon inspection of the ratings of Congressmen on liberalism and conservatism was the following: is the regression line of liberalism on level of education unidirectional, or does the slope change directions after education reaches a certain level? In substantive terms: is it possible that reaching a certain educational degree is likely to bring about more elitist and, therefore, more conservative attitudes toward society, as compared to the attitudes of individuals whose educational credentials are somewhat lower? Is the holder of a Ph.D. degree more conservative than an individual with a master's degree?

One might be tempted to seek an answer to this question by looking at the well-documented data on the political attitudes of college professors. The 1977 Ladd-Lipset Faculty Survey, as reported by Ladd (1979), indicates that 47 percent of *all* university professors described themselves as "liberal," compared to 43 percent of those with a "postgraduate education" in the general population, and only 39 percent among college graduates. (Comparisons with the 1977 NORC general survey are difficult, because of attitudinal labels.) Breakdowns by academic disciplines show that twice as many professors in the social sciences and humanities (58 percent) consider themselves more liberal than those in law, business, medicine, and engineering (29 percent), but no published comparison is available for the disciplinary breakdown among those with a "postgraduate education" in the general population. While this is a matter of reporting factual information, no matter how similar the distribution across disciplines may turn out to be, it could not answer the question of what it is that we are comparing. While all college professors in the Ladd-Lipset Survey may hold Ph.D. degrees—and again, this is a factual matter that can be ascertained—*college professors are an occupational group and not an educational category*. What ought to be compared are, for example, Ph.D.s and M.A.s, or D.Ed.s and M.Ed.s, *controlling for occupation*. It is, of course, possible that after controlling for disciplines and occupations, a unidirectional relationship between levels of education and levels of liberalism still holds true; until the evidence is available, judgment has to be suspended. U.S. Senators and Congressmen, however, are not a representative sample of the population; they overrepresent, exaggerate, or distort certain characteristics. It is therefore impossible to make inferences from the findings of this study to the general population, even though these findings will be shown to be statistically significant for the population of U.S. Congressmen over a ten-year period.

2. Interest Group Ratings of Congressmen as Measures of Attitudes

While some of the data on college professors—though by no means all the data—consists of self-assigned labels of conservative, middle-of-the-road, or liberal attitudes, the attitudinal data on Congressmen reported here have the distinctive advantage of representing "outside" evaluations of *behavior* by organizations and interest groups with a clearly identified ideological or economic bias. "To rate a Member of Congress, an interest group normally chooses between 10 and 40 votes for each house of Congress from the total set of roll-calls taken during the particular session under study. These votes are chosen for their relevance to whatever interests the group purports to represent. The rating is determined by ascertaining the "correct" vote on each of the chosen roll-calls and calculating the percentage of "correct" to "correct" plus "incorrect" votes (Poole and Daniels, 1982:3).

It may seem that the choice of a relatively small number of roll calls to arrive at the ratings of Congressmen introduces a certain bias; however, as documented in the above-quoted Poole-Daniels study, which covers a period of 22 years (1959 through 1980), interest groups choose issues of ideological relevance to their interests; and they prefer issues that override considerations of party loyalty. This sharpened focus on ideology legitimizes the use of interest group ratings as measures of ideologically "constrained" attitudes for the purposes of the analysis report in this paper, provided, of course, that the ideological positions of the groups are stable and that the roll calls chosen represent all major areas of policy. Poole and Daniels provide the following examples of roll calls chosen for group ratings. For the 1979–1980 House ratings, 31 percent (301) of all votes on which the minority was 10 percent or larger (971) were chosen; and of these 301 votes, 40 were chosen by five or more groups. They consisted primarily of issues in the area of government management (e.g., tax reform, gas and oil price deregulation, pollution control, energy policy), social welfare (e.g., labor relations, food stamps, Social Security, aid to education), and foreign policy (e.g., weapons systems, foreign aid, the Panama Canal Treaty, SALT, Taiwan). The selected roll calls thus represent a wide variety of issues.

As for the stability of group positions, three conclusions of the Poole and Daniels study are relevant. The first refers to the finding that no matter where a group stands on the liberalism/conservatism dimension, they all tend to perceive the same spatial configuration of the Congress and the Senate. Second, most groups maintain very stable positions on that dimension. Finally, although some individuals have displayed changes in ideological patterns during their career (e.g., Senator Schweiker), most Members of Congress show an overall stability on the liberalism dimension, with an average deviation of 13.9 percent of the length of the dimension.

3. Is Liberalism Unidimensional?

Using a metric "unfolding" technique, Poole and Daniels concluded that one single left/right or liberalism/conservatism dimension accounts for 81 percent of the variance in ratings across the 22-year period they had studied. A second dimension, which they identify as "strength of party affiliation," added only 6.1 percent to the average explained variance. No measurement of deviations from linearity has been reported.

In this paper a scrutiny of the assumption of unidimensionality and linearity will be offered. This will involve the ratings of the Americans for Democratic Action (ADA) and of the Committee on

Political Education of the AFL-CIO (COPE) for 681 cases over two five-year periods, 1968–1972 and 1976–1980. Allowing for temporary vacancies and unavailable ratings, a total of approximately 8,000 observations has been included. The purpose of the comparison between ADA and COPE ratings is to explore whether the distinction between economic and cultural liberalism discussed in the 1960s and early 1970s in connection with the concept of a "post-industrial society" and the appearance of "post-bourgeois" values, and documented in Inglehart's "Silent Revolution in Europe" (1971), can be identified in congressional voting. More specifically, it is assumed that the ADA rating criteria are representative indices of cultural liberalism, whereas the COPE ratings represent the economic liberalism of the New Deal era. Any such "labels" are, of course, only approximations and, strictly speaking, the comparison refers to ADA and COPE ratings only.

The terms "cultural" and "economic" liberalism are derived from Bell's typology (1979:186), which uses as distinguishing criteria the areas in which the two ideologies differ. Essentially, Bell's analysis is intended to emphasize that a person can be a liberal in economic matters and a conservative on cultural issues. In attempting to preserve the original meaning of the term "liberal" and emphasizing that a dichotomy is insufficient to do justice to the diversity of attitudes in different areas of life, Bell has classified himself as a socialist in economics, a liberal in politics, and a conservative in culture (Steinfels, 1979:165). The discussion of these ideological differences has revolved primarily around the so-called "neoconservatism." Using Bell's typology, this set of attitudes can be shown to combine liberal welfare-state positions in economic matters (e.g., government intervention) and a conservative attitude in cultural matters (e.g., traditional, small-town values), as opposed to an unrestrained free enterprise ideology in economics on the one hand and a cosmopolitan attitude in cultural matters on the other. Bell identifies the following typical social groups falling into each of the four cells of the matrix:

| | | *Economic Issues* | |
		Left	*Right*
	Liberal	Urban intellectuals	Managers
Cultural Issues			
	Conservative	Working class	Old capitalists

An area not covered by this typology is defense, in which the neoconservative will favor increased defense spending over increased spending on social welfare, if such choices compete with each other, but, unlike the economic right-wing, will not favor the dismantling of the welfare state. In matters concerning the ecology (which are cultural issues) neoconservatives will be, at best, indifferent; and while the neoconservatives agree with the need for affirmative action for "neglected groups" in labor relations or university admission policies, they will oppose quota systems, as well as involuntary busing as a means for school integration. Thus "cultural conservatism" is combined with the welfare-state liberalism of a preceding generation.

Pointing at areas of disagreement between cultural and economic liberalism seems to imply, as does a four-cell typology, that positions on these dimensions are essentially dichotomous: one either does or does not support busing, government-funded abortions, Medicaid, or defense spending. Neither Bell and the neoconservatives nor their "liberal" critics should be suspected of making such oversimplifying assumptions. There are always degrees of agreement or opposition and degrees of compromise between alternative options. Stated otherwise: it is reasonable to conceptualize both types of liberalism as continuous rather than dichotomic dimensions, even if "measurements" of liberal attitudes are, at best, locations on an ordinal scale. The advantage of interest group ratings consists in their conceptualization of attitudes, or rather voting behavior, as measurable on an interval scale, since the ratings represent the percentage of cases, out of all roll calls drawn into the analysis, in which a Member of Congress supported the position a group considered to be closest to its ideologically preferred outcome. One ought to bear in mind, however, that congressional votes are always dichotomous: the choice is only between a "yes" or "no" vote, and absences or abstentions are often considered by interest groups as a vote against their preferred position. Compromises between alternatives, to the extent that such compromises have been made, are already built into the proposed bill or resolution; and it is the interest group which decides whether a compromise takes sufficiently into account the group's ideological preference to warrant a "yes" vote. To sum up: interest group ratings are frequencies of support for positions the group considered congruent with its ideological preference. They are, therefore, only substitutes for interval-scale measurements of attitudinal intensity. However, given the consistency of group ratings over issues and time, they constitute a very reliable measuring instrument.

Some general rating scales (in contradistinction to those of groups with narrowly defined interests) even mutually validate each other; thus, the ratings of the ADA, which is the most liberal group, are generally reversed, "mirror," images of ACA (Americans for Constitutional Action) scores, the latter representing the most conservative group. Moreover, this validation occurs along the entire "length of the dimension." ADA and COPE scores, however, represent two different types of liberalism and cannot be expected to validate each other along the entire length of the rating scale, unless they both are *unidirectional and linear dimensions.* The analysis presented in this paper will identify the range of values within which the ADA and COPE scores are very close to each other and that in which they differ considerably. The range within which the scores differ by approximately one-third of the entire length of the dimension will be interpreted as representing neoconservative positions. Scattergrams displaying the full joint distribution of ADA and COPE scores will demonstrate the rationale for choosing one-third of the length of a dimension for this interpretation.

Education and Liberalism: Congressional Ratings, 1968–1972 and 1976–1980

In order to examine the association between higher education and liberalism, educational categories have been narrowly defined across the spectrum of educational levels. Table 2 displays the distribution of cases by levels of education, indicating the code number used for every educational category in the analysis.

Yearly ADA and COPE ratings, across two five-year periods, were averaged for all cases falling under each educational category, accounting for temporary vacancies and missing ratings. Table 3 displays the average ADA and COPE ratings for this ten-year period.

TABLE 2.
Distribution of Cases by Educational Category

	Category Code	Number of Cases
No higher education	1	45
Some higher education, without a degree	2	103
Baccalaureate degree (B.A., B.S.)	3	159
Some formal education beyond the baccalaureate	4	29
Master's degree (M.A., M.S., M.B.A., M.P.A., M.S.W.)	5	76
Some formal education beyond the master's degree	6	7
An LL.B. law degree	7	274
A. J.D. law degree	8	136
A doctoral degree (Ph.D., Ed.D., M.D.)	9	32
		N = 861

TABLE 3.
Mean ADA and COPE Scores by Educational Category

Educational Category Code	Mean ADA Score	Mean COPE Score
1	27.03	41.41
2	35.54	46.50
3	33.31	41.88
4	44.18	47.69
5	49.95	56.51
6	62.72	68.97
7	42.28	47.35
8	40.77	47.27
9	39.85	41.51
Total population mean	ADA 39.60	COPE 46.69

Analyses of variance were performed for the ADA and the COPE means of educational categories. The F value for the ADA means was statistically significant at a level better than 0.001; that for the COPE means was significant at the 0.017 level. An analysis of variance for 428 cases and observations over the five-year period of 1968–1972, in which categories 3 and 4, and 5 and 6, respectively, had been collapsed, showed education as the main source of variation with an F value significant at the 0.007 level for mean ADA scores and 0.05 for mean COPE scores. The overall means for ADA and COPE for 1968–1972 were 38.31 and 41.95, respectively.

The above findings are statistically strongly convincing evidence that *on neither of the two scales of liberalism are levels of education and liberalism ratings linearly related.* The highest liberalism ratings were those for categories 5 and 6 (M.A. and M.A. +). Liberalism ratings display an upward slope from categories 1 (no higher education) through 5 and 6, but categories 7 and 8 (the law degrees) and 9 (doctoral degrees) show lower ratings than educational levels 5 and 6. The holders of law degrees deserve separate consideration, but the fact that Congressmen with doctoral degrees displayed significantly more conservative attitudes than those with master's degrees constitutes *a finding challenging the prevailing assumption of linearity in the relationship between education and liberalism.* Holders of doctoral degrees had average ratings, comparable to those in the B.A. and B.A. + categories. Educational categories constitute an ordinal scale, but if one were to translate it into an interval scale based on assumptions about the number of years of college education, it would be possible to display the above findings graphically as represented in Figure 1.

The mean ratings on the ADA and COPE scales are, of course, only indicators of central tendencies; they have to be complemented by

FIGURE 1.
Mean ADA and COPE Scores, by Years of Higher Education*

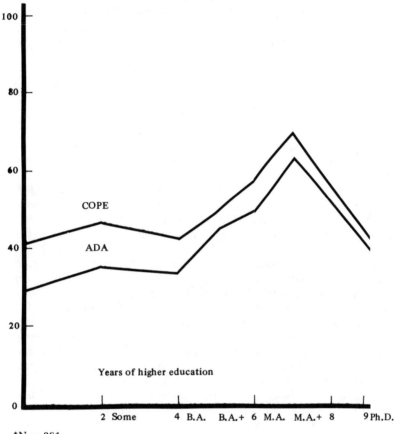

*N = 861

measures of dispersion. Most frequently, the standard deviation is used to convey this information. As will be shown below, the data do not indicate a symmetrical normal distribution; and rather than interpreting a large standard deviation for such a distribution, a categorized distribution of actual scores can be described. Table 4 summarizes this distribution for 1978 ADA ratings. "Negative" scores are those below 50, "positive," those between 51 and 100.

The distribution in the House of Representatives indicates that while "no college" Members have the most conservative distribution, there is no significant difference in the total percentage of conservative ratings between those with "some college education" and those who hold baccalaureate degrees. Yet, it is precisely the group

TABLE 4.
Education and ADA Ratings

	0–29	50–65	80–100	All "Negative"	All "Positive"
U.S. House (Percentages)					
No college	62.5	6.5	—	93.5	6.5
Some college	40.5	21.5	2.7	67.5	32.3
B.A./B.S./+	57.0	15.0	8.2	69.3	30.0
M.A./M.S./+	30.9	21.4	28.5	45.2	54.6
Ph.D./D.Sc./M.D.	53.0	26.5	13.3	59.6	40.0
LL.B.	39.0	17.0	11.0	63.0	37.0
J.D.	37.0	26.0	13.7	53.4	46.6
				N = 357	
U.S. Senate (Percentages)					
No college	—	—	—	—	—
Some college	71.4	—	—	100.0	—
B.A./B.S./+	50.0	16.6	8.3	66.6	33.3
M.A./M.S./M.B.A./+	28.6	42.9	14.3	28.6	71.4
Ph.D./D.Sc./M.D.	40.0	20.0	—	60.0	40.0
LL.B.	30.9	21.4	11.9	52.3	47.7
J.D.	36.0	18.0	9.0	45.0	55.0

with more years of education which has 57 percent of its members in the most conservative category of ratings, as opposed to 40 percent for those with only "some college."

The "lawyers"—generally found to be more conservative than other professions—show slightly lower percentages in the most conservative rating categories than those with baccalaureate degrees or only "some college." Thus an addition of three years of education—even in law school—apparently somewhat increases liberal attitudes, at least among Members of the House; yet, on the ADA scale in 1978, 53 percent of the J.D.s and 63 percent of the LL.B.s were on the conservative side.

Among those with master's degrees, the single most liberal group in the House, 54.6 percent had positive rankings; they also had the highest percentage in the 80–100 category. This is consistent with the expectation of a positive correlation between educational level and liberalism. Yet, at the level of doctoral degrees (not including J.D.s), the percentage of negative (conservative) ratings rises to approximately 60 percent, with more than one-half of the cases in the most conservative category (0–29). In the Senate, where the number of cases is obviously smaller, the same relationship obtains; in fact, those with master's degrees in the Senate are even more liberal than their counterparts in the House.

To introduce some controls into these observations, the cohort of House Members elected in 1974 was analyzed separately. If political

events and the "political climate" of a particular period are important socializing factors, the post-Watergate election certainly constitutes a case worth exploring. In this overwhelmingly Democratic
group (among those brought into this analysis were sixty-two Democrats and fifteen Republicans), one would expect to find in 1974 a
larger percentage of liberals. Table 5 displays the 1978 ratings of the
1974 cohort.

TABLE 5.

Distribution of the 1978 ADA Ratings of the 1974 Cohort
U.S. House of Representatives (Percentages)

	0–29	50–65	80–100	All "Negative"	All "Positive"
No college	66.6	—	—	100.0	—
Some college	22.2	33.3	—	45.5	55.5
B.A./B.S./+	50.0	12.5	18.0	56.0	44.0
M.A./M.S./+	25.0	—	37.5	37.5	62.5
Ph.D.	42.8	42.8	14.3	42.8	57.2
LL.B.	26.6	—	13.3	80.0	20.0
J.D.	26.3	26.3	26.3	36.8	63.2
			N = 77		

With the exception of those with an LL.B. degree, percentages with
a positive (liberal) rating are indeed higher than those for the entire
membership of the House. More interesting, however, is the fact that
the relationship between the M.A.s and the Ph.D.s persists. Actually,
three out of the seven Members with a doctoral degree elected in
1974 were in the most conservative category. The relationship between the scores of the M.A.s and the Ph.D.s is shown even more
explicitly in Table 6 in a comparison of the mean ratings on the 100-
point ADA scale.

TABLE 6.

Mean ADA Ratings, by Educational Category

U.S. House of Representatives, 1974 Cohort, in 1978	
No college (3)	25.00
Some college (9)	46.66
B.A. (16)	44.68
MA. (8)	58.12
Ph.D. (7)	44.30
LL.B. (15)	40.23
J.D. (19)	51.57

The overall 1978 mean rating for the 1974 cohort was 46.36. Thus, neither those with "some college" education nor those with bachelor's or doctoral degrees differ to any significant extent from the overall mean. Only those with master's degrees have a sizeably higher rating. The difference of over eleven percentile points between the ratings of Congressmen with LL.B.s and those with J.D.s deserves some attention.

In recent years, the J.D. has become the substitute for the LL.B. Yet, J.D.s had been available from some law schools in earlier periods, and they were probably higher degrees than the LL.B.s. We still find in Congress cases of "early J.D.s" and "late LL.B.s." Comparing the total 1980 membership with LL.B.s (106) with the total 1980 membership with J.D.s (96) in terms of year of birth, we find that the average LL.B. and the average J.D. are approximately nine years apart. The average LL.B. was born in 1925, i.e., was forty-nine years old at election in 1974, whereas the average J.D. was born in 1933 and was forty years old in 1974; the median J.D. was born in 1935. Stated otherwise, if the difference in law degrees is essentially a difference between "generations of law programs," it is indeed reflected in the age composition of the respective groups of Congressmen. It is, most likely, the difference in "historical generations," rather than stages in the life cycle of a politician, which becomes relevant in an attempt to explain the eleven-point difference between LL.B.s and J.D.s in their mean ADA ratings—the politics and economics of the 1920s and early 1930s, as opposed to the New Deal and the post–New Deal era.

A final observation on the 1974 cohort: it was somewhat less conservative than the entire House; but with a mean rating of 46.36, it was more conservative than the California delegation (47.74), not to mention such liberal states as Michigan (60.93), Wisconsin (60.0), or Massachusetts (75.0). Pennsylvania had an average rating of 38.68. Thus, although predominantly Democratic, the 1974 cohort was moderately conservative, rather than liberal.

The Relationship between Cultural and Economic Liberalism

In this section evidence will be provided for the statements made earlier in this paper concerning the difference between cultural and economic liberalism. Using mean individual ADA and COPE scores as indicators of cultural and economic liberalism, respectively, the joint distribution of these scores for Members of the U.S. Congress was plotted and analyzed for the pooled data set ($N = 861$) over the selected ten-year period; yearly sets of observations were similarly plotted. Figure 2 displays the scattergram for 1976, Figure 3 for

FIGURE 2.
Joint Distribution of ADA and COPE Scores, 1976

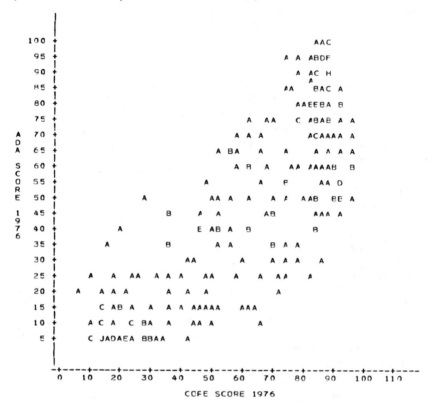

CDFE SCORE 1976

1977, and Figure 4 for the ten-year period. The following analysis refers to the pooled data set.

With COPE scores measured on the abscissa, the scattergram indicates a visually discernible curve created by concentrations of cases in (1) the lowest third of the range of ADA and the middle third of the range of COPE and (2) in the middle third of ADA and upper third of COPE. Since there also were large concentrations of cases in the lowest and in the highest third of the range of both ADA and COPE, R^2—the linearly explained variance—was 0.79. However, the deviation from linearity, statistically significant at the 0.0001 level, improved the explained variance by approximately 15 percent with an Eta^2 of 0.95.

How does one substantively interpret these distributions? Several patterns can be observed.

FIGURE 3.
Joint Distribution of ADA and COPE Scores, 1977

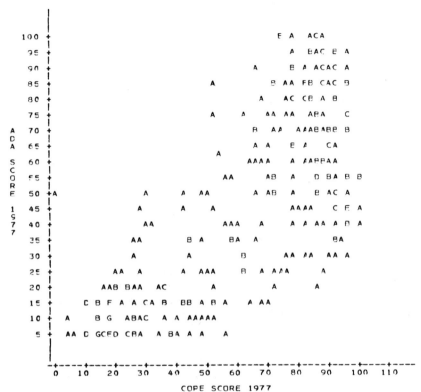

COPE SCORE 1977

1. Conservative Congressmen, those in the lowest third of the range, are "strongly conservative," according to the criteria of both ADA and COPE.

2. A similar overlap obtains for a large part of those in the most liberal third of the COPE range and almost all Congressmen in the highest third of the ADA ratings.

3. There are, however, considerable numbers with COPE ratings in the highest category who received ADA ratings in the middle third of that range. These Congressmen should vote in the same manner as those in category (II) on matters of defense spending and traditionally labor-supported economic policies but vote differently in matters relating to the environment, abortion, and similar "cultural" issues. Thus, category (III) comes closest to the attitudes one would predict on the basis of a "neoconservative" ideology. The data tend

to support this interpretation; it will be illustrated here by a comparison of the ratings and voting records of a House Member in category (II) with those of one in category (III).

	Maryland, 7th district	New Jersey, 15th district
1978 ADA rating	90	50
1978 COPE rating	95	90
Increase defense spending	AGN (against)	FOR
Kemp-Roth tax reduction	AGN	AGN
Alaska lands protection	FOR	AGN
Overriding veto on water project appropriation	AGN	FOR
Prohibition of government-funded abortions	AGN	FOR

4. Another grouping of cases which contributes to the curvilinear relation between ADA and COPE mean ratings can be found in the middle third of the COPE range and the lower third of the ADA range. Here one would expect lesser frequencies of agreement with a COPE and higher frequencies of agreement with positions considered conservative by the ADA. A comparison of the votes of the Congressman for New Jersey's 15th district (category III) with those of two cases falling under category IV will display these differences.

	New Jersey, 15th district	Pennsylvania, 12th district	New York, 28th district
1978 ADA rating	50	25	15
1978 COPE rating	90	65	50
Increase defense spending	FOR	FOR	FOR
Kemp-Roth tax reduction	AGN	AGN	AGN
Consumer Protection Agency	FOR	AGN	AGN
Delay auto pollution control	AGN	FOR	FOR
Prohibit government-funded abortions	FOR	FOR	FOR

5. With three almost empty cells in the 3 × 3 matrix, the only remaining category that deserves brief attention is the middle third on both dimensions, where one would expect to find middle-of-the-road attitudes. Is there any substantively consistent voting pattern in this category? One ought to bear in mind that the category consists, by definition, of cases which support the preferred position of a rating group between 35 percent and 65 percent of the time or, on the average, 50 percent of the time. Thus, on any particular set of

FIGURE 4.
Joint Distribution of Individual Mean ADA and COPE Scores,
1968–1972, 1976–1980

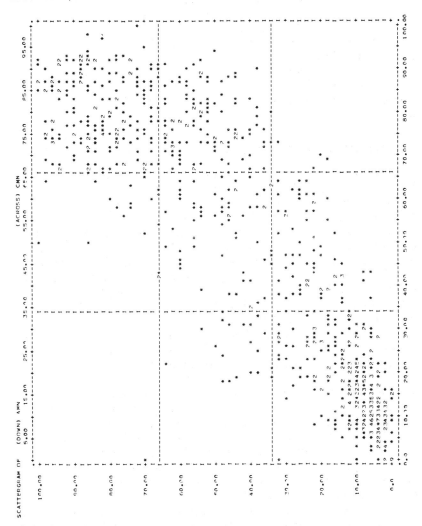

ideologically relevant roll calls no consistent pattern of voting, across
the Congressmen in this category, is likely to be observed. Some
Members in this category will support particular interest-group preferred positions about one-half of the time, while other Members
may support other interest-group preferred positions one-half of the
time. Some overlap may occur, but no specific predictions can be
made. Observations of roll-call behavior in this category do confirm

this absence of a predominant pattern in terms of issue positions. One also notices more frequent cases of abstention or absence when a vote involves taking a clear ideological stand.

To sum up: The shape of the joint distribution of mean ADA and COPE scores provides evidence for the distinction between cultural and economic liberalism and emphasizes the areas in the range of these dimensions in which COPE scores are consistently higher than ADA scores, thus causing a deviation from linearity. The substantive interpretation indicates that these areas of deviation represent the neoconservative components in the patterns of liberal/conservative attitudes.[1]

Higher Education and Congressional Recruitment

With the important exception of a law degree, higher education has not been a recruitment-relevant variable for elective office in the United States. While skills acquired through a college education have been a recruitment criterion for the executive branch—as documented, for example, by Prewitt and McAllister (1976) for federal executive offices between 1930 and 1970—Congressmen, although more highly educated than their constituencies, are neither nominated nor elected because they possess certain educational characteristics or skills. A law degree is certainly an advantage for a legislator, but more than one-half of the Members of the 1980 Congress did not have an LL.B. or a J.D.

One would hypothesize that there is a relationship between the educational level of a congressional district and the education of its congressional representative. The median educational level in rural districts is usually lower than that in the suburbs of a large city. Are such differences of any relevance to the educational level of their representatives in Congress? It is difficult to answer such questions, since many districts are a mixture of urban, suburban, and rural populations; and only a detailed analysis of "who voted for whom" can supply a meaningful answer. At the aggregate district level, the data can be very misleading. Table 7 presents such district-level data, and the results do indeed indicate that a closer look at within-district differences is warranted.

Comparing the distribution of non-law degrees across types of districts indicates that while the largest segment (42 percent) of congressional representatives with baccalaureate degrees was elected in predominantly rural districts, more holders of master's degrees (38 percent) were elected in suburban than in any other type of districts. For Members with Ph.D.s, suburban districts account for 50 percent of all cases. Stated otherwise, the distribution displays the expected directional pattern. However, with 4 out of 16 Ph.D.s elected in predominantly rural districts, one would like to look at lower

TABLE 7.
District Characteristics and Educational Level of the Congress
Holders of Non-law Degrees, 1980
(Percentages)

| | Level of Degree | | | |
	Bachelor's and +	Master's and +	Ph.D.	M.D. and Similar
City	19.1	22.2	12.5	16.6
Suburban	22.3	37.7	50.0	16.6
Rural	42.5	26.6	25.0	49.8
Mixed	15.9	13.3	12.5	16.6
N = 94	N = 45	N = 16	N = 6	

levels of aggregation to determine whether there is a significant re-lationship between the educational level of voters and that of their congressional representative.

Education and Career Patterns

The centrality of law enforcement offices in the careers of politi-cians with law degrees has been amply documented (Schlesinger, 1957 and 1966; Eulau and Sprague, 1964); it still applies to many Congressmen-lawyers today. Since this pattern is well known, there is no need to dwell upon it here. Instead, it may be of interest to look at the other major avenues of access—or *loci* of "apprenticeship"—leading to congressional office. Table 8 displays the relative impor-tance of four of these areas of apprenticeship. The entries are not mutually exclusive, since some Congressmen had held positions in more than one of these areas. Given the increasing number of congressional representatives with non-law degrees, it may be of interest to cross-tabulate educational levels with career patterns. Ta-ble 9 shows these areas of apprenticeship. Again, the entries are not mutually exclusive, since some of the Congressmen had held posi-tions in more than one of these areas.

Comparing the data summarized in Tables 8 and 9 leads to the following observations:

1. *Of seventy former "aides"* to U.S. Senators, Congressmen, and federal executives, thirty-seven—or *over one-half—held non-law degrees*. Most of them (twenty-two) had bachelor's degrees, but within educational categories the Ph.D.s supplied the relatively largest share: *seven out of sixteen*. They also "served" at the high-est levels of political apprenticeship. *Thus, the major contribu-tion of a college education, other than a law degree, to the pattern of careers leading to a congressional seat is to provide skills*

TABLE 8.

Major Avenues of Access to Congress, Excluding Law Enforcement
Officers (Percentages)

State legislatures	43.5
"Aides" to Representatives, Senators, or federal executives	16.0
City government	12.5
Work in, or ownership of, media of communication	6.5

TABLE 9.

Distribution of Major Career Patterns, by Education, Excluding Law
and Medical Degrees (Percentages)

	Level of Degree		
	Bachelor's and +	Master's and +	Ph.D.
"Aides" to Representatives, Senators, and federal executives	22.2	16.6	43.0
City and county government	18.1	14.6	6.25
State legislature	34.3	35.4	6.25
Business	14.1	14.5	6.25
School systems (teachers, principals, etc.)	2.2	14.5	—
College professors	—	—	62.5
"Media"	10.0	8.3	6.25
	N = 99	N = 48	N = 16

needed by incumbent legislators and executive officials, and
thereby offering opportunities for both political apprenticeship
and entry into networks of valuable political acquaintances.
2. Almost two-thirds of the small group of Congressmen with Ph.D.
degrees were recruited from among college professors. (It would
be interesting to determine whether these former college professors did or did not have to give up academic tenure to enter
elective political office.)
3. Of all Congressmen, 43.5 percent have served in their respective
state legislatures. The percentage of former state legislators among
holders of bachelor's and master's degrees is only slightly lower:
35.0 percent. Those Members with Ph.D. degrees did not seek
state legislative careers. Similar distributions hold for careers in
city government.
4. Almost seven times as many Congressmen with master's degrees
have been involved in school systems (as teachers or administrators) compared to holders of bachelor's degrees.
5. Media-related occupations are a relatively small source of
congressional recruitment, with holders of bachelor's degrees
constituting about one-third of that group.

6. Business people are equally "represented" among congressional representatives with B.A. and M.A. degrees. If holders of Ph.D. degrees have also had a business career, they certainly did not publicize it.

Summary and Conclusion

This paper has examined some aspects of the impact of mass higher education on the composition of Congress, on the attitudes of its Members, and on political careers. The findings include statistically significant evidence, for the population of U.S. Congressmen over two five-year periods, that levels of higher education and liberalism are not linearly related and that there is a relatively sharp decline in mean liberalism scores among holders of doctoral degrees. The paper then documented the existence and substantive contents of "neoconservative" attitudes and identified the areas in which the relationship between cultural and economic liberalism deviates from linearity. The curvilinear function explained 95 percent of the variance in liberalism scores. Finally, the paper investigated some associations between levels of higher education, political career patterns, and congressional recruitment.

One cannot extrapolate from findings limited to the membership of Congress to the general population, no matter how large the number of observations and how high the level of statistical significance. However, two sets of findings deserve to be investigated with samples of the general population: the relationship between levels of higher education and liberalism, allowing for more detailed distinctions between educational categories than those currently available in the literature; and the variables—personal or environmental, educational, economic, occupational or generational—that are most frequently associated with the development of "neoconservative" attitudes. While the emergence of this set of attitudes still requires a sociopsychological explanation, there already is at our doorstep a new ideology, currently labeled "neoliberalism."

Note

1. An interesting question, which this paper will not attempt to answer, is whether the stability of liberalism ratings over periods of time shorter than those examined by Poole and Daniel (1982) varies between ADA and COPE ratings. If such differences can be found, are they associated with levels of education, with location on the rating scale, with regional political culture, or with national political trends? An initial inquiry into this matter, relating only to changes in ADA scores between 1976 and 1978—a period when Congress "drifted to the right"—showed that the single most "volatile" educational category consisted of those with baccalaureate degrees but that within each educational category the

largest amount of variance could be accounted for by regional political culture (Czudnowski, 1981).

References

Bell, Daniel (1979) "The New Class: A Muddled Concept." In The New Class?, edited by B. Bruce-Briggs. New Brunswick, N.J.: Transaction Books.

Bruce-Briggs, B. (ed.) (1979) The New Class? New Brunswick, N.J.: Transaction Books.

Brym, Robert J. (1980) Intellectuals and Politics. London: Allen & Unwin.

Eulau, Heinz, and John D. Sprague (1964) Lawyers in Politics. Indianapolis: Bobbs-Merrill.

Hacker, Andrew (1961) "The Elected and the Anointed: Two American Elites." American Political Science Review 55:539–45.

Inglehart, Ronald (1971) "The Silent Revolution in Europe: Intergenerational Change in Post-Industrial Societies." American Political Science Review 65:991–1017.

Ladd, C. Everett (1979) "Pursuing the New Class." In The New Class?, edited by B. Bruce-Briggs. New Brunswick, N.J.: Transaction Books.

Poole, Keith T., and R. Steven Daniels (1982) "Ideology and Voting in the U.S. Congress, 1959–1980." Paper presented at the annual meeting of the Midwest Political Science Association, April 1982, Milwaukee.

Prewitt, Kenneth, and William McAllister (1976) "Changes in the American Executive Elite—1930–1970." In Elite Recruitment in Democratic Polities, edited by Heinz Eulau and Moshe M. Czudnowski. New York: Wiley.

Steinfels, Peter (1979) The Neoconservatives. New York: Simon & Schuster.

Schlesinger, Joseph A. (1957) "Lawyers and American Politics: A Clarified View." Midwest Journal of Political Science 1:26–39.

———. (1966) Ambition and Politics. Chicago: Rand McNally.

Ruling Elites in a Multilingual Society: Quebec within Canada

Jean A. Laponce

Mosca's analysis of social forces focuses on religion, money, class, occupation, education, and nationalism; his typology of ruling classes contrasts warriors, priests, landowners and wealthy strata, conquering nations or races, castes, hereditary families, scientists, and bureaucrats. He deals only incidentally with language, when he states, in the course of a discussion of Taine and Gobineau's racial theories: "Similarity of language, engendering as it does a freer interchange of ideas and feelings between certain peoples, tends to give them a far stronger resemblance in intellectual and moral type than customarily results from mere blood relationships" (1939:21). Note that Mosca says "between people"; the resemblance he has in mind is that between Italian and French or Russian and Ukrainian.

With Canada as my main, but not exclusive, example, my objective in this chapter will be to apply Mosca's categories of social forces, ruling elites, political formula, and juridical defense to the analysis of linguistic cleavages and conflicts in a multilingual society; in other words, to treat language as Mosca treats money or scientific knowledge, since language—like money or knowledge—is a means of communication, a means of exchange, and an instrument of domination.

The analysis will show that language has a particular political dynamic, markedly distinct from that of religion or class. Languages in contact always tend to stratify, and the dominant one seeks to eliminate the others. This elimination can be retarded or prevented only by very specific means of what Mosca would call juridical defense—specifically, by giving the minority language exclusive territorial control over its core area. But giving a minority such exclusive rights is often perceived to run counter to the ideals of a liberal, equalitarian, and individualistic society. It is so perceived by most English Canadian decision makers in elite positions—hence the ideological and structural crisis faced by the Canadian state in the 1970s and 1980s.

Languages in Contact: From Neurophysiology to Political Geography

Man is an irrepressible exchanger of information. Any individual taken at random from the population presently living on the earth is capable of conversing with any other individual taken from that same population, if not directly, at least through interpreters; and, typically, very few intermediaries would be needed in the chain of translations leading from the first to the second of these two randomly chosen individuals. Communication across languages is so frequent that we assume, rightly, that interpreters can always be found to link among themselves the more than two thousand languages that divide us,[1] but it leads us also to assume frequently, and wrongly, that multilingualism is natural, to assume that an individual brought up in a bilingual environment becomes as surely and as easily bilingual as an individual brought up in a monolingual environment becomes monolingual. That it be not in fact quite as natural to become bilingual as to become monolingual has important political consequences that have often been overlooked by analysts and decision makers when they treat linguistic cleavages of a kind with other ethnic cleavages—religious, for example.

The bilingual (I say bilingual rather than multilingual in order to simplify and because nearly all my examples will be taken from bilingual states and societies) does not have two languages as he has two eyes or two hands. We are born with the capacity to learn more than one language, but the average individual has the urge to speak only one. It is inefficient to have two symbols for the same significant. The grammarian's saying that, in a given language, there are no true synonyms identifies a fundamental psychological mechanism with psysioneurological underpinnings: the mind rejects synonymy; unlike a library shelf, it rejects multiple copies. In the 1950s the neurologist Wilder Penfield (1959) proposed the single switch theory of bilingualism. According to that theory, the two different languages of a bilingual are stored in different areas of the brain, and the switch giving access to one automatically closes the access to the other. If it were so, synonymy across languages would not be of the same type as synonymy within a given language. But the Penfield theory is not supported by the common observation that bilinguals—even the most fluent bilinguals—are subject to interference at the level of both vocabulary and syntax, especially the former. It is as if significant and signified were meant for a one-to-one relationship rather than for a kind of *mariage à trois* where two significants compete for the privilege of being the signifier. As a result, the languages of a bilingual are typically arranged hierarchically, according to roles and social contexts (McKay, 1962; Laponce, 1975). In any given role (father, politician, churchgoer, etc) or social context (playground, shop, work, etc.) the bilingual, if given a choice, will prefer to use one language rather than another, one's fluency in the language and the status of that language being the two major factors determining the preference.

The difference in preference and performance between two differ- ent languages, while often undetectable on simple tasks, becomes obvious on complex problems. Experiments by Dornic (1975) have shown that the gap in reaction time of bilinguals asked to resolve problems of increasing complexity in the one and the other of their two languages increases as a very function of the complexity of the problem. The bilingual who shifts easily from one language to an- other when requesting street directions or buying a railway ticket will typically show stress if asked to improvise a speech, plead a case in court, write a poem, or perform difficult mental arithmetic in the less preferred of his languages.

In short, bilingualism—socially beneficial and psychologically gratifying as it may be—is costly in neurophysiological terms, espe- cially for those who did not acquire the two languages in early child- hood;[2] and the cost does not take the form of a one-time investment; to maintain two languages, rather than only one, in a state of readi- ness means an extra expenditure. Hence the ever present pull toward monolingualism. Measured on a single individual, the effect of this pull is rarely dramatic; we notice people acquiring new languages much more often than we notice them losing fluency in a language or losing that language altogether. But if we change our unit of anal- ysis and consider a family stretched over a number of generations, then the effect of the pull toward monolingualism becomes quite obvious, provided, however, that we control for social dominance, since the cost of bilingualism tends to be shifted downward in the social hierarchy.

The universal tendency to seek monolingualism by "taxing" the weak is not always immediately obvious. Indeed, in many societies the elites are multilingual and the masses monolingual (Russia and Den- mark in the nineteenth century; France and Japan in the second part of the twentieth), but that situation results not from the power dif- ferential between the elite and the masses they control but from the fact that the elites of Russia, Denmark, France, or Japan are, linguis- tically, subordinated to more powerful foreign elites that have loaded them with the cost of extra languages.

The universality of the pull toward monolingualism has profound geographical, hence political, consequences. For reasons of greater efficiency and psychological comfort, people tend to form geograph- ically distinct and linguistically homogeneous communities; languages tend to juxtapose rather than superpose themselves in physical space (Laponce, 1980). If and when they become mixed, the tendency toward monolingualism continues to operate, however, and results either in the merging of the languages in contact or in the elimination of the socially weaker of the two (Weinreich, 1963). Whether religions or races mix or do not mix territorially is basically a cultural problem; whether languages mix or not involves culture, of course; but it involves biology in the first place. The embedding of various languages, each in its protective spatial niche, is rooted in the biological cost of maintaining more than one language. If all the individuals of a given closed society were to know the same two languages, one of these languages would die of redundance; hence the law that a language dies with its last unilingual (Fishman, 1966; Dressler, 1977). Typically, in a multilingual society the various languages have different areas of geographical concentration, within the state or within the cities; and the greater the concentration, the more likely the survival of the language concerned. We should thus expect that the multilingual state will often experience territorial, in addition to the usual socioeconomic, cleavages and that these territorial cleavages may cause a minority, caught between the watching of the center and the protection of a periphery, to develop two different elites for the serving of these two purposes.

Canada's Language Zones in Relation to Its Political Capitals and Boundaries

French-speaking Canadians are not the only linguistic minority group to have a claim to a specific piece of the Canadian territory. The Chinese in the first decades of their settlement in British Columbia and, to this day, many Indian bands, as well as the Hutterites of Saskatchewan, have or had such a claim; but the small size of these foreign language "islands" has, except for very short periods of time, caused them to remain local issues. French Canadians are the only linguistic minority in Canada to have the size and the territorial cohesion sufficient to affect the very structure of the whole state. Close to 27 percent of Canadians give French as their mother tongue; and, in the province of Quebec, that percentage stands at 80 percent. But impressive as it is, this last statistic does not give an adequate measure of the territorial cohesion of the French language. There are, in Canada, five major ethnolinguistic zones. The first, in the East, covers the Maritimes and the southern section of New Brunswick and defines an English-speaking area; the second, which consists of Acadia in northern New Brunswick, and the third, which extends from the New Brunswick border to the very center of Montreal, are both francophone; the fourth that comprises the west of Montreal, the area between Montreal and the U.S. border, part of

Ottawa, and the region of Sudbury in Ontario, is a bilingual zone where the two languages are fighting for territorial control (Joy, 1967, 1978; Lieberson, 1970, 1981), a fight which is to the advantage of French on the Quebec side of the border and to the advantage of English on the Ontario side, the side which includes Ottawa. The fifth region, which extends from Ottawa to the Pacific, is anglophone.

The Acadians of area 2, although they have a very specific identity and a long historical consciousness that sets them apart from both anglophones and Quebecois, are not, at present, a social force that markedly affects the Canadian state. The political problems posed by their territorial concentration are contained within the provincial boundaries of New Brunswick. By contrast, areas 3 and 4 pose problems of Canada-wide magnitude. The third area, that which extends from the center of Montreal to the eastern borders of Quebec, is overwhelmingly francophone. French is the language of more than 90 percent of the population and, judging by the rough estimates of the Gendron Commission (1972), it is spoken over 90 percent of the time: the shops, the churches, the street signs, the local government, the universities are as French as Copenhagen is Danish or Norway, Norwegian. In an area vastly greater than Switzerland lives a concentrated French ethnic group of over 4 million people, a group more numerous than the population of Switzerland in the 1920s, if somewhat smaller than today's Swiss population. What matters, however, and needs to be emphasized is not numbers per se but the conjunction of numbers *and* concentration. The home base of the French language does not quite coincide with the boundaries of Quebec province, but French has a distinctive home base. To repeat: the universities of Quebec, Montreal, Sherbrooke, and Laval are as French as the University of Bergen is Norwegian, probably a little more so.

The fourth zone, the bilingual zone that extends from the center of Montreal to Ottawa and northeastern Ontario, is one of insecurity for the French language. The francophones of that area use the Quebec government and, to a lesser extent, the government in Ottawa to reduce that insecurity; the anglophones use the federal and the Ontario governments to retain their advantage.

How do Ottawa and Quebec react to these conflicting linguistic pulls? In the last twenty years French has made remarkable progress in the nation's capital (noticably in the hotels, in the restaurants, in the offices that serve the public), but Ottawa remains nevertheless overwhelmingly English. Seventy percent of its population does not speak French, and nearly all the higher functions of government are transacted in English. By contrast, in Quebec City, the seat of the Quebec provincial government, nearly all the functions of the bureaucracy, at all levels, are transacted in French, even in the ministry of finance (the last ministry to convert from English to French in the late 1960s); only 1 percent of the population speaks English at the exclusion of French, 75 percent speak French at the exclusion of English, and, altogether, more than 95 percent speak French at home. In eastern Montreal, the residence of the overwhelming majority of the city's francophones, the situation is comparable.[3] To most Quebecois, Ottawa is thus, like Bern to a French Swiss, outside the ethnic territory; it is, linguistically, a foreign environment, since in such an environment one cannot assume that one will be understood in one's mother tongue. That situation differs from that of francophone Belgians who, though a numerical minority in their country, like the French Canadians, have an overwhelming majority in their nation's capital. The Belgian francophone can thus easily identify this ethnicity and his language with the central state; the francophone Canadian, like the francophone Swiss, cannot do so as easily. All the efforts of the Trudeau government to make Ottawa bilingual cannot reverse the inexorable fact that mixing French and English territorially or administratively results in their stratification, English dominating and downgrading French. Quebec politicians are at home in Quebec, they are "abroad" in Ottawa—unless they think in Canadian rather than in specifically Quebec terms, and unless they think in English rather than in French. The result has been a bifurcation of Quebec's political class that has no equivalent in English Canada; nor has it an equivalent in the rest of North America. It is as if a single social force—the Quebecois ethnicity—though agreed on its strategy (ethnic survival), had been unable to agree on tactics and had pursued at the very same time the increasingly divergent goals of insuring its protection at "home" in Quebec and "abroad" in Ottawa.

Strategies of Survival: Accommodation "Abroad" and Opposition at "Home"

For sixty-three of the eighty-five years that have passed since a French Canadian, Wilfrid Laurier, became Prime Minister of Canada in 1896, the Canadian state has been governed by the Liberal party, and that party has typically kept its leaders in office for periods of time unmatched in length anywhere in the democratic world. Laurier remained in office for sixteen years, Mackenzie King for twenty-one years, St. Laurent for eight years, Pearson for five years; and Trudeau, who has thus far been prime minister for thirteen years, may reasonably hope to serve as long as Laurier. The main factor behind the Liberal dominance and the durability of that party's leaders is a remarkable concentration of Quebec's votes on Liberal candidates in federal elections. Since the turn of the century the French Canadian percentage of the Canadian population has fluctuated between 27 percent and 30 percent; but the percentage of French Canadians in the Liberal parliamentary caucus has typically been much higher, often very much higher (see Table 1).

TABLE 1.
Percentage of French Canadians among Liberals in the
Canadian House of Commons

Year	Percentage	Year	Percentage
1896	37	1949	34
1900	37	1953	42
1904	34	1957	65
1908	36	1958	61
1911	38	1962*	
1917	67	1963	39
1921	47	1965	46
1925	54	1968	38
1926	49	1972	48
1930	48	1974	41
1935	29	1979	46
1940	30	1980	49
1945	43		

*The Parliament was dissolved before the *Parliamentary Guide,* our source for all other years, could publish the biographies of its members.

This concentration of Quebec's votes on one of the two parties that alternate in office has had the obvious payoff of giving French Canadians the prime ministership three times in the history of Canada and twice since the Second World War; it has also had, probably, economic payoffs in the form of tariffs that are protective of Quebec's declining textile and leather industries, and cultural payoffs in the form of a francophone radio and television network which, although funded by the central state, serves primarily the province of Quebec, where it is based. However, until the 1970s, when serious efforts were made to increase the use of French in the federal administration, the Quebec impact on Ottawa was not particularly visible. The French Canadian in Ottawa, even after the recent moderately successful attempts at making the administration bilingual, is in a milieu that is linguistically foreign, not hostile or unfriendly or even unpleasant—on the contrary, that milieu may be and is often very attractive—but as foreign as New York would be to most civil servants serving at the United Nations. Many French Canadian politicians do not have intuitive, immediate access to English Canadian culture, a culture that is molded by a language and an education system that is not theirs. Pierre Elliott Trudeau and the previous French Canadian prime minister, Louis Stephen St. Laurent are exceptions (English was the tongue of their mothers and thus to a large extent also their mother tongue). Until the 1970s the French Canadian member of parliament typically saw his role in Ottawa as that of an ambassador, as that of a mediator rather than as that of a full participant. He was a mediator between the politics of the Canadian state on the one hand and the interests of Quebec or, more often, the interests of his own electoral district on the other. More recently, since the advent of the so-called French Power in Ottawa in the late 1960s, which advent gave French Canadians not only the prime ministership but the crucial finance and economic ministries as well, the dominant role has shifted from that of mediator to that of international civil servant.

One could make a good political and social history of English Canada from the vantage point of the liberal caucus in Ottawa; making a history of Quebec from that same vantage point would be frustrating and misleading. Take, for example, the two most serious of the crises that have opposed Quebec to Ottawa in the last generation, the conscription crisis of 1944 and the constitutional crisis of 1981. How did the Quebec MPs react toward the end of the Second World War when, under pressure from English Canada, Mackenzie King negated the promises made to the Quebec electorate not to impose conscription? Here is how MacGregor Dawson describes the scene in the caucus chamber when the prime minister submitted to his party the controversial text that was to be put before parliament that very same day: "Throughout the proceedings, the Quebec members, who were naturally the hardest hit, appeared distressed and anxious. Some looked grim and determined, but they stood silent . . ." (1961:115).

Eventually thirty-four French Canadians voted against the legislation and twenty-three supported it; but how could their temporary and partial breaking of party rank and their absence of voice be explained if not by their feeling of marginality? The same absence of voice on the part of Quebec backbenchers—in the ordinary as in the Hirshman (1970) sense of the term—characterized the 1980–1981 debates on the federal government's proposed Charter of Human Rights, a charter that restricts the right of Quebec to legislate on the subject of language and renders unconstitutional some of the provisions of Quebec's language laws that limit the use of English in public schools. A few Quebec federal liberal MPs voiced concern over the weakening of a piece of provincial legislation that is popular with their electors; yet these complaints have been, on the whole, remarkably subdued and only one Quebecois liberal voted against the restrictive amendments. The Liberal party is dependent on the Quebec vote; yet the Liberal members from Quebec behave as if it were the reverse, as if they were the creation of the Liberal party, as if unaware that the fate of the party is in their hands. This may be due to the feeling that the Canadian state and the federal parties— Liberal included—are not truly, completely, and legitimately their creation, a feeling sustained by the fact that the Quebec electorate appears bonded federally with the name of a party rather than with specific Liberal candidates or programs. Quebec votes Liberal as it goes to church, more often out of habit than out of conviction. The concentration of Quebec's vote on the Liberal party, being traditional and taken for granted, has the cunning effect of reducing the power of the Quebec federal parliamentary caucus and of freeing the federal Quebec ministers from Quebec's control. These ministers can then perform unhindered their new role of international civil servants devoted to maximizing the powers of the institution which they serve and which has elevated them. Such is the role of P. E. Trudeau, who used the crisis that arose in 1980 from Quebec's unsuccessful separation attempt in order to reduce the powers of Quebec and increase those of central English Canada. Had Trudeau been elected from Ontario, he would not have acted differently. The fascinating tug of war between Trudeau and Lévesque, between the French Canadian elite in Ottawa and the French Canadian elite in Quebec City, has been affected by personal factors; it has had many of the characteristics of a battle among "frères enemis." But these personal factors cannot explain the increased divergence between the politicians that Quebec elects in federal elections and those it elects provincially. To explain this divergence between Quebec and Ottawa, we need Mosca's notion of social force as well as the more recent, more psychological, notion of "bonding."

A politician's wisdom is normally measured by the boundaries of his political constituency. There is no reason to expect that Canada should be an exception. The wisdom of the Canadian prime minister, whether he be French or English, is thus defined by the boundaries of an overwhelmingly English-speaking nation, an anglophone social force that speaks through him even when he speaks French. But why should the ordinary Quebec backbenchers respond, as does the prime minister, to the pressure of English Canada? Largely, because of the nature of the Canadian party system. The party leader, once in office, has great power over his caucus; if one seeks election to Ottawa, it is normally with the ambition of becoming a cabinet minister.[4] But to achieve that objective one cannot rely exclusively or even principally on a personal party faction; one must be liked by the party leader. Furthermore, the new member of parliament is soon socialized into the policy norms of his party by collegial and friendly ties established across languages. Such, at least, is the convincing explanation given by Rayside (1978b) on the basis of a comparative study of the opinions of Liberal members of parliament in Ottawa and of Liberals in the Quebec National Assembly. He found that the francophone Liberals in Ottawa, on many issues of vital importance to Quebec, were more than halfway between the francophone representatives in Quebec and the English Canadian Liberals. On the question "Quebec should force immigrant children to French schools"

74 percent of Quebec francophone Liberals said "Yes," while only 7 percent of Ottawa anglophone Liberals agreed. Between the two, closer in fact to the anglophones, the francophones elected from Quebec to Ottawa scored at 33 percent. Similarly, on the question "Quebec has a right to a special status" the ranking was 67 percent, 31 percent, and 7 percent, the federal francophone Liberals taking again the near middle position (Rayside, 1978a:515). Yet the Liberals in Quebec and the Liberals in Ottawa—although the provincial and the federal parties are not linked institutionally—were at the time elected by basically the same electorate. We must then consider the explanation that the same voters are prepared to accept that their politicians play two different strategies—a strategy of accommodation in Ottawa and a strategy of opposition in Quebec City. That explanation is reinforced rather than contradicted by the existence of a strong privileged bond between the Quebec electorate and the federal Liberals, a bond that leaves the federal politicians freer to devise their own tactics. Such tribal bonding between a people and a party name will now be considered at the same time as the political formulae used in the contest for allegiance by the two French Canadian political elites, that in Quebec and that in Ottawa.

Images and Political Formulae

Of the three major Canadian federal parties, the Liberals, the Conservatives, and the New Democratic Party (NDP), only the first two have thus far had any chance of winning an election and only one—the Liberals—has ever had French Canadians as leaders; since 1896 the Liberals have, in effect, though not as a result of a stated policy, alternated French and English leaders. Such alternation is unique among Canadian parties. It has no equivalent among Quebec Liberals at the provincial level, although the percentage of anglophones in Quebec (20 percent) is not markedly different from the percentage of French Quebecois in Canada (22 percent). It has no equivalent at the level of municipal politics either: in Montreal, where the anglophones account for 40 percent of the population, the mayor has been French since the First World War. That there be no reciprocity between Quebec and Ottawa in terms of ethnic alternance is understandable: the language on the defensive cannot afford to be as generous as that which dominates. But it is puzzling that one only of the federal parties has ever played such a winning card. In the case of the NDP, a regional party without roots in Quebec and one which has never been a serious contender to the prime ministership, the exclusive recruitment of its leader from among English Canadians is not too surprising. But what of the Conservatives, who were the dominant party in Quebec until 1896, who have maintained a base in that province, and who at times had close links with specifically Quebec parties, such as the Union Nationale? A seemingly obvious winning strategy would have consisted in the Conservatives selecting a French Canadian leader when the Liberals were led by an anglophone. If this did not happen in the first part of the nineteenth century, it is quite simply because the Conservative party was too English and too Protestant not to have shattered its image and lost too much of its electorate by selecting a French-Catholic leader; if this did not happen in the last twenty years, when anti-Catholic and anti-French attitudes had become marginal among the Conservative electorate, it is largely because of an accident caused by the irrational way Canadian parties select their leaders. In the early 1970s the Conservative establishment brought to Ottawa a prominent Quebec judge and politician, Claude Wagner, who had been minister of justice in Quebec (it is rare for Quebec politicians to shift from the provincial to the federal stream); the intention was to prepare him for the leadership. Had the choice of leader of the party been made by the party establishment, Wagner would have almost certainly been selected; but under the system adopted in 1927, the choice of the Conservative leader is made in one day at a party convention, without recess between votes, the lowest candidate being eliminated at each of the successive ballots. Wagner having been the front runner long before the opening of the convention, the pre-convention alliances and vote tradings among the lesser candidates resulted in Wagner's being defeated on the last ballot (Krause and Leduc, 1979). Thus, by accident, the federal Liberals have remained the only Canadian party perceived by the French Canadian electorate to have a French Canadian image. Such ethnic unbalance has no equivalent in Switzerland or Belgium. The bonding of Quebec electors to the Liberal party is the kind of bonding that takes place between self and a mirror, the only mirror available.

If the Quebec electorate is not specifically attached to distinctly Liberal policies, it is attached, however, to some policies that are distinctly federal and to others that are distinctly provincial. The Quebec electorate is one whose attitudes are ambivalent rather than ambiguous—hence its need for a bifurcated elite, each using different political formulae to mobilize electoral support, formulae that can be reduced to a triad: security, freedom, and solidarity.

Security

With the second largest territory in the world after the USSR, Canada, though the neighbor of the two most powerful countries, has a very weak military establishment. Its whole army (navy and air force personnel included) could, at the cost of only moderate discomfort, be fitted into the Montreal Olympic stadium.[5] For its military security, Canada relies on the United States. The federal government is thus deprived of the possibility of using its exclusive control of the armed forces as a means of drawing to it, on security grounds, the attention and loyalty of the citizenry and that of Quebec in particular; all the more so, since, in the Canadian army, except at the lower levels, the language of command is English (by contrast, in Switzerland as in Belgium, not only are the regiments unilingual, but the high command makes effective use of two languages).

The dominant security formula used by the federal government has been that of economic security, and, as evidenced by the referendum campaign of 1980 in Quebec, it is still a winning formula. The Quebec nationalist and separatist elites have sought, in the last generation, to counteract the federal advantage of Ottawa in the economic security field by bringing more and more of the Quebec economy under provincial control. The nationalization of hydroelectric resources, the Bay James project, the takeover of the Asbestos Corporation do not have their roots in socialist philosophy (socialist parties have never succeeded in Quebec) but in ethnic nationalism. For the Quebec political elite such nationalizations are means of "frenchifying" the economy, means of associating the notion of economic power and, hence, security with Quebec rather than Ottawa. This attempt at establishing economic mastery has been only partly successful. The majority of the Quebec electorate still associates economic security with the federal government, more so than English-speaking provinces, such as Alberta, where the federal government is perceived as a threat to the province's economic well-being. (The hostility of Albertans is, however, at present, directed more against the Liberal party in office than against the central institutions per se.)

If the Quebec electorate sends to Ottawa a political class whose function is mainly to provide economic security, it sends to Quebec a political class whose function is to provide emotional security. The psychological studies of language have shown that a mother tongue has a way of involving the emotions that is unavailable to the languages acquired later in life (Kelman, 1972; Deutsch, 1953). Thus, the government in Ottawa, even when it is led by a French Canadian, cannot play on the feelings of Quebecois to the same extent as the government of Quebec, a government that is part of what Quebecois call "le milieu." It is thus not inconsistent that the same electorate could elect Liberals to Ottawa and the Parti Quebecois to Quebec. By both it is reassured.

Freedom and Solidarity

In his latest reflections on the individual and the state, Ralph Dahrendorf (1979) suggests that the evaluation of the performance of a political system be done in terms of *freedom* and of what he calls *ligature*, a notion that Mosca, like Durkheim, would have probably preferred to call "solidarity." In so doing, Dahrendorf has identified two of the second most powerful political formulae (security being the first) by which political elites mobilize their followers. Dahrendorf wonders whether, in democratic regimes, the freedom formula has not reached, lately, the point of diminishing returns, the point where greater freedom is at the expense of solidarity, the point where the removal of the remaining ligatures threatens society with collapse into randomness.

The English Canadian political elites, at both the provincial and the federal level, especially at the federal level, and more particularly under the Liberals, have emphasized civil rights within Canada and sought to develop "ligatures" in the form of a pan-Canadian nationalism (often by means of a nonvirulent form of anti-Americanism).[6] The 1981 Charter of Human Rights (at the time of writing before the Courts on a challenge of its constitutionality by the Quebec government) is an embodiment of that tradition. True, that charter, which establishes freedoms as extensive as those written into the American constitutional amendments, was first opposed by seven of the nine anglophone premiers of the ten Canadian provinces; but that opposition was more tactical than ideological. It was a prelude to bargaining over the sharing of economic and political resources; the anglophone premiers would not have been supported by their electors if they had maintained their objections to making the federal courts the protectors of individual rights—and in particular of the right to move to all sections of the country. Furthermore, on the question of nationalism, the English Canadian provincial and federal elites are in basic agreement: the provincial governments do not see the provinces (Newfoundland being a partial exception) as attracting loyalties of a nationalistic kind. The premiers of Ontario, as well as those of British Columbia, Nova Scotia, or Saskatchewan, have said repeatedly that they are Canadian first, and their actions, as well as the opinion surveys of their own populations, confirm that they could not say differently without losing credibility. In English Canada, the provincial political elite is thought to be in charge of the adaptation or "mother"-functions of government, mostly economic and social functions with a local base (hospitals, police, natural resources), while the national government is seen to be responsible for the "father"-functions of goal setting for the nation as a whole, hence responsible for the political, economic, and social policies tied to nation building and related to the protection of the citizen's fundamental rights. The federal elite is thus led to weaken or at least to prevent the strengthening of the linguistic boundary that separates English from French Canada and to prevent or at least reduce American cultural and economic penetration. The second policy is protective of the French as well as of the English Canadian culture. But the first policy, that which weakens linguistic boundaries, is, on the contrary, antagonistic to the French minority, since the mixing of languages resulting from the right to move across the linguistic boundaries, coupled to the right to obtain education and federal services in one's preferred language, is advantageous to the language with the greater power of assimilation, i.e., English in the Canadian context (Laponce, 1975; Zolberg, 1975).

In French Canada, as distinct from English Canada, the provincial and federal political elites appear less clearly differentiated in terms of father-mother functions. Ottawa is more powerful, but Quebec sets the societal goals. One follows Ottawa more readily in economic than in political matters; Ottawa is both trusted mother and distrusted father. With regard to freedom and solidarity the contrast is clearer: the Quebec federal elite, being physically removed from the French-speaking geographical core area, finds it more difficult, compared to the provincial, to use to its advantage the solidarity formula; inversely, the French Canadian federal elite is in a better position to make itself the protector of civil rights. It need not have been so; the Quebec representatives in Ottawa could have concentrated their actions on the ethnic solidarity function, as did the Irish representatives in the British parliament of the late nineteenth century. That has not happened; the French Quebecois is both European and American, European in the sense of rejecting the ideal of ethnic assimilation and integration that dominates English-speaking North America, but American in his liking for the wide open spaces of a wide open continent.

Interestingly, the Great Canadian debate of the past ten years over the restructuring of the state has been a debate among French Canadians—French Canadians in Quebec and French Canadians in Ottawa. The major laws and projects that have been the focus of that debate (the Quebec law 101 of 1978 that restricts the use of English in education and business; the Parti Quebecois Sovereignty-Association project defeated in the 1980 referendum; the federal Charter of Human Rights of 1981) all have French Canadian origins. The desire to reform the Canadian state is a French Canadian desire; English Canadians have never put strong pressure on their elites to reform the constitution, and their elites have never been, in the past generation, particularly interested in changing the official rules governing the division of powers among the various levels and branches of government. Thus English Canada once again may well wonder what Quebec wants, since the projects for reform originating from the two French Canadian elites (the federal and the provincial) have become increasingly divergent, the federal concentrating on the theme of freedom and the provincial on the theme of linguistic solidarity. Both projects are more extreme than English Canada would have preferred; the federal French project is more centrifugal, the provincial Quebecois project more centripetal. This debate among Girondins and Jacobins has left English Canada somewhat puzzled—but not to the point of not using it to its advantage, since the result of the controversy has been to weaken the powers of Quebec within the Confederation. The loss is particularly serious on the major point of contention, the language of instruction in the schools. The federal side argued that a liberal democracy ought to give to parents the choice of the language in which their children are educated; the provincial side argued that the language of instruction is not a matter for individual decision, that language is a group, not an individual, right since any penetration of the francophone core-area by English-speaking settlers would weaken the francophone minority. The federal dream is of a Canada that would be bilingual from coast to coast, of a Canada where members of either linguistic group (at least among the elite) could find themselves at home in every region of the country; the provincial proposals reject bilingualism by superposition in favor of bilingualism by juxtaposition. The federal proposals emphasize freedom at the cost of solidarity; the provincial does the reverse.

The performing of the solidarity function is traditional to the Quebec government; it predates the 1871 constitution; but, until the 1950s, the provincial government was not the major institution to determine societal goals and to concentrate the attention of Quebec's French-speaking population. Until the so-called Quiet Revolution of the 1960s, the church was the dominant actor, the main protector, the ultimate recourse. The long period of the church's dominance over French Canadian society corresponds to what André Bélanger (1975) calls the phase of minority-nationalism, a phase during which the minority ethnicity accepted its inferior status in the political and economic systems and sought to isolate itself within the religious and the cultural. This old nationalism did not disappear but ceased to be dominant in the 1960s; it was overtaken by what Bélanger—to use his terminology again—calls a form of dominant-territorial-nationalism, one that finds its major institutional support in the provincial government, whether that government be committed to greater autonomy within the Confederation or to some form of independence. This majority-nationalism is no longer specifically Catholic and French Canadian; it is secular and Quebecois.[7] This more aggressive, more assertive ideology, continues in the 1980s to be the major incarnation of Quebec nationalism; but it is, in turn, challenged by the weakly nationalist but strongly individualistic liberalism represented by Claude Ryan and a large segment of the provincial Liberal party (Clift, 1981; Bergeron and Pelletier, 1980), a liberalism which assumes that, the Quebecois ethnicity having achieved security, the time has now come to shift from societal to individual goals and to concentrate on individual success in the economic sector.

Hence the very recent weakening of the two nationalisms that had succeeded each other; hence, also, the greater responsiveness of a large number of Quebecois to the federal themes of individual freedom and civil rights. This evolution from minority-nationalism to majority-nationalism and to liberal-individualism covers another evolution marked by the shift from the notion of an ethnicity defined by religion, language, and family of birth to that of an ethnicity defined solely by language and province of residence. Such a shift—far from being universal—has temporarily weakened the links of solidarity among an ethnicity which is no longer agreed on its own social and institutional boundaries, which is no longer tightly bound by religion, culture, and family in addition to being linked by language. But although less virulent in the early 1980s than in the mid 1970s, Quebec nationalisms—of the majority and minority varieties—remain the major social forces that a Quebec elite has to capture to stay in power; and, as previously, the themes of individual freedom and civil rights remain, in addition to that of economic security, the winning formulae of the Quebec federal elites.

How could elites originating from the same society be so divergent? Is it because Quebec's social forces are in competition and have diverging interests, the business elite seeking economic security from Ottawa while the intelligentsia seeks cultural protection within Quebec? Undoubtedly, that is a factor but not one sufficient to explain the divergence. More fundamentally, the explanation is in the ambivalence of many French Canadians, divided within themselves by the freedom and the solidarity appeals, divided in their being North Americans who reject North America.[8]

The diverging preferences of French Quebec at the provincial and federal levels is not immediately visible in the composition of the political elites sent to Quebec City and to Ottawa. Both are by and large recruited from the same social groups, as indicated by Table 2, which compares the professions of cabinet ministers while controlling for language and, at least in Quebec, for political party.[9] Among francophones as among anglophones, among Liberals as among Parti Quebecois ministers, the modal profession is that of lawyer. The Quebec top political class is slightly more diversified than its homologue in Ottawa, with its doctors and priests, but considering the small size of the groups compared, the dominant impression is one of similarity. The number of lawyers among cabinet ministers may—I can only speculate in the absence of proof—facilitate and exaggerate the divergence noted between the two levels of government. By profession, a lawyer is trained to represent a client, in some ways to overrepresent its interests. It would then be as if Quebec had selected two different lawyers to represent each side of its divided interests and personality.[10] However, at the level of premiers and

TABLE 2.
Comparison of the Quebec and Ottawa Cabinets
by Language and Profession

| | Federal Cabinet (1977) Liberal | | Quebec Cabinet | |
	English Canadians	French Canadians	Liberals (1976)	Parti Quebecois (1977)
Lawyers	38	42	35	20
University professors	12	8	—	16
School teachers	6	—	4	—
Businessmen	25	8	19	4
Media	12	8	—	8
Accountants, economists, brokers	—	8	19	16
Farmers	6	—	—	—
White-collar	8	8	—	4
Blue-collar	—	—	—	—
Foremen	—	8	—	—
Civil servants	—	8	—	8
Engineers	—	—	8	8
Priests	—	—	—	4
Doctors	—	—	12	12
Other	—	—	4	4
	(N = 16)	(N = 12)	(N = 26)	(N = 25)*

*An economist-professor was classified as professor; and economist-lawyer was classified as lawyer; and a worker-priest was classified as priest.

Source: The Canadian Parliamentary Guide and Répertoire des parlementaires québécois, 1867–1978 Québec, Assemblée Nationale, service de documentation, 1980.

prime ministers a notable difference appears. Quebec's premiers and party leaders, while having sometimes had English-speaking ancestors, come from linguistically homogeneous French Canadian families. By contrast, the last two French Canadian prime ministers of Canada have come from mixed parentage; they had French-speaking fathers and English-speaking mothers, and both learned the two languages in childhood. I am told that Prime Minister St. Laurent, having once been asked in what language he prayed, said, "In English, of course"; the "of course," which was meant to indicate that he had learned his prayers from his mother, might have been misunderstood but probably tolerated by his electorate, had his prayer preferences been public knowledge. Would a politician saying his prayers in a language other than French have been so likely to become prime minister of Quebec?

The overlap between the two major incarnations of Quebec's political ambivalence is not, of course, a complete overlap. The difference in the outcome of provincial and federal elections in that province cannot be explained by the sole ambivalence of the voters. The level of electoral participation is lower in Quebec in federal than in provincial elections (while in English-speaking provinces it is usually the reverse, as indicated by Table 3), and the support given to the Conservatives or the Social Credit indicates that not all Quebecois are bonded to the federal Liberals. But the overlap of electorates between parties pursuing opposite strategies is nevertheless remarkably high. A survey done in the last two weeks of November 1981 by the Centre de Sondage of Montreal University (Trudel, 1981) indicates that approximately a quarter of the Parti Quebecois supporters would have voted for the Federal Liberal party (see Table 4). Trudel's report does not distinguish francophones from anglophones; but since the support that the latter give to the Parti Quebecois is known to be minimal, we can assume that the 25 percent of PQ supporters who were prepared to shift to the Liberal Federals represents roughly 15 percent of the voting francophone population of Quebec, a percentage sufficient to orient the political system differently in federal and provincial elections.[11] Note further in Table 4 that only 15 percent of the Parti Quebecois supporters would have abstained in a federal election and that 65 percent of them, representing roughly 30 to 40 percent of the voting francophone population, would have supported one of the three main federal parties in a federal election—three parties that endorsed, a few weeks after the survey, the constitutional revisions described by the Quebec government as so dangerously restrictive of its provincial powers as to be unacceptable.

How have other multilingual societies resolved the problem of

TABLE 3.
Voter Turnout in Quebec and Ontario Elections

| Provincial Elections | | Federal Elections | |
Quebec	Ontario	Quebec	Ontario
1970 84.2	(1971) 73.5	(1972) 67	79
1973 80.5		(1974)* 67	74
1976 85.3	(1975) 68.1	(1979)* 76	78
1981	(1981) 58.2	(1980)* 68	72

*From the mid-seventies on, the voter turnout, taken singly, is a somewhat misleading indicator of participation in Quebec because of the increasing number of spoiled ballots and because of the vote for the Rhinoceros party. If one deducts Rhinoceros votes, spoiled ballots and blanks, the federal election figures become 1974: Ontario 74.1, Quebec 63.7; 1979: Ontario 77.7, Quebec 72.9; 1980: Ontario 71.3, Quebec 65.1.

TABLE 4.
Federal Party Preferences of the Supporters of the Two Major
Provincial Parties in Quebec*

| | | Provincial Preference | |
		Parti Quebecois	Liberal Party
	Liberals	24.5	79.0
	Conservatives	29.3	11.6
Federal preference	NDP	11.8	3.8
	Others	9.3	0.4
	Undecided	9.8	4.0
	No answer	0.5	0.1
	Abstention	14.9	1.1
		100%	100%
		(897)	(728)

*The voting intentions were as follows:
Provincially: PQ, 42.9; Liberals, 34.8; Union Nationale, 1.3; Others, 2.5; Undecided, 5.7; Refused, 7.1; Would not vote, 5.7.
Federally: Liberals, 43.4; Conservatives, 18.5; NDP, 7.5; Others, 5.5; Undecided,
7.8; Refused, 6.4; Would not vote, 11.0. If one does not take the last three categories into account, the Federal Liberal vote stands at 57 percent. By comparison,
the Liberals had obtained 67 percent of the Quebec vote in the previous federal
election of March 1980; the Conservatives, 12.4, the NDP, 8.9; and the Social
Credit, 5.8.
(Survey done by the Centre des Sondages of the University of Montreal, November
1981.)

group and individual rights? One case is particularly interesting to
consider, that of Switzerland, where the balance of ethnic forces
between dominant group and minority is roughly the same as in
Canada. Switzerland has resolved the solidarity-freedom dilemma
by separating clearly the notions of ethnic origin and language use
(McRae, 1975). The federal system guarantees to all Swiss the right
to settle in any of the Swiss cantons, to open businesses where they
want, to vote and to be elected wherever they happen to reside; in
other words, the various ethnic groups are not allowed to erect
boundaries around their territories and to prevent penetration by
members of other ethnicities. (In that sense the Swiss constitution is
similar to the Canadian.) But if ethnicity is geographically transport-
able, language is not; the German Swiss who settles in a French
canton will not find cantonal public services in German and will not
be allowed to send his children to a German school, not even a
private one; and vice versa, of course, for the French Swiss who
settles in a German canton. These differences have profound effects
on elite attitudes. The Swiss practice, which forces linguistic assim-

ilation at the second generation, reassures the minority against being assimilated from within. The Canadian practice, on the contrary, keeps the minority in a permanent state of insecurity. Furthermore, the Swiss practice tends to discourage elite immigration across the linguistic borders since the individual in an elite position will be more sensitive to the loss of status resulting from his having to operate in a lesser known language and will be unable, because of ethnic solidarity, to play a role of political leadership in a linguistically foreign environment. Wisely, the Swiss have used their federal system to allocate to the cantons the performance of the major solidarity functions; they have anticipated the Common Market by separating the cultural from the economic; they have clearly distinguished ethnic origin from language use; and in so doing, they have avoided the conflict, now fought over among French Canadians, hence among other Canadians as well, between freedom and solidarity. Unlike Canadians, the Swiss have recognized that in the multilingual state the traditional individual rights are inadequate: group rights are needed, group rights over specific territories. The 1981 Canadian Charter of Rights treats language as it treats race or religion. But for reasons that lead from neurophysiology (the cost of bilingualism) to geography (the territorial concentration of languages) to politics (the need of a minority language to have strong protective boundaries), language is a social force unlike race or religion; the solidarity it creates within an ethnic group is not only social, it is also, normally, territorial. Consequently, in a multilingual state, it is functional to separate the languages in contact and to link them at the elite level by low visibility institutions (as in a consociational model of elite accommodation) rather than mix the languages territorially and render difficult, or prevent, the performance of the solidarity function by local political elites. Canada is now pursuing such a dysfunctional policy. Like Belgium in the last generation, it may well be led, at some point, to shift to the Swiss model.

Notes

1. Two thousand is an underestimation. Mueller (1964) reports that there are between 2,300 and 2,800 spoken languages, exclusive of dialects, that about 250 extinct languages have been identified, and that over a hundred of them are near death. Ferguson (1964) puts the total of spoken languages at over 4,000.

2. For a short, up-to-date bibliography on the subject of bilingualism and a review of the often conflicting literature on the psychological advantages or disadvantages of bilingualism, see Garfield (1981).

3. In the whole of Montreal only about 60 percent of the population speaks French most of the time. For that reason, Ottawa is less foreign to

the Quebecois from Montreal than to the Quebecois from Sherbrooke, Chicoutimi, or Quebec City; the effect of Quebec's language law of 1978 has already increased the difference between Ottawa and Montreal and brought the latter closer to the situation of Quebec City. Twenty percent of the members of the federal parliament (all from Quebec) represent electoral districts where French is spoken at home by over 80 percent of the population. This 20 percent translates normally into 30 to 40 percent of the Liberal caucus. The difference in linguistic tone between Ottawa and Montreal is measured by the fact that in 1981, while 40 percent of the books in the bookstore of the Montreal-Dorval airport were in French, in Ottawa the percentage was under 1 percent. And by my count, in early September 1981, only 5 percent of the Ottawa movies were in French compared to 60 percent in Montreal.

4. Of Freshman MPs interviewed by Clarke and Price (1980), 61 percent had cabinet ambitions.

5. In 1980, the Canadian armed forces stood at 78,000 men. The Montreal stadium seats 70,000.

6. Presthus (1973) notes that a low level of pan-Canadian nationalism facilitates elite accommodation between English Canada and Quebec, thus making Canada similar to the European "consociational" democracies studied by Lijphart (1969). The attempts made by Pierre Elliott Trudeau to raise the level of pan-Canadian nationalism may well make ethnic accommodation more difficult.

7. Such majority-nationalism has, for its distant ancestor, the nationalism of Papineau that predates the Canadian Confederation. In the 1830s Papineau became the spokesman for the small bourgeoisie of Lower Canada, a bourgeoisie that was secular and democratic as well as national (Monière, 1979: chap. 2). Papineau's nationalism was defeated in the unsuccessful rebellion of 1938; then began the era of what Bélanger characterizes as minority-nationalism. For a study of the various roots of Quebec's nationalism, see McRoberts and Postgate (1980).

8. Both Wilfred Laurier in the nineteenth century and P. E. Trudeau in the 1940s and 1980s started their political careers as "rebels" against the Quebec establishment; both appealed to the theme of freedom from tyranny—the "tyranny" of the clergy, of a "parochial ordre moral," and of its Quebec political "spokesmen."

9. Kornberg and Winsbrough (1968), Kornberg (1969), and Sigelman and Vanderbok (1977) report a weak explanatory power of class and professional background when used to predict the political attitudes of parliamentarians and political leaders.

10. On the importance of lawyers in Canadian politics, especially federal politics, see Brady (1964) and Kornberg and Winsbrough (1968). Brady sees lawyers as a kind of surrogate ruling class. For a recent compilation of background data on Canadian legislators, see Fleming and Mitchinson's study of Canada's members of the House of Commons and of the ten legislative assemblies (1981). That study shows the proportion of lawyers to be higher in Ottawa and Quebec than in the other provinces. In the last House or Assembly for which information was available the proportions of lawyers compared to farmers, businessmen, and educators were as follows:

	Farming	Business	Law	Education	Other	No Information
House of Commons	7.1	16.8	20.8	15.0	30.4	10.0
Quebec	2.7	16.3	21.8	17.2	32.7	9.0
Ontario	10.4	20.8	15.2	16.0	37.6	—
Newfoundland	2.0	16.0	8.0	24.0	22.0	28.0
Prince Edward Island	18.7	34.3	6.2	3.1	18.7	18.7
Nova Scotia	6.5	26.1	13.1	15.2	26.1	13.1
New Brunswick	5.1	36.2	17.2	13.8	22.4	5.1
Manitoba	19.3	17.5	10.5	15.8	28.1	8.8
Saskatchewan	31.2	11.5	13.1	24.6	19.7	—
Alberta	20.0	21.3	13.3	8.0	36.0	1.3
British Columbia	5.5	32.7	10.9	9.1	41.8	—

The dominance of lawyers is, however, more systematic in Ottawa than in Quebec. Over the four previous elections the Ottawa percentages have been 20.8, 25.0, 25.2, and 28.1, while in Quebec they were 21.8, 17.2, 16.6, and 28.7.

11. A survey done the same month by CROP (1982) indicated that the federal party electorates would distribute their support provincially as follows:

	Federal vote intention (%)		
Quebec vote intention	Liberal	PC	NDP
	(264)	(127)	(96)
Liberals led by Ryan	60	24	18
PQ led by Lévesque	31	64	68
Other party	3	5	7
Would not vote	3	5	2
Don't know	2	3	4
No answer	—	—	1

References

Bélanger, André (1975) "Le nationalisme québécois, un nationalisme en voie de se définir." In Le nationalisme québécois à la croisée des chemins, edited by Albert Legault. Quebec: Centre québécois de relations internationales, Université Laval.

Bergeron, Gérard (1978) Ce jour la . . . Le référendum. Montreal: Quinze.

Bergeron, Gérard, and Réjean Pelletier (1980) L'état du Québec en devenir. Montreal: Boréal Express.

Brady, Alexander (1964) "Canada and the Model of Westminster." In The Transfer of Institutions, edited by W. B. Hamilton. Durham, N.C.: Duke University Press.

Cahiers de géographie du Quèbec (1980), vol. 24. Special issue on "La problématique géopolitique du Québec." Québec: Presses de l'Université Laval.

Canadian Parliamentary Guide (1898–1980). Ottawa: G. P. Normandin, Canadian Parliamentary Guide.

Careless, J. M. S. (1969) "Limited Identities in Canada." *Canadian Historical Review* 50:1–10.

Carlos, Serge; Edouard Cloutier; and Daniel Latouche (1973) "L'élection de 1973." *La Presse*, 20 November, p. B4.

Cartwright, D. C. (1976) *Language Zones in Canada.* Ottawa: Bilingual Advisory Board.

Centre du Bilinguisme (1978) *Minorités linguistiques et interventions: essai de typologie.* Quebec: Presses de l'Université Laval.

Clarke, Harold, and Richard Price (1980) "Freshman MPs' Job Images: The Effects of Incumbency, Ambition, and Position." *Canadian Journal of Political Science* 3:583–606.

Clift, Dominique (1981) *Le déclin du nationalisme au Québec.* Montreal: Libre expression.

Centre de Recherche l'Opinion Publique (1982) *Report.* CROP: Montreal, December.

Dahrendorf, Ralf (1979) *Life Chances: Approaches to Social and Political Theory.* Chicago: University of Chicago Press.

Dawson, MacGregor (1961) *The Conscription Crisis of 1944.* Toronto: Toronto University Press.

Deutsch, Karl (1953) *Nationalism and Social Communications.* New York: Wiley.

Dion, Léon (1980) *Le Québec et le Canada: les voies de l'avenir.* Montreal: Québécor.

Dornic, S. (1975) *Human Information Processing in Bilingualism.* Stockholm: Institute of Applied Psychology.

Dressler, Wolfgang, and Ruth Wodak-Leodolter (eds.) (1977) "Language Death." *International Journal of the Sociology of Language* 12:5–114.

Ferguson, C. A. (1964) "On Linguistic Information." *Language and Linguistics* 17:201–8.

Fishman, J. (1972) *Contributions to the Sociology of Language.* The Hague: Mouton.

——— (1966) *Language Loyalty in the United States.* The Hague: Mouton.

——— (1968) "Sociolinguistic Perspective in the Study of Bilingualism." *Linguistics* 39:21–29.

Fleming, R. J., and J. T. Mitchinson (1981) *Canadian Legislatures: The 1981 Comparative Study.* Toronto: Office of the Assembly, Queen's Park.

Garfield, Eugène (1981) "English vs. Spanish vs. French vs. . . . The Problem of Bilingualism." *Current Contents*, 27 July, pp. 5–15.

Gendron Commission (1972) *Rapport de la Commission d'enquête.* Quebec: Government of Quebec.

Groulx, Lionel (1935) *Orientations.* Montreal: Editions du zodiaque.

Hamilton, Richard, and Maurice Pinard (1976) "The Bases of Parti Québécois Support in Recent Quebec Elections." *Canadian Journal of Political Science* 1:3–26.

Hirschman, A. O. (1970) *Exit, Voice and Loyalty.* Cambridge, Mass.: Harvard University Press.

Joy, Richard (1978) *Canada's Official Language Minorities.* Montreal: C. D. Howe Research Institute.

——— (1967) *Languages in Conflict.* Ottawa: Privately printed. Toronto: McClelland & Stewart, 1972 (reprint).

Kelman, H. C. (1972) "Language as Aid and Barrier to Involvement in the

National System." In *Contributions to the Sociology of Language*, edited by J. Fishman. The Hague: Mouton.

Kornberg, Allan; J. Smith; and O. Bromley (1969) "Some Differences in the Political Socialization Patterns of Canadian and American Party Officials: A Preliminary Report." *Canadian Journal of Political Science* 2:64–88.

Kornberg, Allan, and H. H. Winsbrough (1968) "The Recruitment of Canadian Members of Parliament." *American Political Science Review* 63:1242–57.

Krause, Robert, and Lawrence Leduc (1979) "Voting Behaviour and Electoral Strategies in the Progressive Conservative Leadership Convention of 1976." *Canadian Journal of Political Science* 1:97–136.

Languages in Canada (1976). Ottawa: Statistics Canada.

Laponce, J. A. (1980) "Le comportement spatial des groupes linguistiques." *International Political Science Review* 1:478–94.

——— (1975) "Relating Linguistic to Political Conflicts." In *Multilingual Political Systems*, edited by J. C. Savard and R. Vigneault. Quebec: Presses de l'Université Laval.

Latouche, Daniel (1975) "Le Québec et l'Amérique du Nord: une comparaison a partir d'un scenario." In *Le nationalisme québécois a la croisée des chemins*, edited by Albert Legault. Quebec: Centre québécois de relations internationales, Université Laval.

Legault, Albert (ed.) (1975) *Le nationalisme québécois à la croisée des chemins*. Quebec: Centre québécois de relations internationales, Université Laval.

Lemieux, Vincent; Marcel Gilbert; and André Blais (1970) *Une election de realignement: l'élection générale du 29 avril 1970 au Québec*. Montreal: Editions du jour.

Leslie, Peter (1977) "Ethnic Hierarchies and Minority Consciousness in Quebec." In *Must Canada Fail?*, edited by R. Simeon. Montreal: McGill-Queen's University Press.

Lévesque, René (1968) *Option Quebec*. Montreal: Edition de l'homme.

Lieberson, S. (1970) *Language and Ethnic Relations in Canada*. New York: Wiley.

——— (1981) *Language Diversity and Language Contact*. Stanford, Calif.: Stanford University Press.

Lijphart, A. (1969) *Politics in Europe*. New York: Prentice-Hall.

Mackay, W. F. (1962) "The Description of Bilingualism." *Canadian Journal of Linguistics* 7:51–85.

McRae, K. (1974) *Consotiational Democracy*. Toronto: McClellan.

——— (1975) "The Principle of Territoriality and the Principle of Personality in Multilingual States." *International Journal of the Sociology of Language* 4:33–54.

McRoberts, Kenneth, and Dale Postgate (1980) *Quebec: Social Change and Political Crisis*. Toronto: McClelland and Stewart.

Mallea, John (1977) *Quebec's Language Policy: Background and Response*. Quebec: Presses de l'Université Laval.

Milner, Henry (1978) *Politics in the New Quebec*. Toronto: McClelland and Stewart.

Monière, Denis (1979) *Les enjeux du référendum*. Montreal: Québec-Amérique.

Mosca, Gaetano (1939) *The Ruling Class.* Translated by Hannah D. Kahn. New York: McGraw-Hill.

Mueller, Siegfried H. (1964) *The World's Living Languages.* New York: Ungar.

Penfield, Wilder, and L. Roberto (1959) *Speech and Brain Mechanisms.* Princeton, N.J.: Princeton University Press.

Pinard, Maurice (1975) "La dualité des loyautés et les options constitutionnelles des québécois francophones." In *Le nationalisme québécois a la croisée des chemins,* edited by Albert Legault. Quebec: Centre québécois de relations internationales, Université Laval.

Pinard, Maurice, and Richard Hamilton (1978) "Le parti québécois Comes to Power: An Analysis of the 1976 Quebec Election." *Canadian Journal of Political Science* 4:739–76.

——— (1977) "The Independence Issue and the Polarization of the Electorate: The 1973 Quebec Election." *Canadian Journal of Political Science* 2:215–60.

Presthus, Robert (1973) *Elite Accommodation in Canadian Politics.* Toronto: Macmillan.

——— (1974) *Elites in the Policy Process.* Cambridge: At the University Press.

Rayside, David M. (1978a) "Federalism and the Party System: Provincial and Federal Liberals in the Province of Quebec." *Canadian Journal of Political Science* 3:499–528.

——— (1978b) "The Impact of the Linguistic Cleavages on the 'Governing' Parties of Belgium and Canada." *Canadian Journal of Political Science* 1:61–98.

Répertoire des parlementaires québécois, 1867–1978 (1980). Quebec, Assemblée Nationale: Service de documentation.

Rioux, Marcel (1976) *La question du Québec.* Montréal: Parti pris.

St. Pierre, Guy (1975) "Le Canada et le nationalisme québécois." In *Le nationalisme québécois a la croisée des chemins,* edited by Albert Legault. Québec: Centre de relations internationales, Université Laval.

Sigelman, Lee, and W. G. Vanderbok (1977) "Legislators, Bureaucrats, and Canadian Democracy: The Long and the Short of It." *Canadian Journal of Political Science* 3:615–24.

Trudeau, Pierre Elliott (1968) *Federalism and the French Canadians.* New York: St. Martin's Press.

Trudel, G. (1982) "Trois Sondages sur le Québec." *Le Devoir,* 20 January, p. 13.

Wade, Mason (1966) *Les canadiens français de 1760 à nos jours.* Montreal: Cercle du livre.

Weinreich, U. (1963) *Languages in Contact.* The Hague: Mouton.

Zolberg, Aristide (1975) "Les nationalismes et le nationalisme québécois." In *La nationalisme québécois a la croisée des chemins,* edited by Albert Legault. Quebec: Centre de relations internationales, Université Laval.

Zukowsky, Ronald James (1981) *Struggle over the Constitution: From the Quebec Referendum to the Supreme Court.* Kingston, Ontario: Queen's University, Institute of Intergovernmental Relations.

Party Activists in Los Angeles, 1963–1978: How Well-Matched Rivals Shape Election Options

Dwaine Marvick

In modern electoral democracies, the organizational workers of rival political parties are actively and consciously engaged in shaping the election day choices available to the voters in their locality. To be effective, the campaigns they mount must be reasonably well matched in scope and impact. To be significant, the election day alternatives they pose must be meaningfully different. To be responsive, the choices they enable voters to make must reflect the changing preferences and political attitudes of the citizenry (Lindsay, 1947; Schumpeter, 1943; Dahl, 1956; Thompson, 1970; Key, 1961).

This paper reports findings from a sequence of seven surveys of Republican and Democratic party activists in Los Angeles County. Over a span of fifteen years, it can be shown that the rival party organizations were closely matched in social credentials, organizational effort, political experience, and competitive flexibility. At the same time, the ideological commitments of party activists are persistent and sharply contrasting. Yet their stands on public issues are also shaped in predictable ways by tactical considerations—by how they see the voters lining up on specific issues and shifting over time. These issue alignment perspectives, in short, reflect both ideological constraint and contextual realism.

It should be noted that in 1963 and 1968, the Los Angeles survey objectives permitted relatively little attention to issues and attitudes, compared with later years. Since 1969 the format of the interview schedule has been largely unchanged. Hence, longitudinal comparisons over the last five biennial surveys are readily made, and most of our attention will center on changes and recurrent patterns in the 1970s. For benchmark purposes, comparisons in terms of social characteristics and political experience are based on all seven waves, from 1963 through 1978.

The findings about rival Los Angeles party activists enable us to examine certain problems in understanding how electoral democracy works from an empirical reference point and not merely in terms of conceptual difficulties or institutional complications. The systemic importance of the political substratum as an active force selectively linking the "opinion" of public politics to the "policies" of governments was stressed by V. O. Key as long ago as 1961. Recently, some of the analytical complexities involved in treating democratic elections as linkage processes crucial to the achievement of representative government have been clarified in symposia edited by Lawson (1979) and Eulau and Wahlke (1978). Following these leads, the essential strategy in looking for connections is heuristic. Linkages provide a sensible starting point for inquiry—a search for empirically demonstrable practices by which opinion and governance are brought into a give-and-take relationship—before dealing with more elusive considerations, such as democracy, responsiveness, leadership, or policymaking.

These theoretical questions about how electoral democracy works will occupy us briefly. Thereafter a detailed presentation of the Los Angeles findings will follow. The analysis is organized first to consider how well-matched the rival party organizations have been during these years. A second consideration turns on how ideologically differentiated from each other the contending sides have been. The final question explored is how party activists with different ideological commitments respond to what are believed to be changing opinion alignments among the voters. On specific issues, as a more conservative mood is detected in the public, for example, do the policy perspectives of activists become more intransigent? More flexible? What are here called *issue alignment perspectives* are used to chart empirically the dynamic relationship between what the party activists themselves prefer and what they see the voters as wanting—that is, between their ideological commitments and their political realism.

Some Considerations about How Electoral Democracy Works

Before turning to the Los Angeles findings, it is relevant to consider, even if briefly, what kind of give-and-take relationship between public opinion and governmental policies is said to prevail in a healthy democratic order, what special significance attaches to the thoughts and actions of those in the political substratum, what is meant by well-matched and nevertheless ideologically differentiated rival parties, and what is involved when party activists change their issue alignment perspectives over time.

Out of prudence, all governments probably pay some attention to opinion patterns among the public. In democracies, political leaders are expected to defer to public preferences and to reconcile public wishes with government policy wherever possible because it is right to do so and not merely because it might seem expedient. Of course, alternative sets of leaders capable of governing and waiting to do so sharpen the sense of vulnerability felt by those in power. As Key observed: "Governments may pay heed to public wishes and preferences in part because of the norms of value and behavior internalized by the impact of the political culture on the political activists. They may also pay heed because of the fear that if they do not do so, another crowd of politicians will" (1961:456).

More problematic is the question of whether political brokers must always assess public opinion, not simply yield to it. Given a cumulative buildup of public sentiment for certain solutions to complex policy breakdowns, leaders may make placatory moves in the short run. But sometimes, the public presses for unrealistic and dangerous actions while many in that same public simultaneously expect their leaders to be prudent and not to accept uncritically an attractive and popular course of action. What is posed is an intricate task, that of "estimating what kinds of people have what opinions and searching for a decision that will give appropriate weights to conflicting equities and interests" (Key, 1961:412). Faced with the puzzle of how democratic regimes manage to work, Key found it plausible to give pivotal weight to the political substratum, its beliefs and its competence:

> The critical element for the health of a democratic order consists in the beliefs, standards and competence of those who constitute the influentials, the opinion leaders, the political activists in the order. . . . the motives that actuate the leadership echelon, the rules of the political game to which it adheres, the expectations which it entertains about its own status in society, and perhaps some of the objective circumstances . . . in which it functions. (1961:558, 537)

It is important that the political substratum includes those who are out of power as well as those defending the government of the day. Governments try to conceal their errors and shortcomings; they try to present their policies and performance in the best light possible. Those in out parties have an adversary role to play—to break the government's information monopoly, to put a different interpretation on events, to expose misdeeds and mistakes, and to stand ready to take over. Moreover, what they stress and what they pass over cumulatively has the consequence of shifting the grounds of political debate. The spokesmen for out parties, by silently or grudgingly accepting a certain policy as a political given after years of calling for a different approach, provide the cues that establish de facto consensus:

Party leaders focus their attention on the attainment of office and are not much disposed to fight for lost causes. They tend to abandon positions that have clearly been rejected by majority opinion. As they do so, they also tend to bring their followers around to acceptance of that which has prevailed. In this manner the minority leadership plays a part in the reconciliation of its followers to the new order of things. (Key, 1961:457)

V. O. Key's discussion of the linkage process centered on institutionalized linkage mechanisms like elections, pressure group tactics, and partisan events. He stressed the contributions of the men and women who provide the personnel for the ancillary machinery of politics, and especially the clumsy far-flung apparatuses of rival political parties. Those at the grass-roots level should not be seen as passive or neutral figures. Typically, they are actively trying to shape opinion, as well as to assess it. Sometimes the opinion configurations of relevant publics on particular issues are remarkably persistent; sometimes they fluctuate. It is up to those who are active in politics to interpret what is happening. The appraisals they make are not necessarily prudent or thoughtful: they are necessarily intuitive, and sometimes they are wrong. In contemporary America, those appraisals are keyed both to calculations about electoral risks and to respect for democratic norms. Commonly, too, the substantive preferences of the political activists and leaders themselves enter significantly into the equation.

At least since Joseph Schumpeter's formulation of how electoral democracy works, it is widely appreciated that reasonably well-matched parties must contend for votes. It is further held that the election day alternatives provided by the rival camps of active partisans must be meaningfully different. A third requirement is commonly added. The options made available to the voters on election day—the issues espoused and the candidates who champion them—should have been fashioned with an eye to what the electorate wants. Serious contenders, genuine options, and thoughtful responsiveness: these are familiar desiderata in rhetorical affirmations of what it takes to make democracy work (1943).

In the arenas of electoral democracy, rival parties typically perform parallel functions; they sponsor candidates for legislative seats and key executive posts in government, and they formulate basic programs calling for government action on various fronts. The key point of such functional redundancy is to create a choice situation—to vest with the electorate the power to hire and fire their leaders. Typically, the election day choice comes to be seen in terms of the leadership styles and policy alternatives for which the rival candidates and contending parties stand. As Schumpeter incisively pointed out many years ago, the electorate possesses this hiring and firing power whenever the rivals compete seriously from roughly equivalent resource positions.

To compete seriously, the rival organizations must be well matched, though to be sure one side may compensate for a lack of money by an abundance of voluntary help. Or when an incumbent legislator can effectively claim to have helped secure popular governmental programs benefitting his constituency, those who want to defeat him may look for a candidate whose personal magnetism and community stature will be effective counterweights. Given these considerations, something that can be called *performance symmetry* is approximated; the election day outcome is doubtful as the day approaches when people go to the polls.

In any constituency there are reasons that rival party organizations will look somewhat alike. Functional grounds exist for expecting considerable performance symmetry. One party's workers are likely to be preoccupied with the same electoral calculations that concern the other party's workers. Tactical questions are posed. What issue publics are worth targeting in this constituency? How can potential support from some visible population segment be translated into actual votes? What campaign appeals are feasible in this locality, and what appeals are likely to fall flat or to boomerang and actually benefit the other side?

Activists who are instrumentally oriented toward winning the election probably tend to become more professional in their outlook. They have reason to value and want to acquire the basic skills of the practicing politician—namely, as Lasswell emphasized, the ability to trace influence relationships and to anticipate changes in what influential people want (1977). More prosaically, a practical politician cultivates three key skills: how to organize events, how to communicate arguments, and how to analyze political realities.

For rival party activists to be effective, then, the campaigns they mount must be reasonably well matched in scope and impact. The election has to be seriously in doubt.

But this does not necessarily mean that the election day choice will be meaningful or significant. The rival candidates may be very much alike; their programs on many counts may be quite similar. Once in power, the former outs may and sometimes do behave very much as did the now former ins. It is necessary to ask whether the rival parties stand for alternative styles of governing, for alternative philosophies of conserving and changing society, for alternative programs of public policy.

It is necessary, in short, to establish in what sense the rival parties are asymmetrical. In part, the answer can be found by tracing the stable coalitions of support that back the winning and losing sides. If it is true that one party finds its core support in certain strata and segments of the community, while its rival champions the interests and aspirations of other subcommunities, compositional asymmetry can be said to persist. The social composition of each party mirrors its strong ties to certain geographic, ethnic, and social status groupings. Eldersveld, in his Detroit investigations, has noted how both parties there sought to compensate for their weakness in certain "social credentials" by bringing forward to make the party's case spokesmen with the right speech habits, life-style, and community access (1964, chaps. 3–5).

When attention turns to the substance of policy alternatives, as pressed for by those actively bent on shaping the election day choice to their liking, ideological asymmetry may emerge. It is quite possible for rival parties to be well matched in social credentials and campaign resources and nevertheless to be weighted sharply in opposite directions when it comes to philosophies of public policy. In a political community where rival parties draw significant support from many of the same groupings and segments of the population, each may reasonably claim the energies of a representative cross section. In democratic politics, however, ideological considerations commonly cause political activists of roughly the same social background and status to become advocates of quite different philosophies of government. One party tends to be dominated by defenders of the established interests of the political community; the other comes to include many who champion the needs of subordinate groups.

Just as the probability of closely contested elections is greater when the rival camps of activists are well-matched contending forces, so too it can be said that the probability of meaningful choices for the voters is heightened when each rival party organization is a distinctive ideological rallying point.

A third consideration must be raised. Are party activists with strongly held ideological views able to be responsive to what they acknowledge are changes in voter opinion on current issues of public policy? Alternatively, how thoughtfully aware of the long-run implications of revamping one's stand to make it more popular are those party activists whose ideological commitments are not strong? Political brokers hold policy views that are flexible and that offer the possibility of reconciling and harmonizing the interests of different groups. They are found among the activists in most seriously contending party organizations. They are called opportunists, temporizers, self-centered, and worse by those who think of themselves as political ideologues. By the same token, those who strive for a logically defensible and internally consistent philosophy about the scope of government, the priority of conflicting values, and the utility of principles applied to real cases—whether conservative or liberal in conventional American parlance—are likely to be called stubborn, unfeeling, doctrinaire, and worse by those who think of themselves as pragmatists. As McClosky and others have noted, two contrasting views of American parties prevail. Some see them as ideological vehicles driven by zealots; others view them as brokerage organizations run by opportunists. In many cases, no doubt, the organizational roster includes men and women whose outlook comes close to one pole or the other, as well as many whose perspectives are more complicated, more cluttered, and less conventional than these extremes suggest (McClosky, Hoffman, and O'Hara, 1960).

Sizing up the electorate, no doubt some activists feel themselves to be isolated and out of step. What all the voters seem to want, they feel, is wrong and should be opposed. Others might find themselves elated as they see a popular consensus develop that calls for action which they have long advocated and tried to mobilize support for in vain. Still others may see the electorate increasingly split along partisan lines, with their side largely taking one stand on the issue in question but opposed by the ranks of the rival party, most of whom take the opposite view. Finally, too, there must be those who could be called conflicted advocates of a policy, because they find it is opposed by most of their own party followers but liked and championed by the rival group.

These are what will be called issue alignment perspectives characterized as leftist or rightist and measured empirically over a ten-year period in the Los Angeles project. Operationally defined, such issue alignment perspectives are the personal policy preferences (for or against more governmental action on a given issue) of party activists when interpreted in light of the expectations of those same activists about the current issue preferences of "most" Republican voters and "most" Democratic voters in their locality.

In each party, how to adjust to changing voter preferences on the issues of the day is a recurrent problem that pits pragmatists against ideologues and creates dissension and controversy. Throughout the 1970s in Los Angeles County, it can be shown that the rival party apparatuses were closely matched in social credentials, organizational resources, and competitive flexibility. Typically, they also provided quite different ideological rallying points. In each party, a dominant ideology was apparent in the issue positions taken by most activists on a wide range of policy questions. At the same time, the ideological commitments of party activists did not prevent them from adjusting to the fact that voters in their locality were changing their stance on public issues over time.

The Los Angeles Party Activist Project: 1963–1978

Over a period of more than fifteen years, a sequence of systematic interview surveys has been carried out in the Los Angeles area, monitoring the backgrounds, activities, and views of Republican and

Democratic activists. Although each survey was in part addressed to research questions that became dated and were not subsequently raised, a conscious effort was made to plan the investigations in ways that would cumulatively facilitate longitudinal and panel analysis.

From the earliest stages, the activists interviewed were asked to characterize their social backgrounds, rearing experiences, and political involvements in various ways. They were asked to classify themselves ideologically—as liberals, moderates, conservatives, radicals, or whatever. In the sequence of five biennial inquiries between 1969 and 1978, what are here called *issue alignment data* were gathered, using virtually the same interview forms. On each occasion, informants were asked to express their policy preferences on the same set of policy issues. They were also asked to say what they believed most voters—Republican and Democratic—in their state assembly district wanted the federal government to do about these same public issues.

An effort has been made to be systematically comparative, trying each year to consider the campaign experiences and political perspectives found among a sample of active Democrats in light of the equivalent phenomena found among a counterpart sample of active Republicans. In all surveys made since 1963, the samples of rival party activists have been matched by using the legal grid imposed by California law on major parties, defining the makeup of their county central committees. For Los Angeles County, the apportionment formula requires equal representation for each of the thirty-one state assembly-district party elements into which the county has been divided. This legal grid ensures geographic diversity. Moreover, the resulting samples give equivalent weight in each party to the currently prevailing range of interparty competition and intraparty factionalism. Technically weighted to eliminate distortions due to minor differences in response rates from particular districts, the completed interviews each time provide well-matched twin samples of "the middlemen of politics" (Marvick, 1967) in Los Angeles— those men and women who have been significantly active in the rival party organizational structures at district and countywide levels in recent years.[1]

Party organizations in Los Angeles are loosely knit structures. At the locality or neighborhood level, voluntary political clubs flourish in both parties. At the state assembly and congressional district levels, there are persistent nuclei of organizational activity. Except for campaign finances to some degree, virtually no direction or control is exercised by either party's countywide structure (Wilson, 1962; Crouch, Bollens, and Scott, 1978).

Under such conditions, grass-roots workers are indispensable to partisan campaign efforts, especially for legislative posts in constituencies too small geographically to permit reliance on the media-centered campaign technology that came to dominate statewide races in the 1970s. They add a personal touch to the standardized campaign themes stressed in mailouts, handouts, billboards, and spot announcements. Whether they make speeches, contact voters face-to-face or by phone, or simply engage in informal politicking with their daily associates, these party activists to convey more than the basic campaign messages. Inevitably, by their appearance, words, and gestures, they indicate the kinds of people who support the candidate in question. They also add their own ethical and ideological commentary. The social and political credentials they convey in face-to-face contacts with voters are credentials intertwined and fused with their personal style and status.

Despite noteworthy differences, both parties have been staffed largely by upper-middle-class volunteers. Neither has been able to boast of a roster that could be called a representative cross section of occupations, income levels, educational attainments, or ethnicity. From Table 1, which reports selected social characteristics of party activists from 1963 through 1978, certain conclusions can be drawn.

In each party, three-fourths are married with dependent-age children. About the same percent are men, although this is less true in the more recent years. On average, both committees are coming to include larger segments past the age of forty. In family terms, both parties show steadily greater reliance on parents in their fifties and sixties rather than on younger couples. It appears in the Republican party especially that a good many people under fifty have been opting out of organized involvement at the county level in recent years.

Other contrasts—as well as some similarities—can be found. More than two-thirds of each party's committee roster are college graduates today. But throughout the seventies, nearly half of the Democrats had either professional or graduate-school experience, compared with about two-fifths of the Republicans.

In both parties a mix of executive and professional occupations predominates. Few sales or clerical workers and even fewer blue-collar workers are found. But among Republicans there is a rough balance between the numbers of professional people and business executives; among Democrats the ratio favors those in professional careers by more than two to one. Republicans are somewhat better off financially. Their incomes averaged $23,000 in 1972 and rose by 1978 to $33,000. The corresponding figures for Democrats show a lower average—$20,000 in 1972—and a less dramatic rise—to $27,000—by 1978.

The Republican party is the party of Protestants; Jews make up a substantial segment of the Democratic roster. In the Democratic party, also, the proportion who claim no religious affiliation rose sharply in 1974 and 1976 but declined somewhat in 1978. Only the Democrats have a full complement of Blacks, and neither party is well represented by Chicano activists. It should be noted that since certain assembly districts are overwhelmingly Black or Chicano in Los Angeles County, delegations from these areas do include quite a few minority-group spokesmen to each party's county committee. About 20 percent of our informants say their home districts have no minority voter blocs. Still, at the other extreme, 40 percent in each party report the presence of "large minority blocs" in their home districts, a fact that is seldom reflected in the composition of their delegations.

In 1978 the average Republican activist claimed 36 years of California residence, 14 in his or her current abode. For the average Democrat, the figures were 31 years in the state, 13 at the current address. Since on average the Republicans are somewhat older, these slight residential differences probably are side effects of that fact. Again, about half the Republicans and two-fifths of the Democrats had grown up in a western state. As for those from other regions, a slightly disporportionate number of Democrats from the South and Republicans from the Midwest could be discerned. Only in big-city backgrounds did the parties differ much: 50 percent of the Democrats and only 30 percent of the Republicans reported having grown up in such places.

There are, then, a few persistent differences that create special advantages in social access for one party and handicap its rival, especially when it comes to religious and ethnic credentials. But the basic similarity of the organization roster of the two rival parties is quite clear—on counts of age, family status, length of residence, amount of education, and even in terms of jobs and income levels.

Party organizations that depend heavily upon volunteers for their manpower needs are probably more likely to draw middle-class participants than do party organizations that operate on a patronage and spoils basis, as do the older urban machines of the East and the Midwest. Early studies of Chicago (Wilson, 1962; Forthal, 1946; Gosnell, 1937), of upstate New York (Mosher, 1935), and of New York City (Peel, 1935; Blank, Hirschfield, and Swanson, 1962) all indicated that party workers were drawn more heavily from lower segments of the social structure. Politics was formerly a career avenue neglected by the middle classes, so to speak. Nor was it often a middle-class hobby. Recent studies of campaign volunteers tend to reverse this staffing picture (Conway and Feigert, 1968). In Detroit, however, Eldersveld's 1956 data showed a sharp contrast between the working-class ranks of the Democratic party and the middle-class composition of its Republican rival (1964).

It is one thing for the organizational rosters of rival parties to be well matched in the social credentials they can boast—even if both were similarly handicapped by the absence of, say, working-class activists, as is the case in the Los Angeles area. It is a different and

TABLE 1.
Selected Social Characteristics of Rival Party Activists
Los Angeles County, 1963–1978

Cases:	Republican Activists								Democratic Activists							
	L78	L76	L74	L72	L69	L68	L63	Total	L78	L76	L74	L72	L69	L68	L63	Total
	88	173	144	183	216	198	275	1275	119	186	130	178	222	194	160	1190
	(%)	(%)	(%)	(%)	(%)	(%)	(%)	(%)	(%)	(%)	(%)	(%)	(%)	(%)	(%)	(%)
1. Age:																
To 40	26	25	25	31	31	37	42	33	40	33	40	41	40	36	40	38
41–50	18	34	38	33	37	33	32	33	24	29	24	29	37	41	33	32
51 plus	55	41	37	36	32	30	26	34	36	38	36	30	23	23	27	30
Average	50	48	47	45	47	46	44	46	45	46	44	44	44	44	44	44
2. Sex:																
Male	61	76	75	67	81	79	78	75	68	70	71	77	79	75	82	75
3. Family:																
Nonparents under 46	13	16	17	14	10	12	14	14	30	22	23	22	15	14	10	19
Parents, in 30s	12	12	11	15	19	21	25	18	10	12	19	17	22	24	29	19
Parents, in 40s	20	25	33	36	33	34	33	31	21	19	22	27	34	40	29	28
Parents, in 50s+	47	39	33	32	30	25	15	29	31	37	27	29	26	19	18	27
Older nonparents: 46+	8	8	6	3	8	8	13	8	8	10	9	5	3	3	14	7
4. California residence:																
Average years	36	34	34	33	*	32	*	33	31	31	30	29	*	29	*	30
5. Current abode:																
Average years	14	14	13	*	*	*	*	13	13	13	13	*	*	*	*	13

	C1	C2	C3	C4	C5	C6	C7	C8	C9	C10	C11	C12	C13	C14	C15	C16	C17
6. Religion:																	
Protestant	69	67	69	77	69	73	75	72	28	27	27	27	37	35	37	39	33
Catholic	19	19	19	15	13	12	14	15	22	20	18	20	19	20	25	27	22
Jewish	3	2	2	3	2	4	2	3	27	22	23	23	23	24	21	23	23
Other	6	2	5	2	10	5	6	5	8	10	7	7	3	7	6	3	6
None	3	10	5	3	6	6	3	5	15	21	25	21	18	14	11	8	16
7. Income (000s)																	
Average	$33	29	25	23	*	*	$25	$27	25	23	20	*	*	*	*		$24
8. Education:																	
Only some college	31	43	35	43	40	35	38	31	31	30	35				41	43	36
Full college	26	20	26	18	31	23	24	18	21	21	10				23	11	17
Graduate or professional schooling	43	37	39	39	29	42	38	51	49	55	44					46	47
9. Occupation:																	
Professional	42	37	39	38	53	*	39	55	46	47	48				68	47	53
Executive–Business	47	32	45	41	25		36	24	23	35	32				14	28	25
Other	11	31	16	21	22		25	21	31	18	20				18	25	22
10. Socio-economic Status:†																	
High	13	13	9	8	14	8	11	11	12	11	12				12	9	11
High middle	48	28	51	39	37	42	41	46	43	42	41				37	45	42
Low middle	35	48	33	36	32	43	38	29	32	38	34				35	36	34
Low	4	11	7	17	17	7	10	14	13	9	13				16	10	13

*Data not available in comparable form.

†SES index gives equal weight to measures of income, education, and occupation.

more immediately relevant and practical question to ask how well-matched the Republicans and the Democrats have been in the amount and quality of campaign effort and political experience they have been able to mobilize. Table 2 reports a number of pertinent features for the Los Angeles rival organizations, covering the years 1963 to 1978.

In Los Angeles both parties continue to draw heavily upon middle-aged, middle-class men and women whose voluntary commitment to party work both during and between campaigns is often constant and great, although their ranks have thinned in recent years. Over the fifteen-year period, about half in each party have been active for more than twelve years; and that proportion has risen somewhat in recent campaigns. At the same time, the proportion of novices, with no more than eight years experience, has declined in both parties—steadily in the Republican case, more erratically for the Democrats.

In each party, fewer than half reported themselves "very active" in 1976 in voluntary club work, despite the fact that they were elected delegates from their areas to the county committee. And this figure is down from over 60 percent in 1972 and over 70 percent in 1968. Year after year, about half report they have "regularly" been involved in party fundraising work.

The rival party rosters do include some public officeholders: about one in every eight or nine persons has held some public elected office, although often it has been a nonpartisan school board or city council post. Perhaps more surprising is the fact that year in and year out, about one in four reports that he or she has held appointed non–civil service governmental jobs at some time since becoming an activist.

But the most striking trend is recorded in the fourth item (under "Cases") of Table 2, where the proportion of those who have ever held a translocal party position, either at the district, county, or state organizational levels (county committee membership of course excluded), shows a precipitate decline in both parties.

In 1968 more than 80 percent in each party had firsthand experience with the planning and coordinating efforts made at a constituency-wide level. Ten years later, fewer than 30 percent could claim equivalent experience. In both parties, the decline is steady from one survey year to the next. Probably it reflects the increasingly nominal role of the countywide party organizations in the conduct of statewide campaigns and also the mounting of legislative contests in particular districts by teams organized by campaign management firms.

Both county committees, to be sure, include many persons with political ambitions. One-third have sought a public office at some time; of these, one third have been successful. Nearly half declare-

they are willing to take "a position of responsibility in the party organization" if asked. But in both parties this figure is down to roughly one-third in the most recent survey (1978).

Asked why people like themselves have been active in organizational party politics, our Republican and Democratic informants were much alike in the reasons stressed: to influence election results (86 percent Republicans, 82 percent Democrats); to shape public policies (70 percent Republicans, 71 percent Democrats); and to gain a voice in party affairs (58 percent Republicans, 57 percent Democrats). Although three other reasons are much less often stressed, it is noteworthy that on all three of these possibly minor considerations, twice as many Democrats as Republicans did acknowledge their importance: to achieve community recognition (14 percent Republicans, 29 percent Democrats); to build one's own political career (14 percent Republicans, 28 percent Democrats); and to make social contacts (9 percent Republicans, 20 percent Democrats).

These patterns and trends in the kind of political experience and effort mobilized by the rival parties over the last twelve year in Los Angeles at the countywide level are not easy to interpret. Evidently some major changes in the kinds of activists who serve on their party's countywide body are occurring in both parties. Both the Republican and Democratic organizations are undergoing similar declines in the number of activists who have had—or are willing to take—translocal positions of party responsibility. At the same time, there are fewer activists with relatively brief records of party experience available; fewer seem to want such experience. But the rival organizations appear to be suffering in equal measure.

Moreover, these changes are apparently not related to partisan constituency level advantages, which have remained almost unchanged during these years. By law, all parts of Los Angeles County are represented on each party's county committee. As noted above, each of the thirty-one assembly districts sends a delegation elected at primary time for two-year terms. Year after year, our surveys show that about one-third in each party describe their home districts as Republican territory while just under 60 percent say they live in Democratic terrain. About one in six consider their home districts to be competitive ground. From aggregate statistics of the winners of each of the assembly contests in the thirty-one districts over the 1963–1978 period, a similar distribution emerges when the winning margin is set at plus or minus ten percentage points. These two measures—one a subjective assessment, the other from voting statistics—permit us to distinguish year by year each party's strongholds, lost ground, and competitive turf. None of the measures of political experience or organizational participation and campaign effort varied discernibly by the political character of these home districts.

TABLE 2.

Selected Political Attributes of Rival Party Activists
Los Angeles County, 1963–1978

Cases:	Republican Activists								Democratic Activists							
	L78	L76	L74	L72	L69	L68	L63	Total	L78	L76	L74	L72	L69	L68	L63	Total
	88	173	144	183	216	198	275	1275	119	186	130	178	222	194	160	1190
	(%)	(%)	(%)	(%)	(%)	(%)	(%)	(%)	(%)	(%)	(%)	(%)	(%)	(%)	(%)	(%)
1. Years active in politics																
Up to 8 years	16	22	20	24	29	38	48	31	20	31	32	26	27	27	40	29
Nine to 12	19	23	21	25	26	14	14	20	16	14	20	25	23	20	14	19
More than 12	65	55	59	51	45	48	38	49	64	55	48	49	50	53	46	52
Average (years)	11	16	16	16	15	16	13	15	19	15	15	16	15	16	15	16
2. Has held public elected office	14	14	7	10	13	13	*	12	9	7	9	13	23	15	*	14
3. Has held appointed governmental position	26	21	27	28	*	19	*	24	25	31	24	28	*	30	*	28
4. Has held translocal party position	30	37	40	46	67	80	*	53	15	30	40	45	69	83	*	51
5. Is "very active" in voluntary party clubs	52	45	54	60	56	70	*	47	63	50	49	63	53	74	*	59

6. "Regularly" helps in party fundraising work	52	40	37	57	76	54	*	54	43	44	36	43	55	70	*	50
7. Hours per week spent on party work																
Up to 10	48	76	73	40	75	46		59	49	62	65	41	63	44		54
Eleven to 20	16	17	17	21	15	24		19	16	20	21	22	24	21		21
Over 20	36	7	10	39	10	30		22	35	18	14	37	13	35		25
Average	20	9	11	20	9	18		14	19	13	14	20	12	20		16
8. Public offices ever sought																
None	66	65	70	70	65	72	*	68	67	73	71	62	57	70	*	66
Once	25	24	20	24	22	21		22	29	23	21	28	30	26		27
Repeatedly	9	11	10	6	13	7		10	4	4	8	10	13	4		7
9. Willing to take responsible party post:																
Definitely	35	33	48	48	57	56	*	48	32	42	45	56	51	51	*	47
Probably	28	39	27	28	17	19		25	39	33	41	27	20	23		29
No	37	28	25	24	26	25		27	29	25	14	17	29	26		24

*Data not available in comparable form.

The Ideological Wings of Rival Major Parties in Los Angeles

It is one of the distinctive features of American politics that we have maintained a two-party system despite many changes in our social and economic order and despite the political tensions created by those underlying processes of change. Europeans have often acknowledged the role of ideology as a force maintaining the identity of parties and sparking competition between them, a practice which in turn makes election day choice more meaningful. For a long time, American political parties have been seen as essentially non-ideological in character.

Cooperation with certain enduring special interests, rather than political convictions about complex issues, is said to be the basic characteristic of American parties. Another common view is that the characteristics are emotional attachment to symbols of party, which often have regional or ethnic loyalties fused with them. Maurice Duverger, in his comparative study of political parties, discussed the non-principled nature of American parties:

> The two parties are rival teams, one occupying office and the other seeking to dislodge it. It is a struggle between the ins and the outs, which never becomes fanatical, and creates no deep cleavage in the country. (1952:15)

Duverger concluded that the result was to take from the election outcome any valid claim to be a popular choice between policies. Apart from the ambiguity of his particular conception of ideology, his conclusion continues to be widely accepted by many political scientists and observers of the American party system. These views, however, bear little relationship to the findings in our Los Angeles surveys. Each party has a dominant ideological wing and a moderate, pragmatic alternative wing. Within each party those who belong in each wing hold strikingly different views on a broad spectrum of public issues. Between the two parties, moreover, the contrast is not only striking when the policy preferences of Republican conservatives are compared with those of Democratic liberals; it is also quite apparent when moderate Republicans and moderate Democrats are contrasted.

When party activists were asked what differences they felt existed between parties, they regularly answered in rudimentary ideological terms. They were quite willing to characterize themselves as liberals, moderates, or conservatives. They found no difficulty comparing their own ideological position with the same position held by their friends, families, job associates, neighbors, or fellow party activists. These were conventional terms, used matter-of-factly by our informants. As a term of self-description, the man or woman using the word *liberal* means something left of moderate; preferring the term *con-servative* meant something right of moderate. Yet only a handful of Democrats called themselves conservatives, and only a handful of Republicans were willing to use the term *liberal* about themselves. In each party, *moderate* was the preferred term used by those who felt they did not share the dominant ideological viewpoint.

In each Los Angeles survey, informants were asked to express their personal policy preferences on a set of public issues. In form, they were asked whether they wanted to see more, less, or the current level of federal action on each policy front. Since 1969, seven issues have been common to all batteries. Table 3 discloses the pattern, using a composite measure based on those seven issues and trans-forming the ordinal scale posed in the questions themselves into ratio-of-support scores. The positions on this Left-to-Right scale range from a leftist call for more federal action at one pole to a rightist call for less action at the opposite pole; those satisfied with the current level of federal action scored near the midpoint.

Republicans are not like Democrats, ideologically speaking, even when they consider themselves moderates. An average of nineteen points separates them over the ten-year period. To be sure, the con-trast is even greater—50 points—between Republican conservatives and Democratic liberals. Neither party is monolithic, however. An average of seventeen points divides moderates and conservatives in the Republican organization, while liberals and moderates in the

TABLE 3.

Policy Preferences of Activists in Different Ideological Wings of the Rival Major Parties (In ratio-of-support scores from "Rightist" 0.0 to "Leftist" 1.0)

	Republican Conservatives	Republican Moderates	Democratic Moderates	Democratic Liberals
1978	.27	.42	.60	.78
1976	.29	.47	.67	.83
1974	.31	.50	.74	.85
1972	.37	.53	.75	.88
1969	.47	.63	.76	.86
Ten-year average	.34	.51	.70	.84
		Difference RC:RM	Difference RM:DM	Difference DM:DL
1978		.15	.18	.18
1976		.18	.20	.16
1974		.19	.24	.11
1972		.16	.22	.13
1969		.16	.13	.10
Ten-year average		.17	.19	.14

Democratic camp are typically fourteen points apart on these issues. It should be noted also that all four groupings are moving to the right, over time. This trend is quite marked for both wings of the Republican party, less sharp for Democratic moderates, and least evident for Democratic liberals.

More than twenty years ago, in an influential article, "Issue Conflict and Consensus among Party Leaders and Followers," Herbert McClosky and two associates (1960) gathered data from the mid-1950s that enabled them to compare the issue preferences of equivalent sets of Republican and Democratic party leaders—specifically, those who were delegates at the 1956 presidential nominating conventions and who answered their questionnaire. Shortly thereafter, the same questionnaire was administered to a cross section sample of the American electorate who indicated themselves to be "party followers."

The findings in that study established in some detail (a) that there were consistent, substantial, and predictable ideological differences between the rival party leadership groups, thus defined; (b) that ordinary Republican followers in the electorate held views on many issues that were quite similar to the view of ordinary Democratic voters also; and (c) more surprising, that the views of the Democratic leaders were quite close to those held by both Republican followers and Democratic followers among the citizenry, while the views of Republican leaders were quite distant from both kinds of party followers in the electorate. In short, the Republican leadership group was off in right field—out of touch with its own partisan following in the electorate and presumably even more distant from the floating vote needed to carry any closely contested national election. It was, of course, a period of Republican ascendancy under President Eisenhower; in any event, the markedly rightist views on public policies of the Republican leadership group did not affect the 1956 outcome in November. By implication, however, Republican leaders were not filling any brokerage roles by taking policy positions reasonably close to those of the voting groups whose support the party needed. They could be said to have provided an ideological rallying point on the political Right, to which like-minded voters could turn. But in 1956 the Democrats seemingly had successfully combined both objectives, creating a clearly leftist rallying point and finding it relatively attractive not only to Democratic followers but to Republican voters as well. Of course, the 1956 election was not an ideological contest; and Eisenhower did win.

In the Los Angeles party activist surveys (the instrument is reproduced in Figure 1), we have no interviews with ordinary party followers in the electorate. Thus it is not possible to carry out an inquiry strictly parallel to McClosky's. But a somewhat closely related question can be explored with our data, on which bears on a point in

FIGURE 1.
Instrument to Gather Issue Alignment Data: 1969–1978

Selected Public Issues:	YOUR PERSONAL VIEW: In this field, the federal government should do:			YOUR FEELING THAT IN THIS ASSEMBLY DISTRICT					
				probably most DEMOCRATIC VOTERS want the federal government to do:			probably most REPUBLICAN VOTERS want the federal government to do:		
	more	same	less	more	same	less	more	same	less
Work for nuclear disarmament									
Control the cost of living									
Cut defense spending									
Expand opportunities for poor									
Get tough with urban violence									
Stop air and water pollution									
Desegregate housing and schools									
Control illegal traffic in drugs									
Eliminate sex discrimination									
Achieve workable gun-control laws									

political linkage theory that V. O. Key (1961) stressed—namely, the importance of leadership discretion and the need to assess public opinion in the process of taking it into account. Each year, out party activists were asked to say where they believed "most Democratic voters" and "most Republican voters" in their home districts stood on the amount of federal intervention needed to cope with each of the seven public issues. Table 4 reports these data. Paralleling Mc-Closky, we have computed ratio-of-support scores and the ideological distance (on the resulting Left-Right scale) between activists and (perceived) voting blocs measured.

TABLE 4.

Issue Preferences of Party Activists, Their Appraisals of Voter Preferences, and the Ideological Distance between Activists and Voters in 1969, 1972, 1974, 1976, and 1978

(In 'ratio of support' scores from 0.0 to 1.0)

	Issue Preferences of		What Most Demo. Voters Want according to		What Most Repub. Voters Want according to		Ideological Distance Between			
	Demo. Activists	Repub. Activists	Demo. Activists	Repub. Activists	Demo. Activists	Repub. Activists	Demo. Voters and Demo. Activists	Demo. Voters and Repub. Activists	Repub. Voters and Demo. Activists	Repub. Voters and Repub. Activists
Seven Issue Average										
1978	.78	.35	.65	.73	.27	.32	+.13	−.38	+.51	+.03
1976	.72	.33	.62	.65	.25	.29	+.10	−.32	+.47	+.04
1974	.80	.39	.68	.73	.30	.37	+.12	−.34	+.50	+.02
1972	.84	.45	.67	.69	.35	.43	+.17	−.24	+.49	+.02
1969	.83	.51	.63	.70	.39	.49	+.20	−.19	+.44	+.02
Help Poor People										
1978	.85	.45	.64	.82	.13	.29	+.21	−.37	+.72	+.16
1976	.89	.32	.74	.88	.16	.33	+.15	−.56	+.73	−.01
1974	.91	.37	.75	.86	.18	.34	+.16	−.49	+.73	+.03
1972	.94	.53	.72	.85	.20	.50	+.22	−.32	+.74	+.03
1969	.96	.53	.68	.80	.22	.44	+.28	−.27	+.74	+.09
Cut Defense Spending										
1978	.82	.14	.65	.74	.16	.13	+.17	−.60	+.66	+.01
1976	.85	.23	.68	.72	.15	.16	+.17	−.49	+.70	+.07
1974	.89	.34	.74	.74	.20	.27	+.15	−.40	+.69	+.07
1972	.87	.33	.67	.65	.24	.30	+.20	−.32	+.63	+.03
1969	.86	.54	.60	.71	.36	.47	+.26	−.17	+.50	+.07
Speed Desegregation										
1978	.65	.16	.45	.51	.05	.13	+.20	−.35	+.60	+.03
1976	.79	.20	.55	.64	.12	.20	+.24	−.44	+.67	.00
1974	.78	.24	.52	.68	.12	.21	+.26	−.44	+.66	+.03
1972	.86	.29	.50	.59	.18	.28	+.36	−.30	+.68	+.01
1969	.87	.41	.49	.67	.21	.35	+.38	−.26	+.66	+.06

Get Nuclear Disarmament

1978	.83	.40	.74	.70	.19	.37	+.09	−.30	+.64	+.03
1976	.89	.49	.77	.82	.40	.43	+.12	−.33	+.49	+.06
1974	.89	.53	.78	.79	.40	.47	+.11	−.26	+.49	+.06
1972	.90	.49	.79	.77	.42	.46	+.11	−.28	+.48	+.03
1969	.87	.46	.64	.73	.36	.43	+.23	−.27	+.51	+.03

Control Cost of Living

1978	.93	.60	.93	.86	.68	.62	.00	−.26	+.25	−.02
1976	.90	.48	.91	.89	.46	.51	−.01	−.41	+.44	−.03
1974	.93	.54	.96	.91	.56	.62	−.03	−.37	+.37	−.08
1972	.89	.60	.90	.79	.54	.60	−.01	−.19	+.35	.00
1969	.86	.59	.84	.79	.70	.71	+.02	−.20	+.16	−.11

Curb Water & Air Pollution

1978	.83	.47	.82	.67	.44	.40	+.01	−.20	+.39	+.07
1976	.92	.54	.80	.81	.51	.50	+.12	−.27	+.41	+.04
1974	.92	.59	.85	.84	.55	.59	+.07	−.25	+.37	.00
1972	.98	.73	.93	.88	.82	.74	+.05	−.15	+.16	−.01
1969	.99	.86	.92	.89	.81	.84	+.07	−.03	+.18	+.02

(Don't) Get Tough w. Urban Violence

1978	.14	.12	.12	.23	.12	.12	+.02	−.11	+.02	.00
1976	.19	.22	.12	.33	.09	.14	+.07	−.11	−.10	+.08
1974	.25	.15	.13	.31	.09	.10	+.12	−.16	+.16	+.05
1872	.41	.18	.19	.27	.07	.13	+.22	−.09	+.34	+.05
1969	.39	.19	.23	.30	.08	.22	+.16	−.11	+.31	−.03

One issue, whether to "get tough with urban violence," has been reverse-scored.

As that table shows, on virtually every issue there is an impressive degree of cognitive agreement about where the two voting blocs stand. Democratic activists and Republican activists have quite sharply contrasting personal issue preference patterns. But they locate each bloc of voters at much the same point along the Left-Right scale. On the average for seven issues, the ratings given by both party activist panels about where Democratic voters stood hovered between 0.65 and 0.70, year after year, while Republican voters were judged to stand at around 0.33; and year after year the Republican party activists located each set of voters slightly more to the political Left than did the Democratic activists. Close inspection also shows that with only slight exceptions both groups of party activists judged the Republican voters to be moving toward the political Right during these years. As for the Democratic voters, there is little evidence of a trend. On six of the seven issues, it should be noted that both sets of activist judges agree that Democratic voters are not close to Republican voters but instead stand markedly to the left.

Table 4 also measures ideological distance that separates each group of party activists from what they believe to be the typical stand taken by their own party followers and the rival party's followers among the voters in their legislative districts. The patterns show remarkably little variation from question to question, and clear longitudinal patterns hold across many of the issues. Figure 2 provides a graphic picture of how differently the rival activists locate themselves in ideological space relative to the two voting blocs.

Year after year the Democratic activists as a group stand conspicuously to the political left of Republican voters and rather substantially also to the left of Democratic voters. But while the distance separating them from their own party's voters fluctuates slightly from year to year, the Democratic activists see the Republican voting bloc as being far to their political right and moving even farther every year.

Quite a different picture characterizes the political world of Republican activists. Year after year, they themselves are moving to the political Right. Year after year, they also see themselves occupying almost the same ideological position on these seven issues as the modal position which they attribute to Republican voters locally. And year after year, they locate the Democratic voters far to the Left, agreeing with their Democratic counterparts on this point. The net effect, since both they and their party supporters in the local electorate are steadily moving rightward, is for the distance separating them from Democratic voters to increase noticeably.

Four conclusions seem warranted. First, the ideological contrast on issues is sharp between our samples of rival activists. Second, both locate Republican and Democratic voting blocs at roughly the same contrasting places in ideological space. Third, neither sees

FIGURE 2.
Ideological Distance between the Policy Preference Positions of Rival Party
Activists and Where They Believe Democratic and Republican Voters
Stand, on a Composite Index Measuring Seven Policy Issues, in Los An-
geles Assembly Districts, 1969–1978 (in 'ratio of support' scores from 0.0
to 1.0)

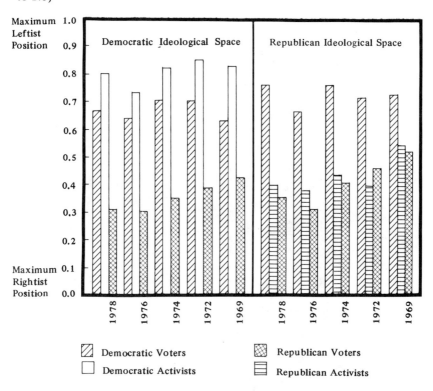

itself as ideologically distant from its own partisan voter following.
Finally, neither appears to see its own ideological position as very
attractive politically to the rival party's local following.

Note that while McClosky's data base permitted him to examine
the coincidence of issues positions modally taken by party leaders
and party followers, the Los Angeles data enable us to say nothing
directly about the electorate. Our data do let us examine the ideological terrain in the electorate as viewed from the perspective of party
activists, however. In Table 4, the modal preferences and perceptions
of rival activists are reported, year by year and issue by issue.

So far, however, we have not looked at the set of scores registered
by a given activist. We have not tried to characterize his or her issue
alignment perspective. Table 5, which presents an eightfold typology
of such perspectives, does this, showing the frequency, year by year,

TABLE 5.
The Issue Alignment Perspectives of Partisan Ideological Types: 1969 to 1978

Pattern: Own View : Own Party Voters : Rival Party Voters	Isolated Leftist Left Right Right (%)	Mainstream Leftist Left Left Left (%)	Conflicted Leftist Left Right Left (%)	Partisan Leftist Left Left Right (%)	Partisan Rightist Right Right Left (%)	Conflicted Rightist Right Left Right (%)	Mainstream Rightist Right Right Right (%)	Isolated Rightist Right Left Left (%)	Total	N
Seven-Issue Average										
Republican conservatives										
1978	2	8	6	6	44	4	22	8	100	43
1976	2	9	4	6	59	1	14	5	100	86
1974	3	9	4	7	54	2	14	7	100	78
1972	3	14	5	7	40	1	24	6	100	91
1969	8	24	7	7	24	2	16	12	100	111
Republican moderates										
1978	6	11	9	13	31	3	22	6	100	26
1976	9	10	12	12	35	2	16	4	100	55
1974	3	18	12	9	33	1	18	6	100	47
1972	4	24	10	10	26	—	22	4	100	62
1969	7	28	15	9	16	3	11	11	100	59

Democratic moderates										
1978	7	10	2	43	11	10	15	2	100	30
1976	9	11	2	42	10	7	16	3	100	45
1974	7	16	1	50	30	11	9	3	100	20
1972	12	22	2	41	5	5	10	3	100	49
1969	21	27	3	27	7	4	8	3	100	66
Democratic liberals										
1978	17	12	4	45	3	9	9	1	100	65
1976	19	11	1	55	3	1	9	1	100	105
1974	17	13	1	57	3	2	6	1	100	82
1972	18	17	1	53	1	1	7	2	100	110
1969	27	24	3	37	2	1	3	3	100	110
Composite Alignment: 7 Issues										
Republican conservatives	4	14	5	6	43	2	18	8	100	396
Republican moderates	6	20	12	10	27	2	17	6	100	246
Democratic moderates	13	19	2	37	7	7	12	3	100	209
Democratic liberals	20	16	2	49	2	2	7	2	100	471

with which self-characterized "conservative," "moderate," and "liberal" party activists look at a set of contemporary issues from each of these possible—and quite independently defined—issue alignment perspectives.

Carried even further, as we shall see at least illustratively, these data permit us to characterize each year the perspective of each individual party activist on each issue. Table 6 gives a separate breakdown of such perspectives for each of the seven issues but omits the year-by-year trends which replicate the patterns.

A perspective, following Lasswell and Kaplan (1950: chap. 2), is "a pattern of identifications, preferences, and supporting expectations." Logically, eight options can be distinguished. In practice, on issue after issue, each activist group tends to by typified by one or two perspectives; but there are always a few colleagues who make quite atypical diagnoses of the issue alignment picture. Half of the logical options involve expecting the electorate to divide along partisan lines; the other four entail the expectation that both Democratic and Republican voters are largely on the same side of an issue. Looked at another way, four options apply to activists who personally take a leftist stand on the issue in question, and the other half are for those who prefer rightist policy.

Consider the combinations. Four otherwise quite different issue alignment perspectives are alike in this: the holder expects the voters of both parties to be largely agreed on the issue stand to be preferred. They come in pairs. On the one hand, a "mainstream rightist" is by definition one who personally prefers a rightist policy and who expects most voters of both parties to agree with him or her. An "isolated leftist" views the electorate the same way, as lined up for a rightist policy. But this activist personally opposes that stand and, hence, is at odds with the electorate, isolated and on the Left. A mirror-image pair of perspectives logically occurs when mainstream leftists are contrasted with isolated rightists. In both cases, the partisan voter blocs are seen as favoring a leftist policy; what varies is the personal preference of the activist— and hence his or her feeling of being supported by the voters or isolated from them.

Four other perspectives include an expectation that the voters will divide along partisan lines in favoring or opposing "more federal action." Again they come in pairs. Persons preferring a leftist policy who see their own party's voting bloc also favoring a leftist policy while also seeing the rival party's voting bloc as taking a rightist stance are said to hold a "partisan leftist" perspective. If the voter alignment were reversed, however, the same persons would hold a "conflicted leftist" view of the issue, seeing more support for their own position coming from the rival camp than from their own party's voters. Again, there is a mirror-image pair of perspectives—those whose view amounts to a "partisan rightist" perspective and those who are "conflicted rightists" on the issue in question.

On some issues, then, certain informants locate both voting blocs on the Left, while other informants place both sets on the Right. Usually when a party-line cleavage is perceived, the Democratic voters are seen on the Left with the Republican voters on the Right. Occasionally, however, it is the other way around.

What do such perspectives tell us? On the one hand, they embody a personal preference; on the other, they entail a voting-bloc appraisal. Over time, either may change; on different issues in the same year, the same activist may hold quite different perspectives. Operationally, these perspectives are defined in purely issue-specific terms, without reference to which party the activists belong to or which way of self-characterizing the ideological stances they adopt. Yet the empirical patterns quite clearly show marked affinities. On most issues, as Table 6 shows, Democratic liberals take a partisan leftist view, while Republican conservatives, viewing the electorate the same way, espouse a partisan rightist perspective. In both cases, their moderate colleagues less often take these partisan viewpoints. Very rarely, a few Republicans take a partisan leftist stance. Even fewer Democrats occasionally take the partisan rightist view on an issue. Although uncommon for any activist, the conflicted leftist perspective is most likely to be espoused by Republican moderates. Similarly, if anyone takes up the conflicted rightist view of an issue, the person is likely to be a Democratic moderate.

When those perspectives that entail consensus among the voters are examined, certain other features come to light. In general, as Table 5 discloses, the mainstream leftist perspective declined sharply from 1969 to 1978, about equally so for all types of activists in both parties. In a less clear-cut manner, the mainstream rightist viewpoint tended to grow somewhat over these same years and for all types of activists. Dovetailed to this, it is noteworthy that the isolated leftist perspective, year after year, and on issue after issue, is adopted most often by Democratic liberals rather than their more moderate colleagues. And the isolated rightist view of issues, if taken up at all, is most likely to be espoused by Republican conservatives.

It is only when specific issues are examined year by year that some of the dynamics of changing perspectives are readily observed. Consider the Democrats on the issue of curbing urban violence; the respondents' percentage of agreement with the statement that "the federal government should do more to get tough on urban violence" is presented in Table 7.

On this issue, the shifts seem to entail the abandonment of personal preference and not any change in what the voters are expected to prefer. Thus Democratic moderates in 1969 were mainstream

TABLE 6.
The Issue Alignment Perspectives of Partisan Ideological Types: Seven Key Issues

Pattern: Own View : Own Party Voters : Rival Party Voters	Isolated Leftist Left Right Right (%)	Mainstream Leftist Left Left Left (%)	Conflicted Leftist Left Right Left (%)	Partisan Leftist Left Left Right (%)	Partisan Rightist Right Right Left (%)	Conflicted Rightist Right Left Right (%)	Mainstream Rightist Right Right Right (%)	Isolated Rightist Right Left Left (%)	Total	N
Alignment on nuclear disarmament policy										
Republican conservatives	3	14	5	6	48	2	14	8	100	394
Republican moderates	7	17	15	14	28	0	14	5	100	249
Democratic moderates	12	19	3	37	5	8	11	6	100	209
Democratic liberals	17	15	2	59	2	2	2	1	100	473
Alignment on cost of living control policy										
Republican conservatives	2	26	5	8	36	3	7	13	100	397
Republican moderates	2	39	7	11	23	2	5	11	100	250
Democratic moderates	4	35	2	38	6	7	1	7	100	207
Democratic liberals	5	39	1	44	2	4	2	4	100	469
Alignment on defense spending cuts policy										
Republican conservatives	3	6	7	7	51	1	17	8	100	400
Republican moderates	6	9	14	14	34	2	18	3	100	251
Democratic moderates	15	9	2	46	13	5	8	3	100	207
Democratic liberals	19	4	3	67	1	2	2	2	100	475

Alignment on policy of more help for poor

Republican conservatives	3	11	6	7	57	2	7	7	: 100	390
Republican moderates	3	16	17	11	36	1	9	6	: 100	244
Democratic moderates	10	8	2	59	9	7	4	1	: 100	214
Democratic liberals	22	6	1	66	2	2	1	0	: 100	487

Alignment on housing/school desegregation policy

Republican conservatives	4	2	3	5	50	2	25	9	: 100	395
Republican moderates	10	8	11	10	30	2	22	7	: 100	239
Democratic moderates	21	6	3	41	8	7	12	2	: 100	211
Democratic liberals	36	3	2	48	4	2	4	1	: 100	473

Alignment on air/water pollution control policy

Republican conservatives	3	35	6	5	29	1	13	8	: 100	396
Republican moderates	4	44	8	4	18	1	11	10	: 100	243
Democratic moderates	6	50	1	32	3	3	2	3	: 100	212
Democratic liberals	13	40	2	40	1	1	2	1	: 100	475

Alignment on policy to curb urban violence

Republican conservatives	9	4	5	7	30	2	40	3	: 100	402
Republican moderates	8	4	9	7	23	3	43	3	: 100	248
Democratic moderates	23	3	3	10	7	7	46	1	: 100	205
Democratic liberals	30	2	3	20	6	3	35	1	: 100	447

Composite alignment: 7 issues

Republican conservatives	4	14	5	6	43	2	18	8	: 100	396
Republican moderates	6	20	12	10	27	2	17	6	: 100	246
Democratic moderates	13	19	2	37	7	7	12	3	: 100	209
Democratic liberals	20	16	2	49	2	2	7	2	: 100	471

TABLE 7.
Changing Democratic Perspectives: "Get Tough with Urban Violence"

| | Democratic Liberals | | | | Democratic Moderates | | | |
	Mainstream Rightists (%)	Isolated Leftists (%)	Other Types (%)	Total	Mainstream Rightists (%)	Isolated Leftists (%)	Other Types (%)	Total
1978	35	30	35	100	71	0	29	100
1976	53	20	27	100	63	12	25	100
1974	35	25	40	100	39	21	25	100
1972	36	30	34	100	36	30	34	100
1969	12	49	39	100	26	40	34	100
	Rises to 1976 peak	Falls to 1976 low			Rises to 1978 peak	Falls to 1978 low		

rightists on this issue in 26 percent of our cases, while only 12 percent of the Democratic liberals held that perspective. In each group, nearly half felt themselves to be isolated leftists. By 1976 the picture is radically reversed for the Democratic liberals, with only 20 percent now classifiable as isolated leftists but with fully 53 percent taking the mainstream rightist viewpoint. Their view of the voters did not change; their personal position did. By 1978, some of the liberals had returned to their pre-1976 outlook, to be sure; but the Democratic moderates had by then completely abandoned the isolated leftist position. In fact, 71 percent had taken up a mainstream rightist posture on urban violence policy. Moderates are said to be more pragmatic and have fewer ideological qualms about changing positions toward stands that are more popular with the voters. Table 7 gives empirical warrant for such a proposition. But what about the Democratic liberals? Presumably they are party activists whose ideological commitments largely shape the policies they want their party to champion and the stands they want it to avoid. Yet in the face of what they also saw as a persistent and widely shared rightist consensus among local voters on this issue, a large fraction of those liberals apparently changed their minds in 1976. To be sure, by 1978 perhaps half of them had once again taken up the isolated leftist perspective on this policy question. Still, it would appear that they too had been swayed by a desire to be responsive to the local electorate, as they saw it.

Consider another issue. This time, in Table 8, we look at Republican adjustments of perspective on the question of providing greater opportunities for poor people. The table lists percent in agreement with the statement that the federal government should do more to expand opportunities for the poor.

Assuming that much of the shifting observed here was done by the same persons, not only does the sharp rise in partisan rightist views and the concomitant fall in mainstream leftist perspectives imply that some activists—conservatives as well as moderates— changed their own views from leftist to rightist, it also implies that they revised their assessment of how the voters lined up; no longer were most Republicans, as well as most Democrats, seen as wanting more federal action to help poor people. The issue was instead cast in terms of party cleavages at the voter level.

Finally, let us consider the full matrix on yet a third issue, federal policy aimed at curbing air and water pollution. As Table 9 shows, more than two thirds of all four partisan ideological types in 1969 held the mainstream leftist perspective on this issue! By 1978, no more than 21 percent of any group looked at the environmental policy question that way. Instead, the issue had been transformed into a partisan Left versus partisan Right alignment, with Democrats and Republicans alike making appropriate adjustments.

TABLE 8.
Changing Republican Perspectives: "Expand Opportunities for the Poor"

| | Republican Conservatives | | | | Republican Moderates | | | |
	Mainstream Leftists (%)	Isolated Rightists (%)	Other Types (%)	Total	Mainstream Leftists (%)	Isolated Rightists (%)	Other Types (%)	Total
1978	6	51	43	100	7	40	53	100
1976	5	79	16	100	2	48	50	100
1974	2	69	29	100	12	58	30	100
1972	19	50	31	100	25	27	48	100
1969	20	39	44	100	28	16	56	100
	Falls after 1972	Rises to 1976 low			Falls to 1976 low	Rises to 1974 peak		

TABLE 9.
Issue Alignment Perspectives of Partisan Ideological Types, 1978–1969

	Isolated Leftist (%)	Mainstream Leftist (%)	Conflicted Leftist (%)	Partisan Leftist (%)	Partisan Rightist (%)	Conflicted Rightist (%)	Mainstream Rightist (%)	Isolated Rightist (%)	Total : N
Stop Air and Water Pollution									
Republican conservatives									
1978	0	16	9	9	27	4	30	5	: 36
1976	3	12	10	6	46	0	15	8	: 85
1974	5	16	5	7	46	1	11	9	: 77
1972	2	36	7	2	26	1	17	10	: 92
1969	4	73	2	4	7	1	2	7	: 106
Republican moderates									
1978	5	21	8	14	30	0	15	7	: 20
1976	11	11	15	9	25	1	20	8	: 54
1974	0	35	5	7	21	0	16	17	: 46
1972	2	60	5	0	17	0	3	13	: 61
1969	3	69	10	0	7	1	6	4	: 62
Democratic moderates									
1978	8	17	0	47	13	8	4	3	: 25
1976	11	18	1	51	6	1	6	6	: 46
1974	0	38	0	46	0	10	5	0	: 20
1972	5	63	2	27	0	1	0	2	: 50
1969	4	77	0	13	2	2	0	2	: 71
Democratic liberals									
1978	8	21	1	50	2	5	12	1	: 58
1976	27	22	2	45	2	0	2	0	: 104
1974	15	28	5	50	0	1	1	0	: 84
1972	8	45	1	41	0	1	1	3	: 112
1969	8	67	3	20	0	1	1	0	: 118

In the transition years, sizeable numbers of Democratic liberals (27 percent in 1976) had completely revised their electoral assessments without changing their personal preferences. They became isolated leftists because they saw both Democratic and Republican voters going over to a rightist stance. By 1978, 12 percent of them had fully capitulated and on this issue took up a mainstream rightist posture.

In the Republican camp, the shift away from the mainstream leftist view held by so many in 1969 to a partisan rightist perspective for the most part entailed a change of personal preference (from Left to Right) and a corresponding reassessment of where Republican voters stood (on the Right instead of on the Left). In the transition years, both moderates and conservatives showed some tendencies to relocate Democratic voters on the Right as well; in 1978, fully 30 percent of the Republican conservatives thus had completely reversed their perspectives and were mainstream rightists on the pollution issue.

The necessarily selective probes here are intended mainly to illustrate the way in which the notion of issue alignment perspectives enables us to monitor empirically the adjustments which party activists of different ideological persuasions must make from time to time, between what they themselves would prefer by way of government policy and what they see the voters as wanting—that is, between their ideological agenda and their political realism.

To a Democratic activist—and all the more so to a self-styled liberal Democratic activist—conscious of his or her identity as such, merely to have a set of personal preferences on issues of public policy is not necessarily a basis for deciding upon political priorities. Activists have entered politics to affect policy, to shape party decisions, to persuade voters. Their views on issues are not academic once they have been linked to supporting expectations about what the voters want. To some extent, the voters may change; but to some extent, too, it may be necessary for the activists to revise their own agendas.

Let us put it another way. To a Republican woman, thinking of her party activist self and of the policy goals she wants to see implemented by effective campaigning and victory at the polls, it presumably makes a difference whether on certain issues she believes the voters are favorably disposed, while on other issues she thinks them to be split along party lines. If she is self-consciously "in" one of the ideological wings of her party—either conservative or moderate—the importance of sizing up the electorate might be largely a matter of indifference. A doctrinaire consistency might prevail through time. But it seems more likely to cause such a party activist to have some second thoughts about each issue. Presumably, some issues thus come to be seen not only as desirable but as ready now for concerted action, popular with both Republican and Democratic voters. Other issues regrettably have to be put on the back burner. Still other issues are beginning to split the voters along party lines and are presumably ripe to champion ideologically in partisan style.

Conclusions

Some highlights from the Los Angeles party activists project have been presented in an effort to clarify in measurable ways certain adjustment problems that would seem to be unavoidable for those who are differentially recruited into party structures which have some of the hallmarks of ideological camps, and who are bent upon trying to win elections, sometimes by catering to voter-held views, sometimes by concerted efforts to change them, sometimes by muting their own ideological priorities, sometimes by seeking to proselytize even more loudly. Following Schumpeter, we view democratic choice as resting with the voters when certain conditions are met:

1. When the campaign has been closely fought by well-matched contenders, a situation that implies both equivalent credentials and resources for the rival organized campaign efforts.
2. When the election day choice is meaningful in terms of issue positions and ideological alternatives publicized by activists who offer rallying points for issue-conscious and programmatically committed voters.
3. When the election day choice is also updated and reformulated to reflect a realistic appreciation on the part of many rival party activists that significant groups of voters have changed their stance on particular issues, shifted from Left to Right perhaps, or from general agreement to a partisan alignment perhaps.

For the most part, party activists are self-recruited to their volunteer efforts. They join typically because they hold strong opinions on political questions. Much of their attention centers on how to change the opinions of their fellow citizens. Inevitably, they often fail to do so. In frustration, presumably they often are tempted to decruit themselves.

Voter opinions are complex and changing things; catering to them in order to increase the electoral chances of a party calls for skill and realism and much hard work. The Los Angeles data suggest that many activists on both sides have been political brokers, either from a sense of pragmatism and relative indifference to ideological consistency or from a need for realistic priorities in pursuing their personal ideological agendas by remaining active in competitive campaign situations. There is evidence too that volunteers do seek ideologically attractive organizations to join and continue to work in; when the function of such organizations is to win elections under rivalry conditions, ideological considerations must be tempered by what is commonly called political realism. One option is to change one's mind; another, to acknowledge how unpopular one's stance on a particular issue is; still another is to shift energies and attention to policy questions where more favorable voter reception seems likely. Lurking behind these adjustment possibilities is one more serious possibility—dropping out of the self-selected party activist role.

Note

1. In California the county committee is the lowest level of official party organization, as prescribed by statutes promulgated around 1910 during the Progressive era. There are no statutory provisions for precinct, ward, or city party units, probably because of the nonpartisan character of city and school board elections. Rank and file party voters, at primary election time, elect county committee members for two-year terms, either by assembly or supervisorial districts. Each of the thirty-one state assembly districts located within Los Angeles County is entitled to seven seats on each major party's county committee. In even-numbered years at the June primary, these district delegations are chosen. Often, rival slates are sponsored by intraparty factions. In both parties, it is not uncommon for ten to fifteen people to compete for these party leadership positions. On the other hand, the ordinary primary voter does not pay much attention to this set of questions. Incumbency practically guarantees retention. Openings arise chiefly because substantial numbers of incumbents fail to file for re-election. Why do we study county committee members? It is not because that body is an authoritative organizational control unit—it is not—but simply because it provides a convenient and comprehensive sample frame to invoke when selecting matched samples of rival party activists.

References

Conway, Margaret, and Frank Feigert (1968) "Motivation, Incentive Systems and the Political Party Organization." *American Political Science Review* 62:1159–73.

Crouch, Winston; John Bollens; and Stanley Scott (1978) *California Government and Politics.* New York: Prentice-Hall.

Dahl, Robert A. (1956) *A Preface to Democratic Theory.* Chicago: University of Chicago Press.

Duverger, Maurice (1952) *Political Parties.* New York: Wiley.

Eldersveld, Samuel (1964) *Political Parties: A Behavioral Analysis.* New York: Rand McNally.

Eulau, Heinz, and John Wahlke, eds. (1978) *The Process of Representation.* Beverly Hills, Calif.: Sage.

Forthal, Sonya (1946) *Cogwheels of Democracy: A Study of the Precinct Captain.* Chicago: University of Chicago Press.

Gosnell, Harold (1937) *Machine Politics: Chicago Model.* Chicago: University of Chicago Press.

Hirschfield, Robert; Bert Swanson; and Blanche Blank (1962) "A Profile of Political Activists in Manhattan." *Western Political Quarterly* 15:489–506.

Key, V. O. (1961) *Public Opinion and American Democracy.* New York: Knopf.

Lasswell, Harold D. (1977) *On Political Sociology.* Edited by Dwaine Marvick. Chicago: University of Chicago Press.

Lasswell, H., and Kaplan, A. (1950) *Power and Society: A Framework for Political Inquiry.* New Haven: Yale University Press.

Lawson, Kay (ed.) (1979) *Political Parties and Linkage.* New Haven, Conn: Yale University Press.

0ecLindsay, A. (1943) *The Modern Democratic State.* London: Oxford University Press.

McClosky, Herbert; Paul Hoffman; and Rosemary O'Hara (1960) "Issue Conflict and Consensus among Party Leaders and Followers." *American Political Science Review* 54:406–27.

Marvick, Dwaine (1967) "The Middlemen of Politics." In *Approaches to the Study of Party Organization,* edited by William J. Crotty. Boston: Allyn & Bacon.

Mosher, W. E. (1935) "Party and Government at the Grass Roots." *National Municipal Review* 24:15–18.

Peel, Roy (1935) *The Political Clubs of New York City.* New York: Putnam.

Schumpeter, Joseph (1947) *Capitalism, Socialism and Democracy.* New York: Harper and Bros.

Thompson, Dennis (1970) *The Democratic Citizen.* New York: Cambridge University Press.

Wilson, James Q. (1962) *The Amateur Democrat: Club Politics in Three Cities.* Chicago: University of Chicago Press.

On Cronyism: Recruitment and Careers in Local Party Organizations in the United States and Canada

Harold D. Clarke and Allan Kornberg

Party Organizations and Cronyism

Even when academic degrees, scientific training, special aptitudes as tested by examinations and competitions, open the way to public office, there is no eliminating that special advantage in favor of certain individuals which the French call the advantage of *positions déjà prises*.

Gaetano Mosca, *The Ruling Class*, p. 61

The past two decades have witnessed the publication of a number of studies of local party organizations in the United States and other Western democracies.[1] A significant proportion of this research has concerned the recruitment of party activists and has focused on three topics. The first of these is the social backgrounds and current status of party workers. In the tradition of much of the literature on political elites, scholars pursuing this line of inquiry have attempted to map the socioeconomic and demographic characteristics of party activists in comparison to other elite groups and/or the general public. A second topic frequently pursued is the motivational basis for initiating and sustaining party work. Viewed in organizational terms, the principal variant of this research has concerned the incentives available to parties for attracting and retaining personnel. A third, less thoroughly studied, subject is party recruitment processes. When such processes have been investigated, the emphasis has been on initial recruitment to party organizations, with relatively less attention given to subsequent political career development.[2] To date, all three types of inquiries have tended to be heavily descriptive in orientation; but to the extent that hypotheses have been generated and tested, there has been a strong tendency to treat initial recruitment phenomena as dependent variables. Much less attention has been given to questions related to consequences of variations in how individuals begin party work. The present inquiry represents a modest attempt to redress this imbalance by focusing on the possible consequences of one aspect of the recruitment processes of local party organizations—namely, the involvement of politically active friends or family members in these processes—in two countries, the United States and Canada.[3] More specifically, we are concerned with cronyism: the initiation and advancement of political careers on the basis of friendship or kinship ties.

Although much has been written about the general decline of patronage and the consequences thereof for local party organizations (e.g., Crotty and Jacobson, 1980; Epstein, 1980, chaps. 5 and 9; Huckshorn, 1980, chap. 12; Ladd, 1978; Burnham, 1970), surprisingly little is known about the extent to which cronyism influences the staffing of higher level party positions or the selection of candidates for elective and appointive offices. Given evidence suggesting the possible significance of "friends and family" centered social networks in party recruitment processes,[4] there would appear to be considerable potential for cronyism within contemporary local party organizations. Certainly, the existence of such recruitment practices would be consistent with the more general tendency for ascriptive criteria to retain their importance in the organizational life of advanced industrial societies (Mayhew, 1968:105–20). In this respect, despite the putative importance of achievement norms in such societies, Schwartz recently has argued that "in no case does the importance of who one is, that is, of ascriptive criteria ever disappear, or ever become unimportant" (Schwartz, 1982:72).

If documented, the widespread existence of cronyism in local parties in polities such as those of the United States and Canada would help to explain why parties in these systems are, in Eldersveld's words, frequently only "minimally efficient" organizations (Eldersveld, 1964:526). By extension, cronyism may be an important factor in explanations of both the *decline* and the *persistence* of local parties. This is so because to the extent that parties rely on cronyism in personnel selection processes, achievement-related criteria will be discounted. The resulting tendency to select individuals who are either incompetent and/or politically unattractive[5] means that parties not only will be minimally efficient, but also that they will be disadvantaged vis-à-vis other political organizations that rely more heavily on politically relevant achievement norms as guides to personnel recruitment. Operating in competitive political milieux, the decline of parties relative to such achievement-oriented organizations is, therefore, an expected long-run outcome of crony-centered (or other politically irrelevant ascriptive) recruitment practices. Somewhat paradoxically, however, cronyism might be important for the *survival* of parties in the sense that it provides a recruitment mechanism to ensure continued personnel availability under adverse political circumstances. For example, during an election when a party's prospects are far from auspicious, reliance on friends and family networks enables it to find candidates willing to run for office and to mobilize the workers needed for conducting a "respectable" campaign. In liberal democratic systems that place a premium on electoral competition, it may be assumed that a party's ability to mount such campaigns is crucial to its long-term survival prospects.

In general, it would seem difficult to predict the consequences of such contradictory effects of cronyism for the viability of *particular* party organizations. Very likely, a blanket *ceteris paribus* assumption would not prove warranted, and contextual variables (e.g., the nature and intensity of interparty competition) characterizing different political environments would dictate the eventual fate of parties relying heavily on cronyism.[6] Assuming this to be the case, the present paper will pursue the more modest prior question, namely, the *existence* of cronyism. To investigate this topic, data gathered in a comparative study of local party organizations in four cities (Minneapolis, Seattle, Winnipeg, and Vancouver) will be employed. The following section of this paper discusses some of the significant characteristics of local parties in the United States and Canada which guided the design of the study. It also reviews some of the study's principal findings pertinent to formulating specific research questions on cronyism.

Research Design and Relevant Findings

The organizational form of constituency level parties in both the United States and Canada is similar in that it tends to resemble a squat, truncated pyramid. The number of positions at higher levels of party organizations is relatively small, and there are few layers between the narrow top and the broad base of these organizations. Because there are so few layers, the possibility of holding important offices is considerably restricted—so much so, in fact, that in one sense the pinnacle of a successful party career in both countries is to exit from the organization proper by becoming a public elective officeholder or securing a judicial or other desirable appointive office. Another similarity is that both United States and Canadian party organizations are populated almost entirely by unpaid "amateurs" who have other positions which normally take precedence over their status as party officials.[7] In addition, parties in both countries view the capture and retention of public elective offices as their principal goal. Thus, party work tends to be episodic, since the parties, as organizations, are relatively dormant in the interim between elections. Regarding recruitment practices, despite less frequent elections and the fact that they are not legally required to accept anyone, democratic norms, party constitutions, and customary practice combine to induce Canadian parties to behave rather like their U.S. counterparts in that they frequently not only accept but actively seek out representative members of a broad spectrum of social groups. As a result, in both countries constituency level party organizations often constitute "alliances of sub-coalitions" (Eldersveld, 1964, chap. 4). In sum, in comparative perspective, there are many more similarities than differences between party organizations and the kinds of people who are party officials in the two countries (Kornberg et al., 1970).

The pattern of these similarities and differences suggested that a comparative study of the political socialization, recruitment, and career patterns of American and Canadian party officials might make a valuable contribution to the understanding of political parties generally and of recruitment to party organizations in particular. We decided to undertake such a study, relying on two major theoretical orientations—the social-structural and political socialization perspectives—to guide our investigation.[8] Although the design and organization of the research is described in detail elsewhere (Kornberg et al., 1979), a brief summary is in order.

We intended to focus our investigation on two question: First, what induces minute percentages of people in the United States and Canada to accept and retain responsible official positions in party organizations?[9] And second, under what conditions will a few members of these already small groups become contenders for elective and appointive public offices or the powers behind those who hold them? Both cost and time factors led us to design a comparative community, rather than a comparative national, study. Having made this decision, it was important to choose communities with organizational and contextual settings that matched across country lines well enough to justify the assumption that they were alike on a number of relevant underlying dimensions.[10] Vancouver, Winnipeg, Seattle, and Minneapolis were selected because their social and demographic characteristics were sufficiently similar to offer reasonable assurance that any cross-national differences observed would be real. Equally important, the two American communities were characterized by flourishing Republican and Democratic party organizations, while the two Canadian cities contained active New Democratic, Social Credit, Liberal, and Progressive Conservative parties.

Ideally, since we were interested in the political socialization and recruitment experiences as well as the career patterns of party officials, we should have monitored the experiences of groups of children into adulthood in order to explain how very small and exclusive subpopulations in the two countries eventually become party officials. However, since it is very difficult to predict who among the hundreds of thousands of people born annually will either join political parties or rise to prominence within them, and since, in any event, time and monetary constraints would have made a long-term panel study impossible, we decided to adopt a relatively conventional cross-sectional survey method to collect developmental information from party officials and two nonparty control groups in the two cities in each country. The first of the nonparty control groups was composed of randomly selected samples of the total adult populations of Seattle, Vancouver, Minneapolis, and Winnipeg. The second consisted of "matched" samples[11] of people similar to the party officials with respect to key characteristics such as sex, age, and current social status but different in that none of them held formal positions in the party organizations of the four cities. Our expectation was that in-depth personal interviews with random samples of population of the four cities would reveal that they differed substantially from party officials with respect to conventional measures of social and economic status, whereas interviews with the matched samples would indicate that variations in political socialization experiences led some but not other members of socially and economically homogeneous subpopulations to enter party organizations (Kornberg et al., 1979, chap. 1).

We were able to secure funding to complete the study, as designed, in Canada but were unable to secure the financial support required to interview the two nonparty control groups in the United States.[12] The results of the Canadian investigation indicated that social structural factors alone cannot explain why a small minority of persons become party officials; political socialization experiences also play a role. By way of illustration, we found that although the party officials and their matching samples (whom we termed "nigh-dwellers") were relatively similar with respect to social backgrounds (Kornberg et al., 1979:82–83), party officials reported developing an initial awareness of politics earlier; identifying with a party and with their present party earlier; having had much more contact (during their childhood and adolescent years) with politically involved individuals; more often having had politically interested and active parents; and having had longer, stronger, and more sustained levels of interest in politics. In general, it appeared that many of the party officials had been reared in considerably more politicized environments than those of their nigh-dweller counterparts (Kornberg et al., 1979:42–52, 83–86).

With respect to recruitment, although none of the nigh-dwellers held formal positions in party organizations, we found that more than two-fifths of them and nearly one-third of the random samples of populations of the two cities at some time in their lives had been approached by political party officials during an electoral campaign with requests to engage in activities such as telephoning and canvassing voters, soliciting funds for party candidates, driving people to voting places, and so forth. Nonetheless, party officials were rather selective about those to whom they turned for assistance. The nigh-dwellers whose assistance had been sought were distinguished by a variety of socioeconomic status attributes. They derived from higher status backgrounds; they were better educated; they more frequently were high-income-producing professionals, executives, or proprietors of businesses; and they more often were "joiners" of social organizations and heavy consumers of printed media than those not approached for help. Equally interesting, those approached were reared in more politicized settings, more often followed politics closely, more often felt politically efficacious, more often considered themselves opinion leaders, and more frequently voted in various types of elections (Kornberg et al., 1979, chap. 3).

Particularly important in the context of an investigation of cronyism, it appears that party officials often have fairly detailed information about the people to whom they turn for assistance. In this regard, slightly over one-half of the nigh-dwellers knew the party official with whom they had been matched; and, although nearly two-fifths of those who did not know their party matches had had their assistance solicited by a party, almost two-thirds of the nigh-dwellers who were "close friends" of the officials had been approached to do something for a party. The role of friends and family as party recruiters was evident among the party officials as well. Approximately one-half of the officials in the two Canadian cities stated, in reconstructing the conditions under which they entered a party organization, that their first party contact was a friend or relative. These data suggest that there is an important social dimension to political recruitment and that if often takes place within a network of personal relationships of varying closeness (Kornberg et al., 1979:76–77).

Implications for the Study of Cronyism

The findings reported above suggest that there are a number of specific questions regarding cronyism in local party organizations that can be addressed using the four cities' data. We will focus our analyses on the following:

1. What is the overall function of prior contact and personal acquaintanceship with party officials in initial recruitment to Canadian and American party organizations?
2. Do cronyism mechanisms operate to elevate the friends and family of party officials to higher party offices when the former commence party work? As a related question, do neophyte party activists recruited by networks of families and friends tend to receive important and prestigious tasks to perform when they join a party organization?[13]
3. To what extent does the incidence of cronyism vary by country and party?
4. What effects do prior contact and personal acquaintanceship

(i.e., cronyism) have on career development in U.S. and Canadian party organizations? More specifically, what are the relationships between cronyism and the tendencies for party officials to: (a) hold higher level party positions; (b) be nominated as influential members of their party; (c) receive nominations as candidates for public elective offices; and (d) hold public appointive offices?

We shall demonstrate that although many officials in all parties in both countries report that they were encouraged to start party work by relatives or friends, and many recall that such persons were their first contact when they decided to join a party, there is little evidence of cronyism. With other pertinent factors controlled, in no party in either country does one find consistent and/or strong relationships between recruitment under the auspices of relatives and friends and either initial party career success or subsequent career development. Indeed, from an organizational perspective, interpersonal networks of relatives and friends often appear to be as exploitative as they are rewarding. Perhaps because these networks are not so perceived by many party workers, parties continue to be able to use interpersonal recruitment mechanisms centering on ties of friendship and kin to attract the labor needed to weather the storms generated by the recurring imperative of electoral competition.

Starting Party Work: The Role of Family and Friends

As noted, previous research has established that substantial numbers of party officials and other types of political activists are reared in families where parents, siblings, or other close relatives were themselves involved in politics. It has been further demonstrated that placement in such politicized milieux influences political socialization processes—raising levels of political knowledge and awareness and accelerating the age at which future party workers acquire partisan attachments. Over and above helping to establish a motivational basis for eventual political activism, it can be hypothesized that family and friendship ties are important elements in sociopolitical networks that lead many future party workers to embark upon their "pathways to politics."

A variety of evidence in the four cities study supports this hypothesis.[14] At the most general level, substantial pluralities of party activists in both countries (43 percent in Canada, 45 percent in the United States) and in every party reported that they had been encouraged to initiate party work in the year or two prior to joining a party.[15] Overwhelming proportions of those who had been encouraged stated that the person or persons who did so were party activists and that the encouragement had been an important factor in their decision to join a party. The idea that family and friends frequently played important roles in encouraging future party workers to become active is suggested by responses to a question asked regarding which experiences, influences, and events were "particularly important" in moving the respondent in the direction of working for a party. In both countries approximately one-third of the activists cited family or friends as providing the crucial impetus for starting party work. In the United States, Democrats and Republicans were equally likely to cite family and friends; in Canada, the proportions doing so varied from one-quarter of the New Democrats to two-fifths of the Liberals. Interestingly, many respondents indicated that the family members or friends were themselves political activists.

The meaning of citing family or friends as important influences in the process leading one to become a party worker is not entirely clear. On the one hand, respondents may be reporting that such persons actually recruited them for party work. On the other hand, they may be indicating that the friend or family member in question played a pivotal, albeit much more subtle, part in a lengthy sequence of events leading to an eventual decision to become politically active. For example, in some instances friends or family members may have been responsible for stimulating an initial interest in party politics. In other cases, they may have done nothing more than introduce the future party worker to people who were politically active; these persons in turn may have done the actual recruiting, the latter act occurring some time after such an introduction had been made. Of course, there are many other possibilities as well.

To learn more about how initial recruitment to parties occurs and the role of family, friends, and others in this process, respondents were questioned regarding the position in the party of the person who was their first contact at the time they joined and their relationship with that person. Regarding the former, the data indicate that although many contacts were high-level party officials or candidates for or holders of public offices, many others were not (see Table 1). In the United States, 34 percent of the officials reported that their first party contact held high-level positions or were public officeholders or candidates. The comparable figure for the two Canadian cities is 47 percent. As Table 1 shows, the source of this cross-national difference is the greater tendency among Canadians to report their first party contact was a public officeholder or candidate. In neither country did the positions of first party contacts vary greatly by party.

The relationship of first party contacts to the neophyte party workers is displayed in Table 2. These data reveal that persons joining parties frequently contact or are contacted by relatives or friends. Slightly over one-third (36 percent) of the American party officials and nearly one-half (49 percent) of the Canadians reported that their first party contact was a relative or friend. Party differences are min-

TABLE 1.
Party Position Held by First Party Contact by Country and Party

	Canada					U.S.		
Party Position	New Democratic Party	Liberal Party	Progressive Conservative Party	Social Credit Party	Total	Democrat	Republican	Total
Position above precinct/poll level Public officeholder or candidate	18%	27%	28%	28%	25%	25%	24%	25%
	24	20	25	18	22	11	7	9
Sub-total	(42)	(47)	(53)	(46)	(47)	(36)	(31)	(34)
Precinct/poll or lower level	12	17	17	21	17	31	37	34
Campaign worker	40	30	25	29	32	19	17	18
Other	3	1	1	1	1	1	3	2
No such person identified	4	4	4	2	4	14	12	13
(N =)*	(151)	(192)	(127)	(89)	(559)	(242)	(284)	(526)

*Missing data excluded.

imal in the former country, but discernible, if not dramatic, in the latter, with members of the two older Canadian parties, the Liberals and Conservatives, being most likely to report that first party contacts were relatives or friends. It is also noteworthy that although the data for all parties in both countries suggest the substantial role of previously established social networks in party recruitment processes, these networks only infrequently appear to be family centered. Indeed, as Table 2 shows, in both countries and in all parties, the overwhelming tendency (by a ratio of 6 to 1 in Canada and 8 to 1 in the United States) is to cite friends rather than nuclear family members or other relatives as first party contacts. Thus, while kinship ties may have important recruitment effects in terms of influencing socialization processes that orient people toward eventual political participation and helping to locate individuals in social networks where contact with party activists may provide recruitment opportunities, seldom do such relationships serve as the proximate routes to party work.

The term "party contact" is ambiguous in the sense that it does not inform one regarding the nature of that contact. Specifically, did the party contact person approach the future activists and "recruit" them for party work, or did the latter approach the former and "volunteer" his or her services? Answering this question can help us understand the role of interpersonal ties in the recruitment process. Prior to investigating this topic, it may be observed that approximately three-fifths of the party activists in both the United States and Canada reported that they had volunteered their services. In the former country Democrats (71 percent) were considerably more likely to volunteer than were Republicans (51 percent). In Canada, New Democrats were the frequent volunteers (69 percent); Liberals did so least often (52 percent). It is also noteworthy that there is a tendency for persons to volunteer for general party work rather than for specific tasks. This is true in both countries and among all parties, the ratio of general work to specific tasks among volunteers ranging from slightly less than 3 to 1 among Democrats in the United States to nearly 6 to 1 among Canadian New Democrats. In contrast, persons approached to begin party work tended to be offered a specific task. Again, this is true in both countries and among all parties. In the United States the ratio of "recruits" offered specific tasks rather than general work is approximately 4 to 1 among both Democrats and Republicans. In Canada the ratio is approximately 2 to 1 for every party except the Social Credit, where it is 4.5 to 1.

The relationships between mode of entry into party work (i.e., approached-volunteered, specific tasks-general work) and nature of first party contact (i.e., contact as a family member or friend, contact as a holder of a high-level party position) are displayed in Table 3. These data illustrate that mode of entry into parties is associated

TABLE 2.
Relationship to First Party Contact by Country and Party

Relationship	Canada					U.S.		
	New Democratic Party	Liberal Party	Progressive Conservative Party	Social Credit Party	Total	Democrat	Republican	Total
Close relative (spouse, parent, sibling)	7%	4%	6%	3%	5%	3%	3%	3%
More distant relative	2	2	1	0	2	1	1	1
Friend	32	50	42	40	42	31	33	32
Sub-total	(41)	(56)	(49)	(43)	(49)	(35)	(37)	(36)
Work associate	2	4	2	3	3	3	4	4
Distant acquaintance	18	13	10	21	15	14	18	16
Co-member of organization	1	1	1	1	1	1	1	1
Others (including stranger)	35	23	35	30	30	35	30	32
No such person identified	4	4	3	2	3	12	11	11
(N =)*	(165)	(205)	(145)	(98)	(613)	(278)	(322)	(600)

*Missing data excluded.

TABLE 3.
Mode of Entry into Party Work by Nature of First Party Contact

	A. United States Nature of First Party Contact						B. Canada Nature of First Party Contact					
Mode of Entry into Party Work	Party Contact Was Friend or Family Member (1)		Party Contact Held High Party Position (2)		Party Contact Was Friend or Family and Held High Party Office (3)		Party Contact Was Friend or Family Member (4)		Party Contact Held High Party Position (5)		Party Contact Was Friend or Family and Held High Party Office (6)	
	Yes	No	Yes	No	Yes	No	Yes	No	Yes	No	Yes	No
Approached, specific task	44%	23%	30%	34%	41%	31%	33%	21%	31%	25%	36%	25%
Approached, general work	13	6	9	9	13	4	19	11	16	14	21	13
Volunteered, specific task	11	21	23	15	15	18	9	10	10	8	10	9
Volunteered, general work	32	50	39	42	31	42	38	58	44	53	33	53
V =	.27*		.11		.11		.21*		.09		.18*	
(N =)†	(216)	(389)	(174)	(352)	(68)	(444)	(295)	(320)	(262)	(297)	(136)	(416)

*p ≤ .05.
†Missing data removed.

with having a close interpersonal relationship with the person serving as the initial party contact. In both countries, those with such interpersonal ties are more likely to report being approached to start party work rather than volunteering their services. Such persons also are more likely than others to perform specific tasks for the party rather than doing general work. Additionally, in Canada, there were discernible (but not strong) tendencies for persons whose party contacts held high party office to be recruited for party work and to engage in specific tasks. In the United States, the relationships between the position held by party contact and mode of entry into party work were virtually nonexistent.

Finally, if cronyism is prevalent in local party organizations, one might expect to find that the relationship between nature of party contact and mode of entry into party work would be strongest for those persons whose party contact was both a friend or family member *and* an occupant of high party office. Such contacts, by virtue of holding higher level party offices, presumably would be more likely than other party workers to be able to offer a potential activist the kinds of party work he or she desired. Equally or more important, such contacts presumably would be motivated (or could be prevailed upon) to offer the requisite assistance. However plausible such an expectation might seem, the data in the two right-hand columns of the two panels of Table 3 do not support it. In neither country do persons with party contacts who were friends or family members holding high-level party offices show strong tendencies to enter party organizations in ways that differ dramatically from those with other types of party contacts. Moreover, comparisons of columns one and five in the two panels again suggest that the stronger factor in differentiating modes of entry into party work is relationship to party contact rather than position held by that contact.

When considering the implications of these findings for understanding how initial recruitment into party organizations occurs, it is important to observe that in no case are the relationships observed very strong (i.e., maximum Cramer's V's for the United States and Canada are .27 and .21, respectively). Thus, it appears that the use of close interpersonal ties (i.e., with family, other relatives, friends) to facilitate the initiation of party work is not a one-way street. Although the data suggest that persons already in the party tend to use such contacts to approach persons for party service more frequently that those outside the party volunteer their labor by contacting relatives or friends who are party workers, the latter is not a rare occurrence.[16] Again, regardless of the relationship with first party contact, large numbers of party workers began their careers by doing general work rather than specific tasks. Moreover, controlling for both the relationship of the party contact to the party official *and* the position held by the party contact does not enable us to isolate a cadre of party officials whose modes of entry into party work differ sharply from those of other persons. In sum, in neither the United States nor Canada does it appear that the nature of initial party contacts provides an adequate basis for comprehending how party careers begin. For some people, such careers begin when they arrive, seemingly unbid, on a party's doorstep. For others, interpersonal ties evidently do play a role in party recruitment; but these ties, even if they are with persons who hold high party offices, do not specify *how* recruitment occurs or the *nature* of the organizational tasks assumed by new party workers.

Family, Friends, and Party Careers

Data presented in the preceding section suggest that family and friendship ties frequently constitute "paths to party work." However, such ties, even if they are with high-ranking party officials, are not strongly associated with *particular* modes of entry into party organizations. Still to be investigated is the question of whether interpersonal family and friendship networks tend to constitute cronyism systems that facilitate political careers. As noted earlier, when conducting an inquiry into this subject, it is necessary to be cognizant of an alternative possibility, namely, that persons already active in local party organizations frequently use family members and friends to provide the foot soldiers needed to fight a party's political battles. Stated otherwise, it is possible that the social ties to party organizations provided by family and friendship networks are primarily exploitative rather than rewarding. Of course, it also is conceivable that both types of processes are at work simultaneously. Data gathered in the four cities project will enable us to investigate these possibilities in some detail.

First to be considered are what might be termed the initial outcomes of the party recruitment process. Only small minorities of neophyte party workers (7 percent in the United States, 13 percent in Canada) begin their careers with a position at or above the district (constituency) level; and as Table 4 indicates, there is virtually no evidence to suggest that close interpersonal ties between new party workers and party recruiters facilitate occupancy of such positions. In neither country for any party are the relationships statistically significant (Table 4, row 3). To the extent that the nature of initial party contact is relevant for obtaining immediate occupancy of a higher level party office, there is some evidence that the position held by the contact may be influential. Such relationships are statistically significant for New Democrats and Progressive Conservatives in Canada and for Republicans in the United States (Table 4, row 6). In all cases, however, the relationships are weak (ϕ = .20, .19, and .14, respectively). Finally, analyzing the data in terms of persons whose party contact was a friend or family member holding higher party office fails to produce any statistically significant results (Table 4, row 9).

A second measure of initial career success is the type of work done by the new party recruits. Some party activists spend their time performing prestigious tasks such as writing speeches and campaign material, giving talks at meetings or rallies, or soliciting financial contributions, while others find themselves relegated to discharging mundane chores such as canvassing, placing party literature in mailboxes, acting as scrutineers, or driving people to the polls. As data in Table 5 indicate, there is a statistically significant positive association for one of the Canadian parties (the Liberals) between having close personal ties with one's first party contact and the performance of prestigious tasks (Table 5, row 3). This is not true, however, for activists in the other three Canadian parties or in either American party. In both countries, there also is some evidence that having a first party contact who holds a high position is positively associated with performing prestigious versus mundane tasks (Table 5, row 6). Even when the combined effects of having a party contact who is both a friend or family member and a high-ranking party official are considered, however, all the relationships remain weak (Table 5, rows 6–9).

The evidence from the bivariate analyses is, therefore, at best mixed. In general, there is little support for the notion that family or friendship ties with party contacts provide payoffs in terms of high-level initial positions in party organizations. However, it does appear that in at least one of the Canadian parties persons with such ties do tend somewhat more frequently than other new party activists to have an opportunity to perform prestigious tasks, particularly if the party contact person held a high-level party office. Of course, personal ties are not the only factors with potential to condition the course of party careers. Previous research has indicated that a variety of socioeconomic and demographic variables, as well as levels of participation in party work, help to determine who will enjoy career success (Kornberg et al., 1979: chaps. 7, 8, 9). In terms of *initial* party positions held and tasks performed, the latter type of variable (i.e., level of intraparty participation) is necessarily irrelevant. However, the other factors might be significant. Thus, we will investigate the relationships between familial and friendship ties with first party contact and holding higher level positions and performing prestigious tasks, controlling for sex, age of entry into party work, and socioeconomic status at time of entry. Other possibly relevant variables considered include early location in a politicized social milieu (as measured by membership in a politically active family and acquaintance with politically involved persons) and mode of entry into party work.[17]

TABLE 4.
Percentages with Initial Party Position at or above District/Constituency
Level by Relationship and Position of First Party Contact

First Contact	Canada					U.S.		
	New Democratic Party	Liberal Party	Progressive Conservative Party	Social Credit Party	Total	Democrat	Republican	Total
Close relationship								
Yes	15	10	11	21	13	4	7	6
No	12	5	19	19	13	11	6	8
φ =	.03	.08	.11	.04	.00	.11	.02	.05
High party position								
Yes	22	9	22	15	17	9	13	11
No	8	8	8	17	10	8	5	6
φ =	.20*	.01	.19*	.03	.10	.03	.14*	.09
Close relationship and high party position								
Yes	20	10	21	17	15	3	10	7
No	11	7	14	16	11	9	6	8
φ =	.10	.05	.09	.01	.05	.07	.05	.01

* p ≤ .05.

TABLE 5.
Percentages with Prestigious Initial Party Task by Relationship
and Position of First Party Contact

First Contact	Canada					U.S.		
	New Democratic Party	Liberal Party	Progressive Conservative Party	Social Credit Party	Total	Democrat	Republican	Total
Close relationship								
Yes	36	32	34	41	35	52	51	51
No	29	13	32	41	27	51	43	47
φ =	.08	.22*	.01	.00	.08	.01	.08	.04
High party position								
Yes	37	29	46	37	36	64	56	60
No	34	20	20	40	27	46	45	44
φ =	.02	.10	.28*	.03	.10*	.19*	.10	.15*
Close relationship and high party position								
Yes	44	35	52	33	40	66	62	63
No	33	19	28	40	29	50	46	48
φ =	.09	.17*	.22*	.06	.11*	.10	.11	.11*

* p ≤ .05.

The results of regressing level of first party position and type of initial task performed onto the first party contact variables (party contact was a friend or family member, party contact held a high position) and the several variables cited above show that for all four Canadian parties the party contact variables do not influence the tendency to occupy a high-level first party position.[18] This also is true for the Democrats in the United States. Only among Republicans is there evidence that, with other factors controlled, having a party contact in a high position enhances the likelihood of holding a high party office (data not shown in tabular form). Even in this case the relationship is weak. As for prestigious tasks, for no party in either country is having a friend or family member as a party contact an influential factor. Having a party contact in a high position is of consequence only for Democrats in the United States; for no party in Canada is this the case. In sum, there is precious little evidence to support the hypothesis that interpersonal networks provide the key to understanding who receives organizational rewards when starting party work. To the extent that such networks have relevance for such matters, it appears that they provide an equally good basis for both rewarding and exploiting one's friends and family if and when they decide (or can be prevailed upon) to become party activists.

It is possible, of course, that the rewards provided by interpersonal networks are deferred rather than immediate. Thus, it is important to investigate relationships between party contacts and career outcome variables. Four of the latter will be considered here: level of current party position, ascribed influence in party affairs, candidacy for public elective office, and public office appointments.[19] Regarding level of current party position, for none of the four Canadian parties does one observe statistically significant relationships with having a first party contact who is a family member or friend (Table 6, rows 3, 9). In terms of patterns of percentage differences, for all parties except the Liberals, relationships are actually negative; i.e., fewer of those reporting their initial party contacts were friends or family currently hold a high party office. In the United States the relationship is statistically significant and positive (as indicated by the percentage difference), albeit very weak ($\phi = .09$), for all party officials. For the parties considered separately, the relationships are positive but not statistically significant. It is also noteworthy that having an initial party contact in high party office is not strongly associated with level of current party position. Indeed, none of the relationships are statistically significant, and few of the relevant percentage differences exceed 10 percent (Table 6, rows 4–6).

The failure of the initial party contact variables to predict career outcomes is again evident when one analyzes the number of nominations party officials receive for being influential in their organizations. For example, if one considers persons with 10 or more

TABLE 6.
Percentages with Current Party Position at or above District/Constituency
Level by Relationship and Position of First Party Contact

First Contact	Canada					U.S.		
	New Democratic Party	Liberal Party	Progressive Conservative Party	Social Credit Party	Total	Democrat	Republican	Total
Close relationship								
Yes	53	69	63	64	63	52	57	54
No	65	63	64	82	67	44	45	45
ϕ =	.12	.07	.01	.20	.04	.07	.11	.09*
High party position								
Yes	70	68	58	69	66	52	52	52
No	56	63	70	75	65	44	46	45
ϕ =	.13	.05	.12	.06	.02	.08	.06	.07
Close relationship and high party position								
Yes	68	69	54	56	64	52	61	57
No	61	63	66	78	66	46	47	47
ϕ =	.06	.06	.11	.20	.02	.03	.10	.07

* $p \leq .05$.

nominations as influential, in no analysis for any party in either country do relevant percentage differences exceed 8 percent. Analyses of the mean number of influence nominations in terms of the nature and position of first party contact yield equally weak, statistically insignificant relationships (data not shown in tabular form).

Occupancy of higher level party positions and influence in party affairs are measures of career success which focus on the internal features of party organizations. In a sense, however, in North American political milieux, party career success can also be measured (perhaps can be best measured) by considering the variables that stand at the interface of the party and the larger polity, namely, candidacy for public elective and appointive offices. In the contemporary era, many traditional forms of patronage are either unavailable to local party organizations or unattractive to the kinds of persons they wish to attract. As a result, public office-holding opportunities are frequently, if not invariably, among the few substantial rewards local parties have at their disposal. Regarding the distribution of such opportunities, there is little evidence that they are given disproportionately to persons who initiated party work by having a recruitment contact with someone who was a family member or friend and/or held high party office. Illustratively, Table 7 presents the results of analyses using candidacy for public elective office as the dependent variable. For the 24 analyses summarized in this table, the largest percentage difference (for Social Credit officials) is 11 percent. None of the relationships is statistically significant. Comparable analyses with appointments to public office as the dependent variable yield equally inconclusive results (data not shown in tabular form).

As a final test of the impact of the party contact variables on eventual career success, multiple regression analysis may be employed to predict level of current party position, number of influence nominations, public elective office candidacy, and occupancy of appointive office. Entered as predictors in these analyses are the party contact variables (relationship of contact to respondent, position of contact in the party), as well as four socioeconomic and demographic variables (income, level of formal education, age, sex).[20] Also entered as predictors are two early life "politicized environment" variables (parental political activity, acquaintance with politically involved persons), two measures of party activity (an index based on the number of hours of party work performed in an average week and the number of weeks of intensive party work in the past two years, and the length of one's party career relative to age cohort median)[21] and the three dummy mode of entry variables.

The results of these analyses are consistent with those of previous research and materials presented above. In a total of 32 analyses (4 for each country and party), in only one instance does the friends-

TABLE 7.
Percentages of Candidates for Any Public Elective Office by Relationship and Position of First Party Contact

First Contact	Canada					U.S.		
	New Democratic Party	Liberal Party	Progressive Conservative Party	Social Credit Party	Total	Democrat	Republican	Total
Close relationship								
Yes	48	26	30	38	34	43	31	37
No	41	28	31	34	34	37	27	32
ϕ =	.07	.03	.02	.04	.00	.06	.04	.05
High party position								
Yes	43	30	34	37	35	38	32	35
No	44	24	25	35	32	41	26	32
ϕ =	.01	.07	.10	.01	.03	.03	.07	.03
Close relationship and high party position								
Yes	36	25	30	44	34	48	26	35
No	45	28	29	33	31	39	28	33
ϕ =	.07	.03	.01	.10	.03	.06	.01	.02

* $p \leq .05$.

family party contact variable have a statistically significant effect. Even in this case (for United States party officials with level of current position as the dependent variable) the effect is small (Beta = +.10).[22] Having an initial party contact in a high-level position has four statistically significant relationships. All of these involve analyses of ascribed influence in party affairs. Having a high-level first party contact has significant positive effects for all Canadian party officials (Beta = +.09); for Progressive Conservatives, Beta = +.21. In the United States, the significant relationships occur for the Republicans (Beta = −.13); and when the officials are analyzed without regard to party, Betas = −.11. As the Betas indicate, none of these effects is large. Moreover, their directions are opposite in the two countries. Among Canadians, having a first party contact with a high-level party office has a positive association with the number of influence nominations received; for the Americans, having such a party contact is inversely related to the receipt of such nominations.

It is also noteworthy that the other initial recruitment variables, i.e., modes of entry into party work, are not consistent predictors of career success. In the 32 analyses, the three mode of entry dummy variables (recruited for specific tasks, recruited for general work, volunteered for specific tasks) have statistical effects in six instances. In Canada, being recruited for specific tasks is positively associated with ascribed influence among New Democrats (Beta = +.18) and positively associated with holding appointive office for Conservatives (Beta = +.23). Being recruited for general work is negatively related to public office candidacy for members of this party (Beta = −.22) and among Canadians as a whole (Beta = −.09). In the United States, recruitment for general work has a negative effect among Democrats (Beta = −.17) and a positive one for Republicans (Beta = +.14). In no case in either country is volunteering for specific tasks related to any of the career outcome variables.

Party contact and other initial recruitment variables aside, both who you are and what you do are important for explaining party career success. Thus, although the several analyses differ in detail, variables with recurring statistically significant effects include measures of socioeconomic status (income, education). demographic characteristics (sex, age), and level of commitment to party work (level of participation in the party organization, length of party career). In contrast, in only two instances do the early life politicized environment variables (parental political activity, knowing politically active persons during childhood or adolescence) achieve statistical significance. Again, this finding, taken in conjunction with previous findings from analyses of the four cities data, suggests that although location in a politicized milieu during childhood and adolescence is part of a complex of forces which influence the likelihood that certain individuals eventually will become party activists, it has little, if any, direct effect on the outcome of party careers.

Conclusion: Inverse Cronyism?

Although the recruitment of political party activists has been studied extensively in the past two decades, surprisingly little systematic research exists on factors which determine party careers. Perhaps as a result, a number of venerable but speculative explanations of career success remain part of the conventional wisdom on party organizations and political recruitment. One of the hardiest of the perennials in this garden of scholarly folklore is the cronyism hypothesis. The idea that career advancement within party organizations frequently is facilitated by the good offices of well-placed friends and relatives is an important aspect of this hypothesis. A second is that, *ceteris paribus*, friends and relatives who are party officials often play key roles in helping individuals to secure candidacies for and appointments to public office. This paper has attempted to examine these matters, using data on party officials in two American and two Canadian cities.

Without reiterating the details of the several analyses, the major finding is that there is precious little evidence to support the cronyism hypothesis. Although friends frequently play important roles in the processes by which party workers are first recruited, such persons cannot be shown to benefit systematically from these interpersonal relationships in terms of either initial or subsequent party career outcomes. Having a friend or relative as one's initial party contact, even if that person occupies a high-level position within a party organization, has little relationship with whether or not an individual begins his or her party career with a higher level office. Nor can the nature of first party contact explain who subsequently occupies high-level party offices, who acquires influence within party organizations, or who becomes an elective or appointive public office nominee. In all parties in both countries, cronyism, at least as that concept has been operationalized here,[23] fails to explain party career success. The only possible exception to this conclusion is the finding that in some parties officials with first party contacts who are friends or relatives and also holders of high party positions tend to receive a disproportionate share of prestigious tasks when they first join a party. Even these relationships are obliterated, however, when controls are applied for other potentially relevant variables, thereby suggesting that, if not wholly spurious, possible cronyism effects are at most indirect.

Also relevant to an assessment of the cronyism hypothesis is the finding that contact with politically active or interested persons during childhood or adolesence does not have direct effects on how party careers begin or progress. Although previous research with the four cities data has indicated that location in such politicized early life environments influences attitudes and beliefs relevant for eventual political recruitment (e.g., by enhancing political awareness and interest and strengthening partisan attachments, Kornberg et al., 1970, chap. 2), it appears that such socialization phenomena seldom directly affect the ways in which political careers unfold. Rather, similar to the initial recruitment variables (relationship with first party contact, position of first party contact, mode of entry into party work), the intensive and atypical political socialization experiences that occur in politicized childhood and adolescent environments are best thought of as forces which move individuals in the direction of eventual political activism. Further, to the extent that location in such environments measures placement in social networks composed of politically active and influential people, the effect of such networks is primarily confined to enhancing the probabilities of initial recruitment. Indeed, the fact that having a friend or relative as first party contact and location in a politicized early life milieu are only very weakly related suggests that even the latter effects may be largely indirect.

The evidence presented here strongly indicates that in both the United States and Canada successful party careers are primarily the result of a combination of who you are and what you do. Simply stated, higher party offices, influence within party organizations, and public office-holding opportunities are primarily the preserves of upper socioeconomic status, middle-aged men who are willing to devote substantial amounts of their leisure time to working for their parties. Although lower status individuals, younger people, and women are active in parties, they are disadvantaged in their attempts to enjoy successful party careers; and, in general, even sustained intensive work for their party organizations does not enable them to obviate these disadvantages.

That socioeconomic status and demographic characteristics account for a substantial part of the explained variance in party career variables is hardly surprising to anyone familiar with the literature on political participation and political recruitment, and it is unnecessary to discuss here the several ways in which such characteristics facilitate political careers (Kornberg et al., 1979; Clarke and Kornberg, 1979; Putnam, 1976, chap. 2). In contemporary Western democracies these characteristics collectively capture much of the meaning of what Mosca designated as "the advantage of *positions déjà prises*" (Mosca, 1939: 61). Thus, although cronyism may explain precious little variance in party careers, ascriptive criteria more generally remain highly relevant for understanding how parties recruit personnel and distribute the organizational rewards at their disposal.

Equally interesting is the finding that party career success as we have measured it in this paper varies with levels of commitment to party work. Having as their primary raison d'etre the capture and retention of public elective offices, local party organizations normally require the services of competent individuals who are willing to expend large amounts of time and energy on behalf of the party. Thus, as long as parties remain sensitive to the electoral imperative, they can ill afford to become completely closed oligarchies which promote individuals strictly on the basis of ascriptive criteria.[24] Rather, to capture and retain public office, party organizations must remain permeable to at least some persons of talent and commitment. Then, too, parties in Western democracies frequently are loose and amorphous entities enmeshed in networks of legal regulations and more general political cultural norms that require a certain degree of organizational openness. This means that even if they so wish, parties often cannot keep persons who are willing to commit themselves to party work from doing so and reaping a certain proportion of the rewards that flow from extended and intensive organizational activity.

Regarding cronyism specifically, as a consequence of the pressures of interparty competition and the resulting need to leave party doors ajar to talented, highly motivated persons, opportunities to employ crony-centered recruitment practices are limited. Indeed, it can be argued that the periodic pressures on contemporary party organizations engendered by electoral battles, combined with the paucity of traditional patronage rewards at their disposal, lead many local parties to practice a form of friends and family recruitment that is the very antithesis of cronyism as that concept is traditionally understood. Rather than rewarding persons recruited through the ties of friendship or family, parties knowingly or, perhaps more often, unwittingly, exploit them. Equally important, however, those who join parties by these mechanisms may not perceive their relationship with the organization in exploitative terms. Party career success as it has been measured here is only one kind of reward and may be considered irrelevant by many party activists. For these persons, other instrumental or intrinsic benefits, ranging from the satisfaction of helping to elect candidates pledged to implement cherished policy goals to the social-psychological gratifications of helping friends and family members who have requested their assistance, prove adequate compensation for their labors.[25] Because they do, many local party organizations survive and, in at least some cases, prosper.

Notes

1. The seminal work in the area is Eldersveld (1964). For a bibliography containing citations of many of the relevant studies see Czudnowski (1975):234–42.

2. Principal findings in all three areas are summarized in Czudnowski (1975):177–220. See also Epstein (1980): chaps. 5–8.

3. For discussions of party organizations in these two countries see Sorauf (1980); and Engelmann and Schwartz (1975): chap. 8.

4. Czudnowski (1975):189 lists references to several relevant studies. Because of the study design used, perhaps the strongest evidence is provided by Kornberg, Smith, and Clarke (1979): chaps. 2, 3.

5. In this context, political incompetents are persons who lack the skills and knowledge needed to make a party organization function effectively. Politically unattractive individuals are those who lack the characteristics that make them strong candidates in particular political milieux.

6. The most obvious contextual variable would be level of interparty competition. Other related variables, such as the size and stability of a party's cohort of identifiers in the electorate, however, would be relevant as well.

7. The term "amateur" has been applied to such people by James Q. Wilson, writing in another context; see Wilson (1962). Also see Soule and Clarke (1970):888–98; Nexon (1971):716—30; Jacek, McDonough, Shimizu, and Smith (1972):190–225; and Clarke, Price, Stewart, and Krause (1978):139–51.

8. As is well known, the former emphasizes the explanatory importance of impersonal forces rooted in social structure and organization while the latter gives precedence to individual experiences accumulated during the course of personal development.

9. Lester Milbrath has estimated that at any particular time about 4 percent of the populations of most Western democracies are actively involved in party organizations. See Milbrath (1965):16. For data suggesting that the total number of individuals who at some point in their lives have done some type of party or related campaign work is considerably larger than the 4 percent cited by Milbrath see Nie and Verba (1975):24–25; and Barnes, Kaase et al. (1979). For data on political participation in Canada see Burke, Clarke, and LeDuc (1978):61–75; and Kornberg, Clarke, and Mishler (1982): chap. 4.

10. Societal similarities and differences pertinent to the design of the research are discussed in Smith and Kornberg (1969):341–57.

11. The importance of using matched samples in political recruitment research has been noted by others. See, for example, Prewitt (1965); Czudnowski (1975):189.

12. The primary sources of support for our study were the National Science Foundation (GS-1134) and the Canada Council (68-0434, 69-1415, and 70-0527).

13. For a more limited test of this aspect of the cronyism hypothesis see Kornberg et al. (1979):102–03. The measures and analyses used in this earlier test were somewhat different from those employed here, but the general thrust of the findings is similar.

14. The base N's for the analyses reported here are: United States Democrats = 294, Republicans = 333; Canadian New Democratic Party = 169, Liberals = 210, Progressive Conservatives = 147, and Social Credit = 99. The N's for specific analyses vary somewhat because of differences in the amount of missing data.

15. Because of space considerations, the actual questions posed to the party officials in our survey will not be reported here. Interested readers may obtain this information from the authors upon request.

16. In this regard, it is necessary to recognize the limitations of available data. Specifically, if one had a sample of all those who joined a party

during some specified time period, it is conceivable that one would find that volunteers have higher drop-out rates than recruits. A number of these retired volunteers might have had an initial party contact who was a friend or relative. Such a finding, however, would strengthen the conclusion that a substantial proportion of those wishing to volunteer for party work use interpersonal networks to facilitate their entry into party organizations.

17. In these analyses the variables are as follows: first party contact was friend or family member—yes = 1, no = 0; first party contact held high-level (district (constituency) level or above) party position—yes = 1, no = 0; sex—men = 1, women = 0; age of entry into party work—measured in years; socioeconomic status at time of entry—respondent's Duncan SEI score; location in a politically active family—both parents active = 2, one parent active = 1, neither parent active = 0; acquaintance with politically involved persons—number of politically active or interested persons known during childhood and adolescence; mode of entry into party work—three dummy variables based on combinations of the approached-volunteered and specific tasks—general work variables. Volunteering for general work is the suppressed category.

18. The analyses described here are stepwise multiple regressions performed using the SPSS package (release 8.1). This technique is described in Nie et al. (1975): chap. 20.

19. These variables are measured as follows: level of current party position—district (constituency) level or above = 1, others = 0; ascribed influence in party affairs—number of nominations received as an influential member of one's party organization; candidacy for public elective office—candidates (at any time since joining the party) = 1, non-candidates = 0; held appointive public office (at any time since joining the party) = 1, non-appointees = 0.

20. Income is measured as a 10 category variable with categories ranging from under $5,000 per year to $25,000 or greater per year; level of formal education = number of years of formal education; age = age in years.

21. The index of intraparty activity is the sum of the Z scores for individual party workers with these scores being calculated using the distribution of all party workers' reports of the number of hours of party work performed in an average week and the number of weeks of intensive work in the past two years. Length of party career relative to age cohort median is a dichotomous variable—career is longer than age cohort median = 1, career is equal to or less than age cohort median = 0.

22. The Betas reported here are the standardized regression coefficients yielded by the multiple regression analyses.

23. A variant of the cronyism hypothesis that was not tested due to limitations of available data is that friendship networks established *after* one becomes a party worker facilitate party careers.

24. In some instances, parties do abandon electoral competition in particular milieux and rest content with reaping patronage rewards generated elsewhere. Classic examples are the Republican party organizations in the southern United States, described by Key (1949:34).

25. In fact, a great many party activists do report that they remain active

in party affairs because of such social-psychological rewards. See Clarke et al. (1978:135–51) and the several studies cited therein.

References

Barnes, Samuel H., and Max Kaase et al. (1979) *Political Action*. Beverly Hills, Calif.: Sage Publications.

Burke, Mike, Harold D. Clarke, and Lawrence L. LeDuc (1978) "Federal and Provincial Political Participation in Canada: Some Methodological and Substantive Considerations." *Canadian Review of Sociology and Anthropology* 15:61–75.

Burnham, Walter Dean (1970) *Critical Elections and the Mainsprings of American Politics*. New York: Norton.

Clarke, Harold D., and Allan Kornberg (1979) "Moving up the Political Escalator: Women Party Officials in the United States and Canada." *Journal of Politics* 41:442–47.

Clarke, Harold D., Richard G. Price, Marianne C. Stewart, and Robert Krause (1978) "Motivational Patterns and Differential Participation in a Canadian Party: The Ontario Liberals." *American Journal of Political Science* 22:139–51.

Crotty, William J., and Gary C. Jacobson (1980) *American Parties in Decline*. Boston: Little, Brown.

Czudnowski, Moshe M. (1975) "Political Recruitment." In *Handbook of Political Science*, vol. 2, edited by Fred I. Greenstein and Nelson W. Polsby. Reading, Mass.: Addison-Wesley.

Eldersveld, Samuel J. (1964) *Political Parties: A Behavior Analysis*. Chicago: Rand McNally.

Englemann, Frederick C., and Mildred A. Schwartz (1975) *Canadian Political Parties: Origin, Character, Impact*. Scarborough, N.J.: Prentice-Hall.

Epstein, Leon D. (1980) *Political Parties in Western Democracies*. New Brunswick, N.J.: Transaction Books.

Huckshorn, Robert (1980) *Political Parties in America*. North Scituate, Mass.: Duxbury Press.

Jacek, Henry, John McDonough, Ronald Shimizu, and Patrick Smith (1972) "The Congruence of Federal-Provincial Campaign Activity in Party Organizations: The Influence of Recruitment Patterns in Three Hamilton Ridings." *Canadian Journal of Political Science* 5:190–225.

Key, V. O., Jr. (1949) *Southern Politics in State and Nation*. New York: Knopf.

Kornberg, Allan, Harold D. Clarke, and William Mishler (1982) *Representative Democracy in the Canadian Provinces*. Scarborough, On.: Prentice-Hall.

Kornberg, Allan, Joel Smith, and Harold Clarke (1979) *Citizen Politicians-Canada*. Durham, N.C.: Carolina Academic Press.

——— (1970) "Semi-Careers in Political Work: The Dilemma of Party Organizations." In *Sage Professional Papers: Comparative Politics* Series, no. 01-008, vol. 3, edited by Harry Eckstein and Ted Robert Gurr. Beverly Hills, Calif.: Sage Publications.

Ladd, Everett Carll, Jr. (1978) *Where Have All the Voters Gone?* New York: Norton.

Mayhew, Leon (1968) "Ascription in Modern Societies." *Sociological Inquiry* 38:105–20.

Milbrath, Lester (1965) *Political Participation.* Chicago: Rand McNally.

Mosca, Gaetano (1939) *The Ruling Class.* Edited and revised by Arthur Livingston. Translated by Hannah D. Kahn. Toronto: McGraw-Hill.

Nexon, David (1971) "Asymmetry in the Political System: Occasional Activists in the Republican and Democratic Parties, 1956–1964." *American Political Science Review* 65:716–30.

Nie, Norman H., et al. (1975) *Statistical Package for the Social Sciences.* 2d ed. New York: McGraw-Hill.

Nie, Norman H., and Sidney Verba (1975) "Political Participation." In *Handbook of Political Science,* vol. 4, edited by Fred I. Greenstein and Nelson W. Polsby. Reading, Mass.: Addison-Wesley.

Prewitt, Kenneth (1965) "Political Socialization and Leadership Selection." *Annals of the American Academy of Political and Social Science* 361:91–111.

Putnam, Robert (1976) *The Comparative Study of Political Elites.* Englewood Cliffs, N.J.: Prentice-Hall.

Schwartz, Mildred A. (1982) "Political Support and Group Dominance." In *Political Support in Canada: The Crisis Years,* edited by Allan Kornberg and Harold D. Clarke. Durham, N.C.: Duke University Press.

Smith, Joel, and Allan Kornberg (1969) "Some Considerations Bearing upon Comparative Research in Canada and the United States." *Sociology* 3:341–57.

Sorauf, Frank J. (1980) *Party Politics in America.* 4th ed. Boston: Little, Brown.

Soule, John W., and James W. Clarke (1970) "Amateurs and Professionals: A Study of Delegates to the 1968 Democratic National Convention." *American Political Science Review* 64:888–98.

Wilson, James Q. (1962). *The Amateur Democrat.* Chicago: University of Chicago Press.

—— (1973) *Political Organizations.* New York: Basic Books.

Ben Gurion and the Intellectuals: A Study of Elite Interaction

Michael Keren

"Those who occupy high office," Mosca (1939:453) wrote, "are almost never the 'best' in an absolute sense, but rather individuals who possess the qualities that are best suited to directing and dominating men." Mosca's (1939:452) rejection of Plato's coupling of political rule with "the highest qualities of mind and character" is of utmost importance to an understanding of his notion of the ruling class. The fact that the ruling classes rule shows, of course, that they contain the individuals who are best fitted to do so. Mosca insisted, however, that such fitness by no means implies that they are the "best" individuals intellectually, much less the "best" individuals morally.

This distinction is immanent to Mosca's overall thinking. He realized that once it is assumed that the "best" in an intellectual or moral sense ought to govern, then, in his words (1939:448): "good souls go looking for a political system that will make the concept a reality." Mosca was concerned about the common tendency to attribute to rulers superior intellectual and moral qualities and ventured to show that the "philosopher king," that is, the person who combines knowledge and power, is an impossibility. To Mosca, the philosopher and the king were two distinct roles, associated with wholly different recruitment patterns. "There is little likelihood," he contended (1939:452): "that in normal times the philosopher, as Plato conceived of him, would win out in the struggle for preeminence among the many who are scrambling for high station."

The urge to draw a line between the king and the philosopher had distracted Mosca, and much of elite theory since, from serious anal-

This paper is part of a larger study, *Ben Gurion and the Intellectuals*, based on David Ben Gurion's private papers. The author wishes to thank the Ben Gurion Research Institute and Archives at Sde Boker, Israel, for granting him access to previously unpublished documents there.

ysis of their interaction; the question of the relationship between knowledge and power received little attention. Mosca stated that as long as the intellectual level of the ruling class is high enough for its members to understand and appreciate the ideas of political thinkers, it is not necessary for the latter to attain power in order to have their programs carried out. He felt that the intellectual pressure that the ruling class as a whole exerts is sufficient to force the politicians "to suit their policies more or less to the views of those who represent the best that the intelligence of a people can produce" (1939:452).

Interestingly, however, even Pareto, who granted knowledge a major role in his theory of the elite, had, in the words of one critic, "never presented anything like a complete statement of the interrelation of knowledge and power" (Samuels, 1974:134). The person of power, in Pareto's thinking, manipulates knowledge in order to sustain his position: "The powerful, instead of saying simply that they want a thing, go to the trouble of devising sophistries to show that they 'have a right' to it: they imitate the wolf's palaver with the lamb" (Samuels, 1974:128). But Pareto had never been explicit as to whether or not the lamb deliberately cooperates in its abuse, how it relates to the wolf, and what its ultimate fate was expected to be.

The failure to elaborate, on a theoretical level, the relationship between knowledge and power stemmed from an inbuilt difficulty to incorporate the knowledge-power dimension into elite theory. It had rightly been assumed by Mills (1956:352) and others that this dimension could be reduced to "the problem of the relations between men of knowledge and men of power," that is, to the problem of interaction among elites. It had long been taken for granted that persons of knowledge (intellectuals) constitute an elite or are part of one (Gouldner, 1979). And yet the conceptualization of intellectuals as members of an elite had also to account for their often remote or critical stance vis-à-vis the social order. One could expect intellectuals, as incumbents of elite roles, to rationalize these roles; but it is impossible to tell what elite roles are being rationalized by intellectual deliberation and critique. Suzanne Keller had remarked on this difficulty in her discussion (1979:291) of intellectual elites, noting that they are definitely members in good standing among the "strategic elites" in society but that their outlook and values are neither carbon copies of the values of other strategic elites nor reflections of an independent social role. It had been hard to conceptualize such a role, if only because intellectuals had been conceived as giving primacy to cultural considerations over societal ones. (See Mannheim, 1949; Parsons, 1969; Nettl, 1969.) The difficulty of relating intellectuals' cultural (and political) output to their location in society has been noted in a recent study by Brym (1980), who proposes to examine intellectuals' shifting social ties, thus abandoning the conception of a static relationship between social ties and intellectuals' politics.

In light of the difficulty of constructing a political sociology of intellectuals, Edward Shils's attempt to locate intellectuals institutionally by reference to intellectual "traditions" stands out as an important theoretical contribution. An intellectual tradition, according to Shils (1973), is a set or pattern of beliefs, conceptions of form, sets of verbal (and other symbolic) usages, and rules of procedure, recurrently linked with each other through time. An important intellectual tradition stressed by Shils is the one which defines intellectual activity as being concerned with fundamental, or in his words, "charismatic," things. Shils wrote (1973:29): "The ethos of intellectual activity has defined the highest performance as being endowed with charismatic properties. The conception of 'genius,' the notion of 'inspiration,' both bespeak the charismatic overtones which are oriented to the greatest intellectual accomplishments. Accordingly, intellectual roles of the most creative intellectuals have been defined as correspondingly endowed with charisma; their incumbents have been correspondingly perceived." Other traditions of intellectuals, those concerned with authority, had dealt with the locus of the charismatic and its institutional manifestations. These traditions assert that charisma is located in a particular part of society or in a particular kind of activity.

The belief in the charismatic qualifications of intellectual works and their producers on one hand and the concern with the location of "charisma" in society on the other had brought intellectuals into "unavoidable contact with earthly authorities." According to Shils, even if such factors as common class, common social origin, or mutual need had not been operative, intellectuals would have been in contact with the mighty because they were fascinated by them. "Intellectual activities are 'serious,' the charismatic is 'serious,' and intellectuals being concerned with the charismatic have, willy-nilly, been drawn into preoccupation with those in authority because all great, very powerful authority is believed by those who possess and those who contemplate it to have a charismatic element resident in it" (1973:30).

At this point some explication of Shils's use of "charisma" is in order. Contrary to Max Weber's use of the term as referring to a particular constellation of personality qualities, Shils contended that the charismatic quality of an individual, as perceived by others or himself, lies in what is thought to be his connection with "some very central feature of man's existence and the cosmos in which he lives" (1965:201). The centrality is constituted by its formative power in initiating, creating, governing, transforming, maintaining, or destroying what is vital in man's life. Thus, "charisma," in this meaning, no longer refers to an extraordinary property of an individual but to a recurrent process whereby the social order is being maintained through the attribution of charismatic qualities.

Attributing charismatic qualities to individuals in vital social positions is part of the process whereby societal power is being legitimized. Shils noted that all effective rulers possess charismatic qualities, i.e., have charismatic qualities attributed to them, unless it is known that they are "*fainéants*," who have abdicated their responsibilities out of moral weakness or are otherwise incompetent. This legitimizing process cuts across all political regimes, including those conceived by Weber as "rational-legal," since, to Shils, authority, by its mere existence, calls forth the attribution of charisma.

Shils's conception of "charisma" as a sociological phenomenon related to the functional need for social order, rather than to the occasional intervention by divinely gifted individuals in that order, has allowed for a new look at the social-institutional role of intellectuals. In this conception, intellectuals participate, by nature of their works and traditions, in "the charismatic construction of reality," that is, the construction of a meaningful social and cultural environment. In that process of construction, elaborated by Eisenstadt as a process involving both symbolic and institutional activities, the intellectual finds himself operating side by side with other social elites. "Symbolic and institutional responses to the quest for the charismatic order," Eisenstadt explained, "tend to become, in any society, centered in some specific institutional loci that are important from the point of view of the construction of tradition in general and that of the place of intellectuals in it in particular. Among these loci the most important are the so-called centers of society" (1973:4). Eisenstadt's notion of the center corresponds to that of Shils. In such (charismatic) centers, the major spheres of social and cultural identity are crystallized, and the sources of authority and power are established and legitimized.

This notion provides a partial answer to the problem of the consideration of intellectuals as a social elite. All forms of intellectual activity (as well as such other symbolic activities as religion or the arts), whether affirmative or critical of the social order, are located at the charismatic center. The charismatic construction of reality, one may assume, involves a variety of beliefs, forms, and traditions. Even intellectual remoteness has its function in the construction, maintenance, and orderly transformation of the social order; and the ivory tower could easily be conceived in light of its legitimizing role. One important question remains, however. Given this institutional location of the intellectuals and its source, how does one explain frequent breakdowns of knowledge-power cooperation in charismatic centers? If intellectuals are indeed drawn into contact with the mighty because of their fascination with power and charisma, why had the frequent call upon intellectuals (Feuer, 1969:57) "to transform themselves psychologically, to rid themselves of their liberal individualism, and to prepare themselves for the role of dictatorial, authoritarian rulers" not been responded to more enthusiastically?

True, intellectuals have often been partners in unholy alliances involving the abuse of intellectual activity for the sake of legitimizing and promoting the preeminence of other elites and their own (see Chomsky, 1967; Nieburg, 1970). The "betrayal" of the intellectuals is a much favored subject by modern social critics (Benda, 1955). But what about the frequent finding in empirical research (Wilensky, 1956; Barnes, 1971; Nelkin, 1979; Szanton, 1981) that intellectuals tend to maintain a freewheeling status within organizational and political settings in which they participate in elite roles? And, given the institutional and symbolic rewards associated with the affiliation, why is there tension at all within charismatic centers? (see Zuckerman, 1977).

The question of the sources of tension between intellectuals and power has not received proper attention. It has generally been explained by reference to structural variables. A typical statement by Raymond Aron (1957:215) describes the relationship between intellectuals and the ruling classes as "reciprocal." The more remote intellectuals seem to be from the preoccupations of those who govern, the more Aron expects the latter to give vent to their innate hostility and contempt for the "word spinners." The more recalcitrant to modern ideas the privileged classes appear, the more incapable of ensuring the nation's power and economic progress, the more the intellectuals incline to dissidence. Such a structural explanation does not really explain why "innate hostility and contempt" should be expected in the first place. A somewhat more satisfactory explanation was provided by Eisenstadt (1973), who stressed the very competition between various elites engaged in the construction of cultural reality, a rivalry which implies that each elite, on its part, poses certain types of questions and answers about the social order, thus excluding the questions and answers posed by others. However, one who ignores the content of these questions and answers is left with no clues as to when tension could be expected or what variety of forms it might take and why.

It seems that a fuller explanation of the sources of tension requires three conditions:

1. A transfer of the level of analysis from structural interactions among elites to their exchange of ideas.
2. A consideration of the exchange within specific societal and political contexts.
3. A consideration of political traditions as well as intellectual ones.

The "power" side of the knowledge-power equation cannot be ignored.

In my study of David Ben Gurion and the intellectuals, I attempted to fulfill all three conditions in order to find an explanation to a knowledge-power conflict which constituted a major breakdown in a charismatic center. I refer to a Gogmagog clash in the early 1960s between David Ben Gurion, Israel's first prime minister, and the country's intellectual elite. This clash was interesting for two reasons. First, it involved a charismatic center indeed: On the one side, Ben Gurion, a master statesman associated in everybody's mind with Israel's struggle for independence in the 1940s and its nation-building efforts in the 1950s; on the other side, most of the country's prominent men of letters, scientists, scholars, philosophers, and writers—including persons of world fame. Second, the conflict between Ben Gurion and the intellectuals could not be explained in structural terms. On a structural level it was all but unpredictable, since the conflict occurred within the framework of close cooperation between knowledge and power. Rarely have intellectuals had such direct access to a meaningful center of power. Furthermore, Ben Gurion, a Polish-born Jew, belonged to a political elite composed of many autodidacts like himself who placed much emphasis on the intelligentsia and its societal role. Ben Gurion's files are filled with fascinating exchanges with intellectuals over essential questions concerning the nation-building process. The sources of tension had to be found in the content of these exchanges.

Indeed, Ben Gurion's files reveal an interesting challenge posed to the intellectuals. In 1949, with the end of the war of independence, the new state of Israel faced severe problems, especially in light of mass immigration into the country. Ben Gurion's program of nation building, as he often declared, assigned a leading role to the intellectuals. The scientist, in Ben Gurion's (1951) thought, was expected to explore the secrets of nature in order to overcome the country's natural limitations; the philosopher was expected to reveal and promote the hidden sources of human strength needed to accomplish the impossible; the scholar was expected to inspire the nation-building mission by stressing its ancient ties; and the writer was expected to produce the great epic of the times. And while these demands remained within the sphere of political and ideological rhetoric, the challenge had to be taken seriously.

The challenge to the intellectuals, many of whom played major roles in the vast projects undertaken under Ben Gurion's leadership, lay in the prime minister's genuine belief that their leading role in the material and spiritual transformation of the Jewish people required not blind obedience to the state but rather "the true reflection of the conscience and vision in their hearts" (1951:7). In other words, Ben Gurion expected pure and applied science, as well as all forms of intellectual work, to confirm and inspire a definite social message. Ben Gurion's endless preoccupation with knowledge, his thorough scrutiny of intellectual works and long debates with persons of letters, reflected a persistent effort to establish that tie. As the effort continued and knowledge became interwoven with power in a complex and dangerous way, the intellectuals were gradually forced to define a group position in opposition to their patron. This became apparent in January 1961, when the intellectuals, never before active as a group, almost unanimously supported a public statement calling for the dissociation between "any one individual" and the destiny of the state.

Significantly, however, this political expression of group consciousness by the intellectuals did not occur in the late fifties, when the debates over knowledge and power were at their height. In those years, though often in opposition to Ben Gurion, the intellectuals willingly accepted their nominal role in a charismatic center that he dominated, in both its cultural and political domains. As one of them (Avinery, 1965:29) later admitted, Israel's intellectuals in the fifties "were outdone in their own 'métier' by a politician who, for this reason, could not just be ordinary." Only during a major political-constitutional crisis in the early sixties, known as "the Affair," when Ben Gurion, for the first time in his political career, was perceived to play an ordinary, partisan, noncharismatic role, when for the first time he no longer represented the "raison d'etre" of the state, did the use and abuse of knowledge become a political issue. The fading of Ben Gurion's charisma in the early 1960s and the rise of a powerful but gray and faceless party apparatus instead gave substance to the scientists' worries about the political misuse of science and technology, the philosophers' fears regarding the creation overnight of new ideological orientations, the scholars' concern about selective uses of symbols, and the writers' fatigue with the constant burden of supplying norms. By a dialectical process, the contrasts between knowledge and power which had evolved during Ben Gurion's extraordinary reign, and which remained latent as long as the charismatic center was dominated by him, were now becoming sources of deep political conflict.

This leads me to propose, as a general hypothesis, that *while intellectuals are often willing to play a nominal role in the charismatic center of society, there seem to exist underlying conflicts of principle between knowledge and power whose political saliency varies with the degree to which intellectuals perceive their political patrons as endowed with charisma.* In what follows I shall try to expose two underlying conflicts of this kind which may seem to exceed the boundaries of my case study. The first concerns the relationship between science and values. The second concerns the role of "vision" in policy making. It goes without saying that these intellectual conflicts are not expected to surface in every routine interaction between intellectual and political elites. Ben Gurion's towering personality and unusual concern with knowledge (which earned him the label of "philosopher king") no doubt contributed to the fact that these conflicts were expressed in this special context at this special time. At the same time, the scrutiny of questions concerning the relationship between knowledge and power during the Ben Gurion era revealed what could be much more general conflicts. Ben Gurion's files provide a rare opportunity to observe the evolution of tension between intellectual and political elites in the nation-building process.

It should be noted again that the interaction described here involved incumbents of elite roles in Israeli society. The intellectual conflicts between Ben Gurion and the intellectuals evolved within the context of cooperation between elites. Ben Gurion's main adversaries in debates over the nature of science, described below, were "insiders" who cooperated with him closely and intimately in the scientific and technological projects of the time. Price (1965:83) defined insiders as "eminent scientists who hold important positions in the institutional structure by which government and science are closely connected," and expected them to accept the subordination of science to the value systems established by the nation's tradition and interpreted by the authority of the government. This was true only up to a point. Ben Gurion continuously challenged the scientists to scrutinize the social and political implications of their trade, and he himself had clear views on these implications; his views were often inconsistent with important scientific traditions. Thus, subordination of science to power could have meant—on the level of principles—giving up the essence of scientific inquiry as perceived at the time; and the more precisely the principles were defined, the more subtle the conflict became. Also, Ben Gurion's adversaries in debates over the role of "vision" in policy making, described below, were men of letters who, in the fifties, helped enhance Ben Gurion's notion of "messianic vision" as guide for action on the national level. Gradually, however, the idiosyncratic nature of "vision," and its close association with power, worried the intellectuals, who began to demand adherence to clear principles of policy making instead.

The Conflict over Science

Like most statesmen, Ben Gurion was never a philosopher of science; but it is impossible to derive a rather coherent set of principles from his fragmentary declarations on science. One principle stands out—a strong belief in the primacy of intuition over observation as the source of scientific and moral truth. In his speeches before scientific conferences, Ben Gurion never failed to note "the all-embracing unit of existence, the one-ness of matter and mind." A great admirer of Plato and Spinoza, he believed that humanity, as an organic part of existence, which is both material and spiritual, has the gift of recognizing its deepest nature. Ben Gurion believed in the power of mind to penetrate and explore the secrets of nature and the human conscience; he was often quite explicit about the lessons to be learned from such an exploration.

Ben Gurion's theory of knowledge was articulated in the 1950s before audiences equally fascinated by the power of the mind, although from a wholly different perspective. Israel's scientists, like their peers elsewhere, believed in experimental science and the new horizons it was opening to mankind. They objected to Ben Gurion's notion that "true" reality can be grasped through immediate experience and insisted that science can only flourish if nothing is taken as an absolute truth, especially when there is new evidence to contradict it. "Absolute truth," they believed, is merely the result of fragmentary observations—a notion scientists in the 1950s often tried to apply to the sphere of ethics and politics as well. The following entry in Ben Gurion's diary, describing a conversation with a young physicist, is instructive in this regard:

> In the evening we had dinner, as usual, at Renana's place. Amos Deshalit and Aharon Kazir came—and Amos tried to prove that theoretically there isn't any difference between machine and man, and a machine can be designed which fully resembles man. He does not admit there is knowledge—only physical processes exist, and there is no difference between a living individual and a perfect machine. I wonder whether two machines could exchange letters in matters of philosophy, morality, or science. He admitted there is a difference between non-living and living features, but not an absolute one. (4 January 1957)

The discussion Ben Gurion described in his diary continued to preoccupy the prime minister all that week. "Our conversation in Renana's apartment does not leave my mind," he wrote Deshalit on 13 January.

> I am troubled by your stand as physicist in matters of human reason and condition. Does specialization in the science of physics really prevent one from recognizing the spiritual powers and reason of man? Do you believe that two machines could be designed to exchange letters on matters of art, philosophy and science, such as Spinoza's treatise, or that a machine could be conceived which, while traveling all over the globe, would collect facts and deduce Darwin's theory from them? Don't you realize the entirely different nature of spiritual processes (which are of course related to physical processes in the human body) but differ completely from mere

mechanical processes? Do you conceive of a machine which would compose the book of Job, or Plato's *Symposium*, or Einstein's relativity theory? The perfect machine would perhaps obey the will of its designer, but there is almost no limit to man's reason and intellectual ability.

Debates among scientists and laymen over the simulation of the human mind are usually of little importance. The rhetoric involved is enormous and the low feasibility of such simulation makes the question of its possibility or desirability look quite remote. The same debate, however, since it concerns a major normative question, is of extraordinary importance when conducted between scientists and statesmen. The question has been accurately defined by Goodall (1970:17):

> We can regard the question "Can machines think?" as essentially empty. The relevant one, as a politician ought well to understand, is "Who controls whom, and how, and for what is this going to be done?"

The question of control has been too simply operationalized by Goodall and others. Control was taken literally, and the politician was taken to fear the loss of actual political power presumably implied by automation. "Automation and data processing," wrote Goodall (1970:65) "could very easily deprive the existing political blocks of their meaning, leaving power in a kind of technical no man's land. . . . One can see perhaps what this could mean. Government will no longer be able to manage technical committees and will have to consider expert assessments of various situations. . . ." This approach suffers from a stereotypical view of the politician. Rather than attributing to him a general fear of the machine, investigators should determine which specific political ideas and values are affected by the notion of simulation and which types of political options such a notion opens or closes. In a study of the computer revolution in philosophy, Aaron Sloman proposed the model for such an investigation. Sloman (1978:272) elaborated the basic features of intelligent machines and showed the dilemmas they suggest. For instance, it is impossible to devise really helpful mechanical servants without giving them desires, attitudes, and emotions.

> They will sometimes have to feel the need for great urgency when things are going wrong and something has to be done about it. Some of them will need to have the ability to *develop* their motives in the light of experience, if they are to cope with changing situations (including changing personal relations), with real intelligence and wisdom. This raises the possibility of their acquiring aims and desires not foreseen by their designers. Will people be prepared to take account of their desires?

Ben Gurion's debates with Deshalit over the simulation of the mind concerned a major normative question. Both extended their philosophy of science to the sphere of values. The statesman, in line with his notion of intuition, implied that the creative mind can derive absolute and eternal values from the laws of nature. The scientist implied that values, like truth, are none but predictable (and hence artificially reproducible) human constructs derived from experience with no objective (or "natural") ontological status.

This focus of the debate was set by Deshalit in his 3 February answer to Ben Gurion's previously mentioned letter. Deshalit distinguished between three functions of the brain: receiving, decoding, and encoding information. He limited the debate to the decoding function. As far as receiving was concerned, he saw no difference between Darwin's travels in the world and a computer fed with data on the size, weight, color, and other characteristics of the species. He dismissed the common argument regarding the lack of initiative by machines by claiming that the human initiative to travel and collect specific data is also the outgrowth of former conditioning. As the computer does not work by its own initiative, neither does a person born and raised in a secluded, dark room. And since encoding is also a mere matter of communication, Deshalit focused on the similarities between the mind and the machine in fulfilling the decoding function; that is, the conversion of input into a different kind of output.

Deshalit argued that the equivalence between the mind and the machine could be demonstrated by showing that every logical calculus can be expressed in exact mathematical language.

> I do not mean, of course, that a computer would print, for instance, the statement: "A wise son makes a glad father, but a foolish man despises his mother," but that a machine could easily deduce the folk wisdom involved in that statement [by] other means, such as . . . finding a correlation between the parent's happiness and the childrens' wisdom. True, such folk wisdom sounds disgustingly dry, but this is only because the machine speaks its language and not ours. And let's not forget that from the point of view of the truth of that statement, there is no principle difference whether it is expressed in King Solomon's grandiloquent language or in the form of a dry chart of numbers.

Deshalit's task was, of course, made easy once he argued that the source of knowledge (the "receiving" function) did not have to be considered. It is rather trivial that normative statements can be deduced from other normative statements. It is, after all, the source of these statements which determines their uniqueness and which sparks the question of equivalence between man and machine. At the same time, Deshalit did not wholly ignore the question of the source of knowledge. In the above example, he attributed ethical statements to cumulative experience which provided the justification for their consideration in algorithmic terms. In his later correspondence, it became even clearer that the debate was not over the feasibility of reducing logical statements into mathematical symbols but over the source of values. To Deshalit, observation was the only means to acquire any "truth," including the moral truth Ben Gurion derived by intuition.

For this very reason Ben Gurion insisted upon the distinction between the mind and the machine. Noting that "I have friends, gifted scientists in the Weizmann Institute—physicists and chemists—who laugh at my view on this," he wrote Hans Kreitler, a psychologist, that "the distinct mark of human thinking is the thinker's consciousness about it, and since man knows he thinks, he is the master of his thought and its creator." He objected to the behaviorists' attempts in the 1950s to reduce human behavior to algorithmic dimensions: "Let behaviorists ignore as much as they wish the individual's consciousness, and observe merely his motions and reactions—but they cannot escape recognizing their own consciousness" (Letter, 17 February 1963).

Two years after his conversation with Deshalit, he found a quotation in Niels Bohr's *Atomic Physics and Human Knowledge* which he deemed appropriate to send to the physicist: " 'The existence of life itself should be considered both as regards its definition and observation, as a basic postulate of biology, not susceptible of further analysis, in the same way as the existence of the quantum of action forms the elementary basis of atomic physics; such a viewpoint condemns as irrelevant any comparison of living organism[s] with machines' " (Letter, 10 June 1959).

Deshalit responded at length on 3 July 1959. He first explained that Professor Bohr revised the argument, derived from his complementary principle, that the explanation of life requires wholly new concepts. Deshalit noted recent developments in molecular biology blurring the distinction between living and non-living phenomena. He noted, for instance, attempts to "teach" electronic machines to distinguish between geometrical forms, by storing relevant but partial information in their memory and reinforcing desirable answers. "Let's not forget," he wrote the socialist prime minister, "under what hard conditions the machine has to operate. . . . Let's try and imagine what would have happened to a child who forgets every morning all the information he was fed the day before." He insisted, however, that a physical system consisting of millions and millions of memory units, and whose various centers are independent, could in principle create new ideas by the intrapolation and extrapolation of former ideas and possibly the mutations of former ideas.

And now Deshalit reached the core of the debate. Aware of Ben Gurion's fascination with the objective harmony of nature, he cast doubts about that harmony and left no doubts about the ethical implications of his approach. "If I may," he wrote,

I shall add a remark about the order and harmony we witness in nature and the feelings of wonder with which they fill our hearts. I believe that under slightly deeper scrutiny we might realize that we are not enchanted by the fact that nature is what it is. After all, what are order and harmony if not those things to which we are conditioned since our childhood? The eye and ear react, as is well known, to waves—the one to electric waves and the other to acoustic waves. While the ear distinguishes between different wave lengths even when they are interwoven, the eye observes only an average effect of the waves. Thus, for example, the ear hears two sounds played simultaneously as two sounds, while the eye sees two colors placed on each other as a new color. If one day these characteristics were changed, the Ninth symphony would sound to our new ears as a tasteless and boring mixture of strange sounds while the greatest landscapes would disintegrate into strange and uninteresting sets of separate colors. Our fascination with sounds and colors is thus the outgrowth of certain life habits and is affected to a great extent by the "education" we are constantly exposed to from our environment. When I sometimes realize how many times a day I repeat in my little boy's ears what is just and unjust in the world, I am not surprised that people, (at least some of them . . .) later distinguish between good and evil; I am only wondering why they are doing it so inefficiently. I am sure that every machine would have learned such matters much faster and more profoundly. It was, I believe, Helmholtz who said that if a worker in his artisan shop had approached him with as incomplete a tool as the human eye, he would have fired him. I am afraid that in the not so distant future someone will say the same about the human brain.

Ben Gurion responded quickly: "Nature's order and harmony are not the outgrowth of habit but of reason and cognition. Had there not existed such order, there would have been no habit, or human being, just hurly burly, and we would not have even known it." And he added: "The machine is incapable of wondering. It does not ask questions. The (relative) greatness of man is his ability to ask questions, and sometimes also answering them—while no machine in the world would ever try and explain *by itself* that there is no difference between itself and Amos Deshalit's brain" (Letter, 27 July 1959).

The statesman was indeed fighting for control, but it was the control of the human mind over its environment, not the control of man over machine. He attempted to derive both intelligence and conscience from the universal laws of nature and attributed absolute validity to both. And if modern physics did not yield support to this position, the ancient Prophets certainly did:

> Our Prophets demanded justice in the life of man and envisaged justice in the cosmos. Isaiah, one of the greatest of our Prophets, said "Drop down, ye heavens, from above, and let the skies pour down righteousness; let the earth open, and let them bring forth salvation, and let righteousness spring up together. . . ." And when the Psalmist seeks in one short verse to catalogue supreme values, he says: "Mercy and truth are met together; righteousness and peace have kissed each other." And he adds: "Truth shall spring out of the earth; and righteousness shall look down from heaven. . . ." In the words of our prophets, the moral content is inherent not only in man but in the whole of nature. And I say that only by the guidance of prophetic ethics can we direct the tremendous power of science along fruitful paths, so that it becomes a blessing to mankind. Science unguided by moral values can lead to catastrophe. (In Pearlman, 1965:200)

Here lies the solution to an apparent contradiction between the belief of many statesmen in free science as a lever for human perfection and their frequent call for moral values to guide the scientist in his work. To the statesman, science and values are not separate entities but two aspects of the same "cosmos" to be revealed by the human mind. The demand to integrate intelligence and conscience stems from a belief that one is not possible without the other. In the eyes of the man of action, the scientist who wishes to flourish and make a contribution must be part of a well-defined normative and political structure. To the scientist, the reverse is true. While he recognizes that he is part of a normative and political reality, he also recognizes the need to overcome biases stemming from it. He aims at intersubjectivity; the organic link between science and values is to him a hindrance rather than a blessing. As long as he operates within a normative consensus, one may expect only little consciousness over questions of science and values. But when the consensus breaks down, the underlying intellectual conflict may turn into a gigantic political dispute.

The Conflict over Policy Making

The most recurrent theme in Ben Gurion's debates with intellectuals was the role of vision in policy making. In the context of policy making, vision may be operationalized as a set of goals exceeding the obvious parameters of systems of resources. This is what Ben Gurion referred to when he stressed the need to use "messianic" vision as a guide for policy making. There was a strong realistic element involved in that demand. Ben Gurion felt that the whole endeavor in the state of Israel would fail if "normal" social, economic, and political conditions were relied upon. He also understood that the policies exceeding the normal path involve a cost which can only be borne in a specific state of mind. The intellectuals were assigned an important role in both regards; exploring extraordinary alternatives and creating the state of mind necessary for their pursuit. The challenge worried them mainly because of the arbitrary nature of vision. Vision translated into action cannot keep up with established sets of principles. Calculations of economic costs must be ignored, and many other constraints must be overlooked. Utopian thinking opens the door to very earthly modes of behavior, such as "doism"—the tendency to pursue desired policy in disregard of systemic consequences (which principles are intended to guard). Great projects are undertaken both as monuments of nation building and as the fulfillments of historical missions. If the drying of swamps, inhabitation of the desert, or absorption of immigrants has messianic meaning, then no other considerations should stand in the way. This entails a specific policy-making process, one based on "big" decisions, great determination, centralization, and much improvisation when things go wrong. Planners, economists, and other representatives of rational decision making become a hindrance to the tasks at hand. They are neutralized by the carriers of faith.

The person of vision and the person of principle can hardly coexist in the policy-making system. Both have a claim to the "long range"; but the first considers its benefits, the second, its costs. Their relationship becomes even more complex because of the difficulty of deciding in every specific situation who is right and who is wrong—or what path to follow when both are right. That difficulty came to light in a meeting of Ben Gurion and eleven men of letters assembled in a private home on 4 July 1961. "Strange as it may sound to you," Ben Gurion opened the meeting (recorded by a stenographer), "this has nothing to do with politics." Ben Gurion described at length the major goals for the country and the conditions under which they might be fulfilled. National goals, such as security, education, inhabitation of the land, absorption of immigration, and economic independence, he argued, have no solid economic and sociological ground. The pursuit of these goals on the basis of routine policy procedures is thus impossible. Furthermore, the demand for such procedures may prevent the recruitment of the nonroutine resources needed. The intellectuals' claim that the messianic era is over, Ben Gurion added, endangers the nation-building effort, which depends on their willingness to combine scientific and literary work with messianic vision.

In their reply, the intellectuals acknowledged the important function of visionary statements to the setting of societal tasks and to the recruitment of support for their accomplishment. They strongly objected, however, to their use as standards of performance. It is necessary at times to give up vision, they argued, in order to achieve a better picture of discrepancies between desired goals and existing reality.

A leading economist was mainly concerned with the negative correlation between vision and efficiency. Vision allows one to ignore necessary considerations of resources. With vision as a guide, important goals are considered; but their systemic implications are not. Inhabitation of the desert is important, but so is education; and the trade-off has to be calculated. Has anyone even considered how many schools have not been built as a result of the decision to construct the national water carrier, he asked. And if a decision is made to avoid considerations of cost in light of a policy's expected benefit, it should still be asked whether this particular policy justifies such a costly decision. Furthermore, vision prevents an operationalization of goals. Should the desert be inhabited by 50,000, 100,000, or 200,000 people? What are the implications of any of these alternative models to agriculture in other regions of the land, to industry, to the overall quality of life? Hinting at a possible division of labor, he claimed that while the man of vision may not pay attention to questions of resources, the economist must.

Ben Gurion's reply included a surprise. To him, inhabitation of the desert went far beyond the obvious goals mentioned. The desert, if inhabited, would serve as Israel's strategic gate to the awakening third world in Asia and Africa—a goal the distinguished economist did not even consider. Vision, Ben Gurion argued, consists of the observation of conditions that are non-existing but which might exist. Everything the experts have told us not to do for lack of resources, he added, we have done, and successfully so. Ben Gurion admitted that the experts trying to prevent him from supposedly irrational acts adhered to their professional duty. If one considers all scientific data and nothing else, the experts' position is justified. But science rarely goes out of its way, while the individual qua individual does. Man, Ben Gurion argued, is capable of vision.

Ben Gurion stressed the compartmentalized nature of systematic knowledge that prevents the intellectuals from sensing reality as a whole. The setting of national goals, however, requires an overall picture. For instance, the Israeli economy, Ben Gurion argued, will not flourish as long as it is oriented merely toward the European market. The Europeans can produce their needs by themselves; the millions of people in Asia and Africa cannot. Reaching new markets of this kind is a goal derived neither from calculus by the economist, nor from the word of God, but from man's intuition—from his ability to consider the whole scope of things and their future development. How the Jews would reach the people of Asia, Ben Gurion concluded, and why inhabitation of the desert is relevant to this task, is not written in the books; it has nothing to do with economics, or with sociology, philosophy, biology, or physics. There just is no such science.

Ben Gurion's point was well taken. Most social thinkers rarely go out of their way to evaluate societal performance by comparing it to extraordinary goals of the kind he proposed in the meeting. The division of labor according to which the statesman supposedly determines the goals and the person of knowledge the means is strictly kept. It was the alliance between behavioral positivism and political inactivism that Ben Gurion hoped to avoid. He understood, in principle, the importance of the intellectual's participation in the policy-making process. The perfect society required intellectuals to point the way. Socialist thought always acknowledged the need to expose internal faults and make efforts to mend them. The intellectual, as teacher, was expected to have vision in order to teach it to the generations of the future.

It must be noted, however, that vision had a very specific meaning to Ben Gurion; the goals were predetermined. Nowhere did he consider institutionalization of the intellectual's participation in the determination or evaluation of goals. The intellectual was not to concern himself merely with means, but the goals were not really open to debate. This was never too clear when Ben Gurion referred to the intellectual in Israel, who was expected to operate anyway within the right state of mind; but it can be detected in his references to intellectuals in general. For instance, in response to a letter his daughter sent him from France, in which she noted the intellectuals' objection to de Gaulle, Ben Gurion simply associated those intellectuals with communism. He labelled them "doctrinaires" who acquired their patterns of thought by dictation from Moscow and who were incapable of observing reality as it is (Letter, 15 October 1958).

To the modern political scientist this sounds familiar. Few statesmen are known to accept the intellectual's critical role as a contributor to society. The intellectual is expected to carry a vision and disseminate it but not to determine its content. This is often a convenient status quo for both the statesman and the intellectual; but when conditions change, the intellectual conflict may turn into political dispute.

Conclusion

Ben Gurion's interaction with intellectuals provides initial insights into the evolvement of tension between intellectuals and power *within* the context of knowledge-power cooperation. And since such cooperation is often claimed to characterize the emerging technological state (Ellul, 1964; Galbraith, 1967; Toffler, 1981), this case study may provide an important lesson for the future. The lesson is that in spite of the tight collaboration between intellectual and political elites, which Mosca was so suspicious of, and the emergence of complex knowledge-power structures resembling the model of the "philosopher king," there always exists an underlying conflict between knowledge and power. And while the saliency of this conflict varies, its probability may be a major source of vitality for the modern technological state. As the state develops, more and more knowledge is being acquired from a variety of sources, including sophisticated intelligence systems. However, the intellectual possesses one quality which no intelligence system could ever match: the ability to think freely; that is, to exceed predetermined guidelines altogether. Free thinking by individuals brings up the inherent conflicts between knowledge and power which systems of any kind are programmed to suppress. And it is these conflicts which seem to assure societal and political vitality. It is intellectual conflict, not blind commitment, which makes society aware that there are alternatives, there exists a periphery, there is always the possibility of a mistake. As committed as the intellectual may be, as unwilling to play the role of free thinker, the preoccupation with knowledge inevitably turns him into social critic.

References

Aron, Raymond (1957) The Opium of the Intellectuals. Garden City, N.Y.: Doubleday.

Avinery, Shlomo (1965) "Israel in the Post Ben Gurion Era: The Nemesis of Messianism." Midstream 11: 16–32.

Barnes, S. P. (1971) "Making Out in Industrial Research." Science Studies 1: 157–75.

Benda, Julien (1955) The Betrayal of the Intellectuals. Boston: Beacon.

Ben Gurion, David (1951) "Ha'medina Ve'hama'amatz Ha'ruhani." Molad 7: 3–11.

Brym, Robert (1980) Intellectuals and Politics. London: Allen.

Chomsky, Noam (1967) American Power and the New Mandarins. New York: Vintage.

Eisenstadt, S. N. (1973) "Intellectuals and Tradition." In Intellectuals and Tradition, edited by S. N. Eisenstadt and S. R. Graubard. New York: Humanities.

Ellul, Jacques (1964) The Technological Society. New York: Vintage.

Feuer, Lewis S. (1969) Marx and the Intellectuals. Garden City, N.Y.: Doubleday.

Galbraith, John K. (1967) The New Industrial State. New York: New American Library.

Gella, Alexander (ed.) (1967) The Intelligentsia and the Intellectuals: Theory, Method and Case Study. Beverly Hills, Calif.: Sage.

Goodall, Marcus (1970) Science, Logic and Political Action. Cambridge, Mass.: Schenkman.

Gouldner, Alvin (1979) *The Future of Intellectuals and the Rise of the New Class*. New York: Seabury.

Keller, Suzanne (1979) *Beyond the Ruling Class*. New York: Arno.

Mannheim, Karl (1949) *Ideology and Utopia*. New York: Harcourt.

Mills, C. W. (1956) *The Power Elite*. London: Oxford University Press.

Mosca, Gaetano (1939) *The Ruling Class*. New York: McGraw-Hill.

Nelkin, Dorothy (ed.) (1939) *Controversy: Politics of Technical Decisions*. Beverly Hills, Calif.: Sage.

Nettl, J. P. (1969) "Ideas, Intellectuals and Structures of Dissent." In *On Intellectuals*, edited by Philip Reiff. Garden City, N.Y.: Doubleday.

Nieburg, H. L. (1970) *In the Name of Science*. Chicago: Quadrangle.

Parsons, Talcott (1969) "The Intellectual: A Social Role Category." In *On Intellectuals*, edited by Philip Reiff. Garden City, N.Y.: Doubleday.

Pearlman, Moshe (1965) *Ben Gurion Looks Back in talks with Moshe Pearlman*. New York: Simon & Schuster.

Price, Don K. (1965) *The Scientific Estate*. Cambridge, Mass.: Harvard.

Samuels, Warren J. (1974) *Pareto on Policy*. New York: Elsevier.

Shils, Edward (1965) "Charisma, Order and Status." *American Sociological Review* 30:199–213.

———— (1973) "Intellectuals, Tradition and the Traditions of Intellectuals: Some Preliminary Considerations." In *Intellectuals and Tradition*, edited by S. N. Eisenstadt and S. R. Graubard. New York: Humanities.

Sloman, Aaron (1978) *The Computer Revolution in Philosophy*. Sussex, Eng.: Harvester.

Szanton, Peter (1981) *Not Well Advised*. New York: Russell Sage.

Toffler, Alvin (1981) *The Third Wave*. New York: Bantam.

Wilensky, Harold (1956) *Intellectuals in Labour Unions: Organizational Pressures on Professional Roles*. Glencoe, Ill.: Free Press.

Zuckerman, Harriet (1977) *Scientific Elite*. New York: Free Press.

Elites, Economic Ideologies, and Democracy in Jamaica

Wendell Bell and Juan J. Baldrich

Today, no one would doubt Mosca's principle that in large-scale societies only a few rule; the many do not and never will (Meisel, 1958). Yet political analysts are now less ready than Mosca and his followers, such as Robert Michels, to reach the pessimistic conclusion that such minority rule necessarily makes democracy inoperative. Ruling classes vary in how open and closed they are, in their responsiveness to the needs and wishes of the ruled class, and in the constraints on their powers. Moreover, the concept of democracy, as well as the forms and processes of regimes aspiring to be democratic, has continued to evolve (Dahl, 1971).

We are more aware than Mosca was of a wide range of possibilities and of approximating democratic principles through representation and indirection. Moreover, political regimes exist today that are based upon widespread adult participation in the political system, public contestation or political competition, and the maintenance of public liberties. How effective, efficient, and equitable such regimes

We gratefully acknowledge financial assistance from the National Institute of Mental Health (Grant No. 5-TO1-MH12133) that supported the Yale Comparative Sociology Training Program of which this study is part; from the Concilium on International and Area Studies, Yale University; and from the Social Science Research Council for a grant to the first author that permitted him to reinterview elites in Jamaica again in 1979. We also thank J. William Gibson, Jr., Robert V. Robinson, and David L. Stevenson for their important contributions, including some of the elite interviewing in 1974. Additionally, we thank Charles C. Moskos, Jr., who kindly made his 1961–1962 data available to us for re-analysis; the late Vernon L. Arnett, who gave us advice throughout the project; Vaughan Lewis, who helped in getting election statistics; Carl Stone, who made his survey data available to us; and Leonard Broom, Robert A. Dahl, Gary Gereffi, Juan J. Linz, Ivar Oxaal, Bruce M. Russett, M. G. Smith, John H. Stanfield II, and John and Evelyne Huber Stephens, who made comments on an earlier version of this paper.

are, of course, constitutes an additional set of questions that, while affecting the long-term legitimacy of a regime, do not in themselves determine the classification of a regime as politically democratic or not.

Yet whether or not a regime can be judged objectively to be a democracy—and most regimes cannot—nearly everywhere today the rulers rule in the name of the people. The "political formula," as Mosca called it, of popular sovereignty is everywhere the dominant justification legitimating the structure of political authority. In the late twentieth century, democratic ideology has become *the* myth of the ruling class.

The spread of democratic ideology, for example, was evident during the rise of the new states since the mid-1940s. Nearly all of the 90 or so new states entered the status of political independence with their nationalist leaders voicing the precepts of democracy in opposition to the colonial, mostly European, masters. The vast majority of the new states—about four-fifths—started their new statehood with democratic, that is, pluralist and competitive, regimes. But while the rhetoric remained largely democratic in the sense of justifying rule by recourse to the people's will or welfare, most of the new states actually have become undemocratic. Benin, Burma, Kampuchea, Rwanda, Sierra Leone, Suriname, Togo, Tunisia, and Upper Volta, to mention just a few, come to mind. Because of complex and subtle variations in the degree of competitiveness and opposition on the one hand and in the extent of public liberties on the other, classification is risky. Yet as a rough picture of the fate of democracy in the new states, by 1980 only about one-fourth of the new states remained democratic. A smaller percentage, 19.4, of the new states had multiparty systems that were also considered free (Gastil, 1981:12).

The purpose of this paper is to examine one new state, Jamaica, that has managed to maintain a politically democratic system. Specifically, we (1) explore the beliefs and attitudes of Jamaican elites before and after political independence as both barometer and cause of elite behavior with consequences for the maintenance or breakdown of the democratic regime, (2) give a causal explanation of variations in elite attitudes, and (3) briefly discuss the sources of recent and future threats to Jamaican democracy.

Basic Data

For this report we used a variety of data: government reports and documents, census materials, research articles and books written by other scholars, and informal discussions with other Caribbeanists. Also, we used interviews with Jamaican elites done by Moskos (1967) in 1961–1962 (henceforth cited as "the 1962 study"); and we interviewed Jamaican leaders ourselves during a re-study in 1974, twelve years after the country received political independence. These data are augmented by interviews with key informants and leaders done by Bell on repeated research trips to Jamaica, beginning in the summer of 1956 and ending in June 1979. The last, for example, included interviews with then-Prime Minister Michael Manley and then-Leader of the Opposition Edward Seaga.

Moskos interviewed twenty-four Jamaican leaders. First, he interviewed five persons, each representing a different institutional sector in the society, who had considerable influence in Jamaica based on their positions alone. The five institutional sectors were: "(1) the incumbent political group, (2) the political opposition, (3) major economic enterprises, (4) the civil service and (5) the mass media" (Moskos, 1967:96).

He asked each of the five persons initially interviewed to name the "most important influential individuals on the entire island," considering all aspects of Jamaican life. That is, he wanted to know the political, economic, social, and cultural elite of Jamaican society, those people "who can influence or control other people's opinions and actions" (Moskos, 1967:113). Thus, the positional method gave way to the reputational method, new respondents being selected from those persons most frequently nominated. The same question regarding societal-wide influence was asked of each subsequent respondent.

In the 1962 study, a total of 61 leaders received 2 or more nominations, and of these 24 were interviewed. Using exactly the same procedure in 1974, we found that 158 leaders were nominated, and we interviewed 83 of them.[1] In both years, priority was given to obtaining interviews with the persons receiving the largest number of nominations who had not yet been interviewed.

The fact that a smaller number of leaders was nominated in 1962 than in 1974 raises a question about the comparability of the two sets of data. The larger number of leaders nominated in 1974 represents an actual increase in the size of the Jamaican elite group since independence. This conclusion is supported by the fact that 121 leaders had been nominated in 1974 when we reached Moskos's sample size of 24, in contrast to the 61 leaders who were mentioned in 1962 when the same number of leaders had been interviewed.[2]

Moskos identified as a tentative universe of the top Jamaican elite those leaders who had received one-third or more of the total possible nominations. In 1962 he interviewed 84.2 percent of the leaders who constituted this universe. The remaining persons interviewed were those leaders he chose because they were next in line in reputed influence or because they would make the interviewed group more representative of all Jamaican elites. In 1974, we interviewed 84.1 percent of the 82 leaders who received one-third or more of the total possible nominations. The remaining persons in our sample were those who were immediately below the top leaders on the list.

Admittedly, we are dealing with a small number of cases. Yet more confidence can be placed in the results than the mere number of cases seems to merit. First, the fact that Moskos was able to interview a high proportion—84 percent—of the leaders who had received one-third or more of the total possible nominations means that his "sample" approaches a universe of top reputational leaders in Jamaica. This is also true of the 83 leaders we interviewed in 1974. And this near-universe at each time includes the top Cabinet members, economic leaders, and other elites. Such leaders, of course, are relatively few in number; and we have interviewed most of them.[3]

Second, in 1961–1962 Moskos interviewed not only Jamaican leaders but also similarly selected leaders in some other parts of the then-British West Indies: Barbados, Dominica, Grenada, Guyana, and Trinidad and Tobago. With respect to the distributions of some variables, especially attitudinal, the six territories do show some differences. When they do, however, they are nearly always explained by the degree of advancement toward political independence. For example, Jamaica, being the most advanced, had the smallest percentage of leaders who wished to retain colonial status in preference to political independence, while Dominica, the last of the six territories to become politically independent, had in 1962 the largest percentage of leaders who opposed independence (Moskos, 1967:39). With respect to correlations between variables, the results in the different territories, with only a few minor exceptions, were the same. Thus, the 1961–1962 Jamaican data were replicated in five other similar territories, and the results are for the most part corroborated.[4]

The percentages of Jamaican leaders interviewed having selected social characteristics in 1962 and 1974 are given in Appendix Table 1. Elites in 1974, compared to 1962, included a few women; were more likely to be age forty to forty-nine rather than fifty to fifty-nine; were slightly more likely to be dark brown or black and included a few Chinese; were much better educated; and included relatively fewer political and labor leaders and more elites from the mass media, civil service, education, the church, and ethnic groups.[5]

Jamaica

Jamaica is an island of 2 million people situated in the Caribbean Sea just south of Cuba. A British colony since 1655, Jamaica became a politically independent state on 6 August 1962. With the end of the Second World War in Europe, Jamaica began what was for a new state a relatively long period of transition to nationhood under continued British rule. In November 1944 limited self-government, based on the Westminster model, and, for the first time in the history of Jamaica, based also on universal adult suffrage, was inaugurated. From that time to the date of full political independence in 1962, there were periodic constitutional changes providing for more and more self-government and less and less formal political control by the British. For a few years, from 1958 to near the end of 1961, it appeared that Jamaica would achieve full political independence as part of the West Indies Federation, which included other island ter- ritories in the British Caribbean. A referendum held in Jamaica in September 1961, however, resulted in a go-it-alone decision for Ja- maica. The Federation collapsed and Jamaica became fully indepen- dent as a separate nation-state.

The racial and ethnic composition of Jamaica was established long ago during the period of importation of slaves from Africa. For ex- ample, by 1696, 84 percent of the population was classified as black- or brown-skinned, that is, of African or mixed Afro-European racial origin (Broom, 1954). In 1884, when the first census of Jamaica was taken, 77.7 percent of the population was black, 18.1 percent brown, and 4.2 percent white or of European racial origin (Roberts, 1957). The percentage of Chinese and Afro-Chinese (1.2), East Indian and Afro-East Indian (3.4), and other races (3.2) had increased somewhat (Department of Statistics, 1975). The racial composition appears to be roughly the same today, although with the rise of black conscious- ness there was a shift toward claiming black status during the 1970 census. In 1970, according to the census, 96.7 percent of Jamaicans had African origins to some degree (Census Research Programme, 1976).

The correlation between racial origin and social class remains high and makes it possible to speak loosely of the black lower classes, the brown middle classes, and the light-skinned upper classes. Once this is said, however, caveats must be added: the correlation is not perfect; persons of various colors can be found within each class; and eighteen years of internal self-government and now twenty years of nationhood, during which nonwhite elites came to political power, eroded the correlation. Also, there is a number of very small but ethnically differentiated groups— such as Syrians or Lebanese—that are recognized as having separate identities.

Widespread poverty (72.5 percent of income earners had weekly wages under US $33.30 in October 1974, the medians being US $21.20 for men and US $18.20 for women); a high rate of unemploy- ment (22.4 percent in October 1973 and 26.8 percent by November 1980); and considerable economic inequality (the highest 5 percent of income earners in 1974 accounted for 24 percent of the total income, and, out of 52 countries in the mid-1960s, Jamaica ranked second in income inequality) further characterize the population

(Cumper, 1975; Department of Statistics, 1975; Taylor and Hudson, 1972; Carl Stone, *Jamaican Weekly Gleaner*, 26 Jan. 1981: 11).[6]

Elections

By the end of 1980, there had been nine national elections in Jamaica based on universal adult suffrage, four of them since full political independence. From the data on Jamaican elections given in Table 1, note three facts. First, although independent and third-party candidates received more than a third of the total votes cast in the first election of 1944, they rather quickly lost out after that to the two major parties, the Jamaica Labour party (JLP) and the People's National party (PNP). The percentage of votes cast for independent and third-party candidates was reduced to 13.8 by the second national election in 1949, to 10.5 in the third election in 1955, and to less than 1.0 by 1959. Although in 1962 the percentage of votes cast for candidates other than those of the JLP and PNP rose to 1.4, it was negligible from 1967 on.

Thus, over the three and a half decades of its functioning the modern Jamaican political system has become consolidated and institutionalized as a system dominated by two political parties. There are many explanations for this: (1) the legacy of three hundred years of British rule; (2) two strong, charismatic leaders, Sir Alexander Bustamante and Norman W. Manley, both now deceased, as the founding heads of each of the parties; (3) each major party's links with a mass base, particularly through trade unions; (4) the necessity of getting votes from largely black and uneducated peasants, small farmers, the urban working class, and the poor—a need that meant that some racial and socioeconomic groups, largely white and upper SES groups, didn't have much of a chance to get elected outside the two major parties; and (5) the nature of the electoral laws, since Jamaica has single-member districts and a plurality system in the election of members of the House of Representatives. This type of electoral law has been associated generally with two-party competition except where politically organized minorities are ecologically segregated, as in Canada (Rae, 1971:94). Had a system of proportional representation been instituted in Jamaica in 1944, the island, no doubt, would have developed a multiple-party system.

Second, the percentage of registered voters actually voting has crept up over the years, moving from a low of 52.7 in the first national election of 1944 to a high of 86.1 in the most recent election of 30 October, 1980. This reflects the heightened interest in politics on the part of Jamaicans, the increased polarization of the electorate, and the fact that politics has become one of the biggest—if not the biggest—show on the island.

Third, with somewhat amazing regularity, the winning party

TABLE 1.
Data on Jamaican General Elections, 1944–1980

Year of Election	Number of Registered Voters	Number of Valid Votes Cast	Percentage of Registered Voters Casting Valid Votes	Percentage of Votes Cast for			Number of Parliamentary Seats Won	
				JLP*	PNP†	Independents and Other Parties	JLP*	PNP†
1944	663,069	349,127	52.7	41.4	23.5	35.1	22‡	5
1949	732,217	467,179	63.8	42.7	43.5	13.8	17‡	13
1955	761,238	486,644	63.9	39.0	50.5	10.5	14	18‡
1959	853,539	557,794	65.4	44.3	54.8	0.9	16	29‡
1962	796,540	575,779	72.3	50.0	48.6	1.4	26‡	19
1967	543,307	442,572	81.5	50.6	49.1	0.3	33‡	20
1972	605,662	473,651	78.2	43.4	56.4	0.2	16	37‡
1976	870,972	735,948	84.5	43.2	56.8	0.0	13	47‡
1980	990,417	852,706	86.1	58.9	41.05	0.06	51‡	9

* Jamaica Labour Party.
† People's National Party.
‡ Political party forming the government.
Source: Report of the Director of Elections of Jamaica, General Election 1980, August 1981, Table IV.

changed. The JLP won the first two national elections, the PNP the next two, the JLP the next two, the PNP the next two, and the JLP won again in 1980. On each occasion there was an orderly change of government with a new ruling party taking over.

The picture, however, was clouded by political violence and charges that elections in some districts were not fully free and fair. Obviously, these are serious charges because where the ideology of democracy justifies the ruling class and where it is understood, as it was in Jamaica, that democracy rests upon the ability of the citizen to choose between alternatives at periodic elections, the belief in the integrity of the electoral process is fundamental to acceptance of the authority of the ruling group.

This belief had to withstand quite a lot. For example, as early as the 1959 elections there were charges of systematic "bogus voting." The JLP seized on this after 1962, when they returned to power, to re-enumerate eligible voters. Note from Table 1 that the number of electors on the voters' list dropped substantially from 1962 to 1967. The 1959 and 1962 lists probably were inflated by some names that were listed more than once and by names of people who had died or emigrated. Also, the number of electors on the list in 1967 may have been an under-enumeration as a result of the deliberate efforts of the JLP to keep off known PNP voters. A new enumeration was completed after the PNP returned to power in 1972, and laws were implemented reducing the voting age to include eighteen-year-olds. But the JLP charged that 200,000 eligible voters were excluded largely as a result of deliberate bypassing of JLP supporters (JWG, 14 Nov., 1973:15), a charge that was denied by PNP spokesmen.

Complaints and allegations of abuses continued to be made. Local elections scheduled for 1972 were postponed until 1974 because of incomplete voter registration lists. A parliamentary by-election in one district in 1975 brought forth further charges of electoral malpractice. In 1976 a significant change took place, a move toward systematic and widespread voter intimidation during the general election. Members or supporters of both major parties were involved, acting or reacting, and it is difficult to document who was more guilty of its initiation. Stone (1980:163) says that the JLP was on the offensive during the early period of the campaign, while the PNP initiated aggression in the later period. In fact, the 1976 election had to be held under a "State of Emergency" because of political violence. It was justified by the PNP government as being necessary to maintain order and ensure fair elections but was widely feared and denounced by the JLP as a possible means to put down opposition. Yet the election results, giving the PNP 56.8 percent of the total vote corresponded almost exactly with the results of a public opinion poll. That is, the election results reflected the will of the electorate.

In 1980 the violence escalated. Of 514 killings by gunmen during 1980, Stone (1981) estimates that as many as 152 may have been politically motivated. An informed participant told us it was more like 350. Yet the 1980 election appears to have been reasonably free and fair. A new registration of voters was carried out prior to the election, probably one of the most honest and complete in Jamaican history; and the 1980 election was conducted by an independent body, the Electoral Advisory Committee. Of course, the procedures were not foolproof, and some irregularities did occur: some polling stations did not open on time; at a few stations security broke down and intimidation occurred or open voting was forced; and some ballot boxes may have been stuffed with bogus votes. Although some members of his party openly disagreed, the leader of the losing PNP, Michael Manley, himself told the press that no one could manipulate the election machinery. Moveover, Carl Stone's poll showed that the election results were generally accepted by the Jamaican people as legitimate (JWG, 23 March, 1981:8). In February 1981, Stone asked two relevant questions of a national sample of Jamaican respondents:

"Do you think that the result of this last election in October accurately represents the will of the people?"

Yes	81%
No opinion	4
No	15
Total	100%
Number of cases	(840)

"Do you think that there was any bogus voting or illegal practices on election day in your area?"

Yes	14%
No opinion	8
No	78
Total	100%
Number of cases	(840)

Overall Elite Attitudes toward Democracy

More lasting than momentary reactions to a particular election is the general attitude toward the democratic system, and more sensitively diagnostic than attitudes of the general public are attitudes of the ruling class. In both 1962, prior to political independence, and in 1974, twelve years later, Jamaican elites answered the following question:

"Do you think the democratic form of government, such as the British system, is the best suited for Jamaica?"

Responses	1962	1974
Very suitable	67%	79%
Partially suitable	4	11
Unsuitable	29	10
Total	100%	100%
Number of cases	(24)	(81)
No answer	(0)	(2)

Note that before independence in 1962 fully 67 percent of Jamaica's top leaders judged the democratic form of government to be suitable. This reflects the fact that democracy was not simply imposed by Britain on Jamaica during the transition to self-government. Rather, deep commitments to democratic ideals existed among the local elite, as revealed, for example, in the selected speeches and writings of the preeminent nationalist leader Norman W. Manley (Nettleford, 1971).

By 1974, after twelve years of nationhood, the attitudes of top Jamaican leaders were somewhat more favorable to the democratic form of government than they were in 1962. There remained, however, some leaders, 10 percent of the total, who judged democracy to be unsuitable.

Another measure that permits additional insight into the legitimacy of a democratic regime is the belief about and attitude toward the competence of the electorate. If the electorate is thought to be incompetent, then a major foundation of democratic ideology can be questioned. Thus Moskos and we also asked:

"Do you think the typical Jamaican voter supports leaders who serve the long-range interests of Jamaica? That is, how competent do you feel the average Jamaican voter is?"

Responses	1962	1974
Very competent	48%	49%
Somewhat competent	30	22
Incompetent	22	29
Total	100%	100%
Number of cases	(23)	(81)
No answer	(1)	(2)

Leaders were less sanguine about the competence of average Jamaican voters than they were about the suitability of democracy. Furthermore, the attitudes did not become more favorable. If anything, proportionally more of the leaders—29 to 22 percent—thought the typical Jamaican voter was incompetent in 1974 than in 1962, echoing Tocqueville's (1954:209) observation "that universal suffrage is by no means a guarantee of the wisdom of the popular choice."

Taking the two questions together, one type of attitude is worth discussing further. "Cynical parliamentarians," following Moskos and Bell (1964:321), were leaders who judged democracy to be very suitable while judging the typical Jamaican voter to be incompetent or only somewhat competent. They increased during the first twelve years of nationhood from 26 to 38 percent. Apparently a few leaders, without altering their unfavorable views of the typical voter, changed to a favorable assessment of democracy. Although this was not a large shift, it may reveal a distinctive reaction among some elites who feared, before independence, that their power would be curtailed with the coming of a mass-based representative system but who discovered that they could manipulate the parliamentary system to their own benefit.

Is the Change toward Democratic Attitudes Genuine?

Taking just the "very suitable" responses, one can see that overall change in attitudes toward the suitability of the democratic form of government was 12 percent, 79 in 1974 minus 67 in 1962. Because these attitudes were somewhat correlated with social background characteristics (see Appendix Tables 2 and 3) and because the latter changed, it is conceivable that the overall small difference in democratic attitudes is merely a consequence of changes in the distribution of social background characteristics in the elites of 1974 compared with those of 1962, rather than a consequence of changes in attitudes of particular types of elites. For example, is the change in attitude a result of there being relatively more elites in the forty to forty-nine and fewer in the fifty to fifty-nine age groups in 1974 than in 1962, or have elites of both age groups increased in favorable attitudes toward democracy?

We answered this and similar questions in two ways. The first was to equate the percentage of elites who judged democracy to be very suitable for each subgroup in 1974 to the distributions of each social characteristic in 1962. Then we recomputed the overall change. That is, we asked what the overall change would be if the 1974 overall results were based on distributions of the social characteristics, as they were in 1962. The results are shown in Table 2. Note the overall change controlling for each of the social characteristics does not disappear. The lowest it gets is 10 percent when controlling for institutional sector of major occupation.

The above method broke down when controlling for the back-

TABLE 2.
Standardization of Change in Attitudes toward Democracy,
Controlling for Selected Social Characteristics in
Percentage and Mean Difference

	Standardized Change	
Controlled Social Characteristics	Percentage Difference	Mean Difference
No Variable Controlled	+12*	+.31[†]
Age	+12	+.32
Color or race	+14	+.32
Education	+11	+.35
Institutional sector of major occupation	+10	+.31
Age + color	[‡]	+.32
Age + color + education	[‡]	+.36
Age + color + education + institutional sector	[‡]	+.37

*The percentage of leaders judging democracy to be suitable was 79 in 1974 and 67 in 1962, or a 12 percent increase in favorable attitudes.
[†]The mean attitude toward democracy in 1974 was 2.69 and in 1962 was 2.38, or a difference of +.31.
[‡]The method based on percentages breaks down as variables are added simultaneously because there are too many empty cells to make a meaningful calculation.

ground variables simultaneously because we ran out of sufficient cases to make meaningful computations, so we also used a second method. Following Duncan (1968), we have taken as the quantity to be explained the change in mean democratic attitude from 1962 to 1974. We used all three response categories and scored them as follows: "very suitable" = 3, "partially suitable" = 2, and "unsuitable" = 1. The unstandardized change between democratic attitudes in 1962 ($\overline{X}$ = 2.38) and in 1974 ($\overline{X}$ = 2.69) was +.31. In attempting to explain this change, we first regressed democratic attitudes in 1974 on each of four major background variables: age, color, education, and institutional sector of major occupation. Wealth was omitted because it is not comparable at the two times. In each of the four unstandardized regression equations obtained for 1974, we substituted the 1962 mean of the variable being standardized. Thus we arrived at a set of predictions for mean democratic attitudes in 1974 using the 1962 means of the variables controlled, which can then be compared with the 1962 mean democratic attitude. For example, the regression of democratic attitudes on age gave the following equation: Democratic attitudes$_{1974}$ = 2.44 + .05529 (Age$_{1974}$). Substituting the 1962 mean age, we arrive at a prediction of 2.70 for democratic attitudes, standardizing for age.

Subtracting (2.70 − 2.38), we get a mean difference of +.32. Note from Table 2 that the conclusion is the same as before. The overall difference, as standardized for each of the control variables, holds up; in fact, it is generally a little larger.

Adding the background variables in additional regression equations simultaneously, we can see whether their joint effect reduces the overall change in democratic attitudes. It does not. Thus we can conclude, at least controlling for these variables, that the overall change in Jamaican elites toward more favorable attitudes toward the suitability of democracy from 1962 to 1974, though small, is the result of attitude changes among elites having similar background characteristics rather than merely the result of the changing social composition of elites. In some fundamental sense the change is genuine.

The Role of the State in the Economy

From the end of World War II to 1962, the overriding political issue in Jamaica was the issue of political independence. Many elites—especially white, older elites from the economic sector—opposed political separation from Britain. Others wanted it because it meant no less than a change in the ruling class itself, first its augmentation by new elites and eventually, perhaps, the replacement of one ruling group by another. For the emergent nationalist elite, it meant obtaining the legitimate control of the state as an instrument of power, in order to enhance and consolidate their own position as a new and rising ruling class to be sure, but also—and most publicly proclaimed—to achieve the ends of social justice in the society, especially to raise levels of living for the people and to create more equality.

During the transition to independence, a new ruling class of Jamaicans did begin to take shape—most visibly the new politicians and labor leaders and an expanding cadre of civil servants—slowly pushing the British and the old, established Jamaican colonial elite aside. This trend continued after independence; but, as nationhood was achieved, another political issue moved to the fore: how much of a role should the state play in the society, particularly in the economy? Now that the instrument of state power was in the hands of a new political elite, many of its members wished to increase its power by enlarging its size and the scope of its functions. This was so largely because, while they now controlled the state, the mass-based political parties, and the trade unions, they did not control the commanding heights of the economy.

On this issue, we classified leaders according the their economic views into five groups: reactionaries, conservatives, populists, liberals, and radicals. *Reactionaries* wanted the role of the government in economic life to be confined to basic services, such as a postal system, roads, police and fire protection, and water. *Conservatives* favored the provision of limited social services—health care, education, and unemployment compensation—but thought the government sided too often with the trade unions and far too rarely with the private sector. *Populists* were pragmatists who had no long-term programs, were mainly concerned with "bread and butter issues," and favored a mass-based government. *Liberals* wished the state to play a greater role in social and economic affairs than it was then doing. They also stressed worker's rights, social programs, and other reforms, all of which were to be carried out within the framework of welfare capitalism. *Radicals* favored major changes in the economic structure of society, sometimes to the extreme of advocating abolition of all private property (Moskos, 1967:47–48).

Given below are the distributions of these economic ideologies for elites in 1962 and 1974, along with the comparable results of a general public opinion poll based upon quota sampling carried out in September 1977 (Stone, 1980:186).[7]

Economic Ideologies	Jamaican Elites		General Population
	1962	1974	1977
Radicals	25%	15%	8%
Liberals	17	49	17
Populists	21	1	29
Conservatives	29	27	36
Reactionaries	8	8	10
Total	100%	100%	100%
Number of cases	(24)	(82)	(902)

Comparing the elites before and twelve years after independence, we can see that radicals and, especially, populists lost in relative numbers, conservatives and reactionaries stayed about the same, and liberals increased. Although we may have mistakenly classified some populists as liberals in 1974, we rechecked our coding carefully and believe that the relative increase in liberals—largely a shift toward the social programs of the modern welfare state—reflects the facts.

The relative decline of radicals among elites deserves some comment, since it is well known that Jamaica veered to the left under Manley's PNP government from autumn of 1974, when he proclaimed that Jamaica would become a democratic socialist state, until the sweeping election victory of the JLP on 30 October 1980. There was a *relative* decline in radicals, that is, in extreme left-wingers, including outspoken Communists. But from 1962 to 1974 there was an increase in their absolute numbers, just as the whole Jamaican elite group had expanded, to the point of creating a critical mass of radicals, an increase in their degree of organization, and a heightening of their power as they penetrated the inner circle of the PNP.

Compared with the economic ideologies of elites in 1974, the general population in 1977 was somewhat more to the right, conservatives and reactionaries together accounting for 46 percent of the general population and 35 percent of the elites.[8] One reason the PNP lost the 1980 election was the fact that the electorate—elite and mass alike—perceived it as being overly influenced by extreme leftists. The visible support given to the PNP by the communistic Worker's Party of Jamaica (WPJ) contributed to this view (Stone, 1981).

Between 1962 and 1974 economic ideologies of elites polarized according to their political party preferences. In Table 3 note that 60 percent of the radicals in 1962 were JLP, compared to 40 percent who were PNP. Liberals and populists, and even to some extent conservatives, were more likely to be PNP than JLP. There were only two reactionaries among the leaders in 1962, and one was JLP while the other supported whichever party was in power.

By 1974, however, all the radicals were PNP. None was JLP. Seventy-two percent of the liberals were PNP, compared to only 10 percent who were JLP. Forty-two percent of the conservatives were JLP, compared to 26 percent who were PNP; and 67 percent of the reactionaries were JLP, compared to none who were PNP. Considering that most of our interviewing was completed during the summer of 1974, before Manley's declaration of democratic socialism some weeks later, we assume that after that the ideological polarization of elites by political party preference continued. And it was a matter of everyday observation that the radicals pursued their cause with ardor.

Attitudes toward Democracy and the Role of the State

Even a dedicated democrat such as Michael Manley occasionally had his doubts about the effectiveness of a two-party democratic system. In an interview in June 1979 he told us that the parliamentary system is best suited to Jamaica. "It is not," he continued, "even a subject of debate. It is just part of Jamaican society and it works." Yet, after explaining those aspects of the system that work very well, he went on to say that "there is a problem with economic development. The party system in developing societies is an obstacle to mobilization. . . . How do you mobilize a poor country that needs to change but has a political system that is designed to maximize conflict and disagreement?"

TABLE 3.
Political Party Identification by Economic Ideologies, 1962 and 1974

| Economic Ideologies | Percentage of Jamaican Leaders Who Supported | | | | | | | | | |
| | 1962 | | | | | 1974 | | | | |
	JLP	Party in Power*	PNP	Total	Number of Cases on Which Percentage Is Based	JLP	Party in Power*	PNP	Total	Number of Cases on Which Percentage Is Based
Radical	60	0	40	100	(5)	0	0	100	100	(10)
Liberal	0	25	75	100	(4)	10	18	72	100	(39)
Populist	25	0	75	100	(4)	(1)	0	0	100	(1)
Conservative	28	28	44	100	(7)	42	32	26	100	(19)
Reactionary	(1)	(1)	0	100	(2)	67	33	0	100	(6)

*Includes some civil servants who would not give a political party preference, except to say that they supported whichever party was in power.

If the role of the state in the economy came to be a major subject of political conflict in Jamaica, as it had, then this raises the question of the consequences for the democratic system. Table 4 presents attitudes toward democracy by economic ideologies. Note the curvilinear relationship at each time period. Radicals and reactionaries—the extremes at each end—were least favorable to a democratic regime. An intelligible way of exploring these relationships is to compute the regression equations of economic ideologies (where Radical = 5, Liberal = 4, Populist = 3, Conservative = 2, and Reactionary = 1) as the independent variable with attitudes toward democracy (where "very suitable" = 3, "partially suitable" = 2, and "unsuitable" = 1) as the dependent variable. Since the predicted curve looks like an inverted "U", the simplest mathematical formulation of such relationship is a parabola. This model necessitates a squared independent variable, so that the regression equation has first- and second-degree versions of economic ideologies. The regression equation will estimate coefficients for each of our two versions of economic ideologies. The first degree term, that is, the unsquared version of economic ideologies, is the slope of the curve when it cuts the vertical axis; or put in another way, it is a function of where the uppermost part (the vertex) of our inverted "U" lies in a graph. We have no use for the first-degree term because the coding of economic ideologies is purely arbitrary. We have computed the regression equation subtracting the horizontal coordinate of the vertex from economic ideologies (Tierney, 1968:182-184).

TABLE 4.
Attitudes toward Democracy by Economic Ideologies,
1962 and 1974

Economic Ideologies	Jamaican Leaders Who Think Democracy Is Very Suitable			
	1962		1974	
	Percent	Number of Cases on Which Percentage Is Based	Percent	Number of Cases on Which Percentage Is Based
Radical	33	(6)	54	(11)
Liberal	100	(4)	85	(39)
Populist	100	(5)	(1)	(1)
Conservative	57	(7)	91	(22)
Reactionary	(1)	(2)	43	(7)

So doing, the equation for 1974 is:

$$dmocrt74 = 3.05 + .00(ecideo74 - 3.07) - .22(ecideo74 - 3.07)^2$$

where dmocrt74 = attitudes toward democracy in 1974,

ecideo74 = economic ideologies in 1974, and

3.07 = the horizontal coordinate of the vertex.

For 1962, the equation is:

$$dmocrt62 = 2.87 - .01(ecideo62 - 3.22) - .28(ecideo62 - 3.22)^2.$$

Since subtracting the horizontal coordinate of the vertex of economic ideology arbitrarily sets the contribution of the linear term at zero, any departure being due to rounding error, the multiple correlation (R) is a function of the squared term and is equal to the standardized regression coefficient for the squared term—which in this case is negative. The relationship is roughly the same at both time periods: For 1974, R = .44 and for 1962, R = .46. The estimated and observed means are given in Table 5, with a pictorial representation in Figure 1.

In Table 5, note that the discrepancies between the estimated and observed means of democratic attitudes were somewhat greater for 1962 than for 1974. Thus, the model fits the data better in 1974 than in 1962. A way of summarizing this is to look at the discrepancy between Eta and R, which for 1962 was greater (Eta = .55 and R = .46) than for 1974 (Eta = .45 and R = .44).

Radicals distrusted democracy because they feared that it would not produce the progressive policies and thoroughgoing changes they favored. Reactionaries viewed democracy in Jamaica as a threat, an instrument through which some extreme form of socialism, communism, or other undesirable change (from their viewpoint) might be introduced. Radicals wanted a greater mobilization of Jamaican people and society to achieve national purposes of greater equality and moral solidarity with the elimination of wasteful political conflict and opposition. Reactionaries wanted to pursue business as usual, with guarantees that the rules of the private property game would not be changed.

Finally, pursuing the effects of economic ideologies on democratic attitudes still further, we computed for 1962 and 1974 a stepwise regression with attitudes toward democracy as the dependent variable and age, color, education, institutional sector of major occupation, wealth, economic ideology unsquared, and (economic ideology − vertex)^2 as independent variables. The correlation matrices, means, and standard deviations on which the regressions were based are given in Appendix Table 3.

Turning to Table 6, where the results of the regression analyses are given, note that the squared version of economic ideology had the largest zero-order correlation at both times. Furthermore, looking at the standardized regression coefficients, we can see that the correla-

TABLE 5.

Estimated and Observed Means of Attitudes toward Democracy by
Economic Ideologies, 1962 and 1974

| | Attitudes toward Democracy* | | | | | |
| | 1962 | | | 1974 | | |
Economic Ideologies	Estimated Mean	Observed Mean	Number of Cases	Estimated Mean	Observed Mean	Number of Cases
Radical	1.96	1.83	(6)	2.25	2.27	(11)
Liberal	2.96	3.00	(4)	2.87	2.82	(39)
Populist	2.85	3.00	(5)	3.05	3.00	(1)
Conservative	2.46	2.14	(7)	2.80	2.86	(22)
Reactionary	1.50	2.00	(2)	2.10	2.00	(7)

*Democracy is "very suitable" = 3.00.

FIGURE 1.
Observed and Estimated Values of Attitudes toward Democracy by Economic Ideologies

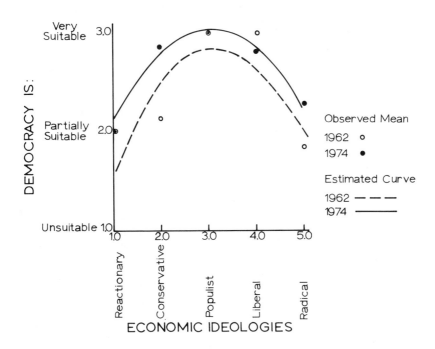

tion was not reduced when all the other variables were controlled; in fact, for 1962 it increased to −.55, while for 1974 it remained the same at −.44. Thus, at both times the curvilinear relationship between economic ideologies and democratic attitudes was the largest relationship we found, and it was not spurious.

Three other independent variables are worth mentioning for 1962: age, color, and institutional sector of major occupation. With the other variables controlled, democratic attitudes increased with age, lightness of skin color, and having one's leadership status based in the political or labor sectors of the economy. In 1974 the relationship with age, controlling for all the other independent variables, had slipped to near zero, the correlation with color had reversed, and that with institutional sector reduced. Also, a small negative relationship between education and democratic attitudes became apparent in 1974. But by far, the most important independent variable was economic ideology as it related curvilinearly to democratic attitudes.[9] The major sources of antidemocratic attitudes among Jamai-

TABLE 6.
Results of the Regression Analysis (Dependent Variable = Attitudes toward Democracy), 1962 and 1974

Independent Variable	Multiple R	R Squared	R Squared Change	Simple r	Regression Coefficient	Standardized Coefficient
1962						
(Economic ideology – vertex)² (radical and reactionary)*	.46	.21	.21	−.46	−.34	−.55
Age (old)	.52	.27	.06	.19	.33	.34
Color (white)	.56	.31	.05	.03	.44	.34
Institutional sector (political, labor, et al.)	.61	.37	.05	.16	.52	.26
Wealth (rich)	.61	.37	.00	−.04	−.02	−.01
Education (high)	.61	.37	.00	.03	.00	.00
Economic ideology (radical)	.61	.37	.00	−.03	.00	.00
[constant]					.30	
1974						
(Economic ideology – vertex)² (radical and reactionary)	.44	.19	.19	−.44	−.22	−.44
Color (white)	.46	.21	.02	−.17	−.10	−.11
Education (high)	.47	.22	.01	−.06	−.10	−.12
Institutional sector (political, labor, et al.)	.49	.24	.01	.14	.18	.13
Age (old)	.49	.24	.00	.08	.03	.05
Economic ideology (radical)	.49	.24	.00	.03	.01	.01
Wealth (rich)	.49	.24	.00	−.10	.00	.00
[constant]					3.23	

*The pole of each variable defined as the high end is given in parentheses. "Vertex" is the horizontal coordinate of the vertex.

can elites, then, were found in the opposite poles of economic ideologies, among elites on the extreme left *and* the extreme right.

Some Implications for Strategies of Dependent Development

For the person who values democracy, one implication is so obvious (and already so well-known) that we are embarrassed to affirm it once again: avoid both extreme left *and* extreme right political solutions to economic and social problems. Each poses a threat to the democratic polity.

There is, however, one thing that cannot be avoided, and it contains a certain irony in the case of conservatives and reactionaries who claim to want minimal government control and intervention: in the modern world, the political system has become accountable for the performance of the economy nearly everywhere. This is no less true for a capitalist system in which the government is trying to stay away from regulation, control, and direct management of the economy as it is for a socialist system in which government control and management of the economy are explicit goals. Today, doing nothing is viewed as one alternative policy and the government shares the blame if the economy, as a consequence, does not thrive or if major sections of the population fail to share in the benefits even if it does. In Jamaica, Manley's democratic socialist regime fell in large part because of the failure of the Jamaican economy (Stone, 1981). Similarly, we are safe in predicting that Edward Seaga's new government also will fall, probably after two terms, in 1988 or 1989 if not sooner, if his capitalist, private-enterprise solutions do not transform Jamaica into a growing economy again.[10]

Why did democratic socialism fail? In addition to simple bad luck— e.g., the worldwide recession and rising costs of oil—we belief there are five chief reasons. (1) The PNP declaration that Jamaica would become a democratic socialist state led to the definition of Jamaica as having a "poor investment climate" among members of the international financial community; the result reduced direct foreign investment in Jamaica. (2) The weakening and demoralization of the Jamaican national bourgeoisie. Both of these factors were exacerbated by three others: (3) the reckless and unnecessarily radical rhetoric in which some of the PNP spokesmen garbed their proposed democratic socialist policies; (4) the growing ties between the PNP and Cuba, including a Cuban presence in Jamaica, which became highly visible manifestations of the leftist direction of the PNP; and (5) the rise of violence, both political and gangster-related, and the corresponding reduction in public safety. A cycle of negative feedback was established: the worse the economy became and the more visible the signs of radicalism, the more validated appeared both the judgment of Jamaica as having a poor investment climate and the fears of communism and the breakdown of public order among the local bourgeoisie. The more validated such judgments and fears, the worse the economy became. The self-fulfilling prophecy was at work.

In their carefully documented and persuasive analysis of direct foreign investment in Mexico and Brazil, Gereffi and Evans (1981) show that, even if foreign investors are making high rates of return, when policies sound too nationalistic or too concerned with the problems of labor and the poor, the flow of direct foreign investment declines immediately. The policies of Echeverría, only mildly reformist by third world standards, reduced capital and profit flows of transnational corporations in Mexico from a positive $179 million in the 1960–1969 period to a negative $349 million in the 1970–1976 period (Gereffi and Evans, 1981:52). In Brazil, the flow of direct foreign investment declined in the nationalistic period of Vargas's second presidency and dropped off even more during Goulart's left-leaning regime. Gereffi and Evans conclude that the band of national policies acceptable to transnational corporations that define a "good investment climate" is exceedingly narrow and question how free dependent states really are to explore even a welfare-oriented version of capitalist development.

The PNP declaration of democratic socialism, then, was taken by some observers to mean a declaration that Jamaica had become a bad place for foreign investment. In a country where foreign capital had been the single most important factor for economic growth since World War II, the resulting falloff in such foreign investment was consequential. Moreover, no one will ever know what investments Jamaica might have received but did not. One informed American source told us that, as a result of the uncertain future created by democratic socialism in Jamaica, for the short run bauxite production was decreased in Jamaica and increased elsewhere, as in Australia, and for the long run a billion-dollar-plus development of bauxite resources in Brazil was begun.

The weakening of the national bourgeoisie was also consequential. It did not come overnight, nor did it rest on a single action nor, more central, perhaps, a single word. While we were interviewing leaders in the summer of 1974, Manley rode a wave of popular support. He received largely favorable local reactions to the bauxite levy act—the brainchild of two Jamaican capitalists (Maingot, 1980)—that passed the Jamaican House of Representatives in June 1974 and that increased government revenues from the aluminum companies by more than 700 percent. Many conservative economic elites were then willing to admit to us that Jamaica's recent moves toward the third world and nonaligned countries were little more than understandable exercises of Jamaica's new national sovereignty, that the links it had forged with new black African states and with Ethiopia were a realistic expression of the African origins of the majority of Jamaica's people, and that the PNP government's efforts to battle poverty, illiteracy, and unemployment through social legislation at home were necessary to keep the ship of state (and, perhaps, the privileges of first class) afloat. Even an American bauxite executive told us that the levy was fair, though he added that he wished Manley would shut up about it and cool the wild rhetoric. He said the latter was already interfering with the transnational aluminum company's ability to raise its own loans for its Jamaican operations in the international market.

By the general election of December 1976, the PNP, even though it won nearly 57 percent of the popular vote, compared with the JLP's 43.2 percent, had lost much elite support—especially among economic elites (Stone, 1981)—and had started the downward slide that would result in its eventual defeat in October 1980. Already, many of the patterns—which would be accentuated later—were clear: extreme rhetoric of class warfare—Marxist, Leninist, socialist, communist; the flamboyant denunciation by key PNP party officials, sometimes by Manley himself, of the capitalists, the middle and upper classes, the U.S. Central Intelligence Agency, and the United States; the increased ties and exchanges with Cuba; the influence of extreme leftists in high places in the PNP and Manley's apparent inability to control them; rabble-rousing speeches in the face of rising political violence in which "the enemy" was identified as "over there" in residential concentrations of JLP supporters; the inability of the security forces to guarantee the safety of the people—or even their own in some cases—and growing uncertainty as to whether the security forces would obey the PNP government; the weakening of the economy, including lack of foreign exchange, inflation, unemployment, increasing foreign debt, negative economic growth, devaluation of the currency, and the many empty shelves in the supermarkets; and, of course, the generally mild economic and social reforms to help the poor, the unemployed, and the landless peasants that were beclouded in radical rhetoric. The JLP leaders, of course, were not blameless, nor was Jamaica's leading newspaper, the *Gleaner*. In their rhetorical counteroffensive, they overdramatized and exaggerated these developments, often portraying them as even more radical than they were or as precursors to a coming Communist or Communist-Cuban take-over.

Thus, despite Manley's numerous assurances that he truly meant Jamaica's democratic socialism to be *democratic*, that there would always be room for a private sector, that Jamaica would have a mixed economy, that foreign capital was welcome, and despite his plea to them to simultaneously develop *and* equalize Jamaica, some members of the national bourgeoisie began to jump ship. The Jamaican business elite, never very strong on productive enterprise since the nature of the colonial economy encouraged import-export trade and housekeeping-like small businesses rather than manufacturing, lost faith. Many, including some PNP supporters, took their money out of Jamaica or kept it out when it was owed to them from abroad. Some sent their families out; and, finally, some of them emigrated themselves. Not just entrepreneurs left; the "professional and technical middle class—doctors, dentists, nurses, architects, engineers, accountants" (Maingot, 1980:2) also went. The desertion of the national bourgeoisie resulted in a further collapse of the economy, and even many of those who stayed sat on their hands and watched.[11] The self-fulfilling prophecy again did its work.

And what Manley learned, as he told us in June 1979, was that, "We can't run the bloody economy without these people." Jamaica was deprived of essential assistance while trying to shift priorities to include social justice as well as economic growth, in part because of the shift itself and especially because of the radical package of talk in which it was presented.

The growing links with Cuba simply functioned to inflame the worst fears of the bourgeoisie, and the inability of the government to maintain public safety and prevent violence lent urgency and further anxieties to the sense of uncertainty and fear about the future.

If we were to have written a book at that time, it would have been entitled *The Coming Breakdown of Democracy in Jamaica.* But the title would have been inaccurate, because Michael Manley and Edward Seaga, committed political democrats both; dedicated and hardworking Jamaican leaders, such as Gladstone E. Mills, who headed the team that planned and carried out the 1980 voter registration; and countless numbers of Jamaicans of all social classes, who, loving Jamaica, fair play, and freedom of choice, channeled their energies into those acts that helped make democracy work. The structure of the situation, obviously, was basic. The Jamaican constitution provides for a leader of the opposition. He was ready, with his shadow cabinet, to offer a political alternative.

If the immediate threat to Jamaican democracy from the radical left was overcome with the 1980 election of the JLP and the inauguration of Edward Seaga as prime minister, what of the threat from the reactionary right? If we were to be consistent with our interpretation of the failure of the PNP, then we must conclude that the Jamaican economy and democracy will both be served if policies are implemented that result in redefining Jamaica as having a good investment climate and in the strengthening of the Jamaican national bourgeoisie. By 1982 it was clear that Prime Minister Seaga's JLP government was doing all that it could to open Jamaica's economy to foreign investment. More difficult, perhaps, will be the reconstruction of the national bourgeoisie.

Can the Jamaican economy be rebuilt with dynamic, thriving business and middle classes as its central element? The answer is not clear. Stone (1981:14–15) believes that the Jamaican middle class and business sector have "lost their confidence in their ability to give national leadership . . ." and "have retreated into an isolationism that seeks to preserve their declining but large share of national wealth. . . ." He says, further, that the JLP is "caught in the precarious situation of relying almost entirely on foreign capital from North America to restore some life to the economy in terms of investment and job creating activity."

In the short run, perhaps, he is correct. In the long term, we think not, *if* government acts to create an environment for the revitalization of the *local* business and middle classes. Sources of support and encouragement might be found for those Jamaican entrepreneurs—and they exist—willing to risk their energies in the creation of Jamaican-owned and operated economic activities. Perhaps a new type of economic elite will arise in Jamaica, a nationalist business class, free from foreign control, manufacturing Jamaican things for local consumption and export rather than mainly bringing foreign things into Jamaica. And in the case of bauxite, sugar, and other exports, where dependency on internationally controlled markets will no doubt continue, new agreements might be written, keeping in Jamaica much of the capital that is, in fact, generated in Jamaica. Furthermore, the local intelligentsia should not be forgotten because its members are an important source of innovation and meaning in a society still struggling to find its identity and to define its future.

Why should this be done? Reasonable observers might give a number of reasons. One, obviously, is the simple fact that the fuller realization of Jamaica's independence and the changes of increasing flows of international exchange that are more in Jamaica's interest would be enhanced by an expanded, dynamic, more autonomous, and more industrially oriented business and middle class.[12]

A second answer follows from the analysis made over a decade ago by the West Indian dependency school and particularly by the Trinidadian economist Lloyd Best. Best and his colleagues had noted that many of the newly independent Caribbean states had entered nationhood during the 1960s with the predominant economic strategy being "industrialization by invitation."[13] Even though in the smaller islands not much industrialization per se occurred, tourist and other developments took place. In Jamaica, "inviting the foreign capitalists in" was pretty much the dominant strategy, first by inviting external capital to produce for export and, second by "import substitution," that is, by producing for local consumption, thereby reducing imports and expenditures of foreign exchange, until the

1974–1980 period of PNP democratic socialism—and even then it was far from abandoned. Although various tax and other concessions did attract foreign capital, the strategy did not produce the employment, savings, and reinvestments anticipated by the underlying theory. It had failed, in other words, to solve the local economic problems and to drive the economy into self-sustained economic growth and prosperity.

Best showed that for Trinidad and Tobago, despite the massive inflow of foreign capital, dependence on such investment was largely counterproductive. Outflows of income from the country exceeded inflows; foreign investment was actually decapitalizing the country.[14] As Oxaal (1975:40) comments, that "policy had not worked because the local share of total profits had simply not been high enough to permit a higher contribution of local savings to investment." Savings generally come from profits, not wages; and where nationals work for wages and capitalists are foreign and take their profits out of the country, "rising national income does not lead to more national ownership of business" (Best, as quoted by Oxaal, 1975:40). One consequence may be that the effects of economic development on democracy may be contingent, becoming a positive force mainly when the development results in some localization of capital and the formation of a robust national class of independent-minded entrepreneurs and managers.[15]

We must at once point out, however, that a thriving national bourgeoisie cannot afford to turn its back on the social question, because the legitimacy of any regime and the loyalty to it on the part of members of all classes depend also on the people's judgment that the regime is just. Everywhere today, social justice importantly includes a judgment of the fairness of the distribution of wealth and income (Bell, 1980). Such fairness, it should be added, is seldom defined as anything like total equality by anyone except by a few intellectuals. That is, there is plenty of room for the existence of *fair inequalities.*

Nor, returning to Best, is localization the same thing as nationalization or expropriation although they are not ruled out as possibilities. It simply does not matter, according to Best, whether the major industries in the Caribbean are "foreign companies or not so long as they performed in the way dictated by local people" (Oxaal, 1975:42). A key part of that performance, of course, is keeping a major share of profits in the Caribbean.[16] Localization includes requiring the transnational companies that dominate the economy to transform themselves into entities having recognizable and bona fide legal status within the host state. Most fundamentally, of course, localization can be achieved by providing inducements for local, private entrepreneurial initiative. Thus, not only capital, but capitalists as well, can be localized (Gereffi, 1978, 1980).[17]

A Marxist critique of these suggestions, of course, is that, although capitalism may be strengthened, no genuine revolutionary transformation of the society and its class relations would occur, and the means of production would not be socialized nor the profit system eliminated (Oxaal, 1975:44–45). True enough. But our answer is that there seems to be no reasonable and acceptable alternative.

The success of the Cuban model relies on Soviet aid. We see little chance of the USSR subsidizing Jamaica the way it has subsidized Cuba. In any event, there is relatively little popular support in Jamaica for accepting a dependent relationship with the Soviet Union or any other socialist state.

Although nationalization and expropriation on a unilateral basis might work in the long run, for the foreseeable future Jamaica would suffer economically. We have already seen the consequences of the reformist policies and radical-left rhetoric of democratic socialism. This is assuming, of course, that the United States would permit a truly revolutionary regime to govern in Jamaica, even if it were elected democratically. No serious student of the Caribbean can doubt the possibility of U.S. intervention in the area.[18]

We cannot, of course, be fully optimistic for the prospects of democracy in Jamaica, even if a strong national bourgeoisie is created, because, as we have shown, this class disproportionately contains elements, though a distinct minority of the class, of reactionary antidemocrats. Furthermore, there is always the risk of the evolution of this class into a "native monopolic bourgeoisie," intimately tied to imperialist capital (Cueva, 1977; Cardoso, 1973). Thus, although a local capitalist state might replace the global capitalist state within Jamaica, new alliances might be forged between local and external business forces with the end result of accelerating reliance upon outside capitalist forces (G. K. Lewis, 1981).

Conclusion

Mosca believed that "the history of all societies, past and future, is the history of its ruling classes" (Meisel, 1958:10). Because we believe that there is much truth in that, we have tried to understand the recent and future history of democracy in Jamaica by investigating the attitudes and beliefs of Jamaican elites.

Jamaica, unlike most new states, has managed to maintain a democratic regime based on a parliamentary system, universal adult suffrage, and public liberties. In nine national elections since self-government began in 1944, there have been five orderly turnovers of government control between the two major political parties. Furthermore, during the first twelve years of independent statehood, attitudes of elites toward the suitability of the parliamentary system, already reasonably favorable before independence, became even more favorable; they became overwhelmingly supportive of a democratic regime.

Yet elites' attitudes toward the competence of the typical Jamaican voters did not increase from 1962 to 1974, less than half at each time judging the voter to be very competent. After twelve years of independence, there was an increase in "cynical parliamentarians," leaders who judged democracy to be suitable but who judged the Jamaican voter to be less than very competent.

Although in the years just before independence, the grand debate in Jamaica centered on the desirability of independence itself, in the years after independence the growing issue dividing elites was how much of a role the state should play in the society, especially in the economy. Radicals decreased in relative numbers between 1962 and 1974, but they increased in absolute numbers as the size of the ruling class grew. Also, they became more powerful, acquiring key positions in the People's National party, one of Jamaica's two major political parties. A related fact was the polarization of the two major parties, with the PNP moving to the left and the Jamaica Labour party moving to the right. With the PNP pronouncement that Jamaica would become a democratic socialist state in the fall of 1974, the stage was set for the further ideological separation of the two parties and a major confrontation between the left on the one hand and the center and right on the other.

Political democracy in Jamaica may have hung in the balance, because if either the extreme Left or the extreme Right had ended up in control of the state, then an authoritarian system of some kind might well have resulted. In a multiple regression equation we showed that economic ideologies were by far the most important factor in explaining attitudes toward democracy, with radicals at one extreme and reactionaries at the other being most antidemocratic.

In the elections of 30 October 1980, the PNP, along with its radical cadres and supporters, was defeated. A key factor was the collapse of the Jamaican economy. There were, of course, unpromising conditions over which the PNP leadership had no control: rising oil prices, a soft bauxite market, and worldwide recessionary trends. But the PNP's declaration of democratic socialism, the radical rhetoric in which they clothed it, the PNP's growing ties to Cuba, and the rise of political violence resulted on the one hand in a definition of Jamaica as having a poor investment climate with the loss of direct foreign investment and on the other hand in the demoralization and defection of the Jamaican national bourgeoisie.

As direct foreign investment fell off and as the national bourgeoisie lost confidence and began deserting Jamaica, the economy went into a tailspin. A negative feedback loop was set up. Everything seemed to amplify everything else negatively. The more the middle classes grumbled and withdrew, the angrier and louder some of the radicals got; the worse the economy got, the more political violence there was; the more foreign investors were scared off, the more the middle classes grumbled and withdrew.

If the radicals were defeated along with Manley and others of the PNP in 1980, it was the moderates—liberals, populists, and conservatives—who largely won, although the reactionaries were lurking somewhere in the picture. As the JLP assumed the reins of government, the socialist and communist alternatives seemed out of the question for the time being and in the short run Jamaica's desperate economic situation required some help in the form of aid, loans, and investment from abroad. Prime Minister Seaga immediately looked to the United States.

By 1982, the JLP government had already achieved some success in changing the definition of the situation. In the eyes of foreign investors, Jamaica was acquiring a good investment climate once again. From our analysis, however, we can question a development strategy that depends primarily on foreign investment without serious efforts to domesticate it.

Democracy would be served better, perhaps, if the strategy of development emphasized both the localization of capital and of capitalists, that is, the strengthening of an independent-minded, production-oriented national business and middle class. For three reasons democracy would thereby benefit. First, economic benefits to the society would be maximized. No party can last at the helm of government without alleviating some of the major problems of unemployment and poverty. Unless economic progress occurs, and is to some extent shared throughout Jamaican society, the democratic regime itself might eventually succumb to the promise of greater effectiveness, efficiency, and equity from either the radical Left or the reactionary Right. Policies aimed at such alleviation should be clearly defined as consistent with welfare capitalism and not as communistic. If this were not done, foreign investors and local capitalists might be frightened off again.

Second, domesticating—i.e., Jamaicanizing—foreign capital, where possible, would minimize the growth of foreign elements of the ruling class of Jamaica, whether present in Jamaica or abroad. Thus, also minimized are the revolutionary groups that form in reaction to such foreign elements, and teeth are drawn from revolutionary acts carried out in the name of nationalism.

Third, a local ruling group in a small society like Jamaica means that, compared with an elite riddled with expatriates or distant foreigners, the fabric of society is more of a single cloth; ruling and ruled groups alike are unified by ties of kinship, long personal acquaintance, and collective conscience. The recruitment, socialization, and performance of elites take place within the national norms of fairness. The consent and discontent of ordinary people can be taken more fully into account. Thus, the conditions for the maintenance of a democratic regime are heightened.

Notes

1. We actually interviewed eighty-two leaders in 1974. The eighty-third person, Prime Minister Michael Manley, who was interviewed in 1962 and again in 1979, had just published a book (Manley, 1974) explaining his political philosophy and his goals. Since we were not able to get an appointment with him during the period of our 1974 field work, we "interviewed" him by finding answers to our questions from his book. Except for a few questions, we were able to garner complete responses.

2. In a personal communication, Gladstone E. Mills, Head, Department of Government, University of the West Indies, estimates that the number of full-time Jamaican civil servants dealt with by the Public Service Commission increased from 8,570 in 1962–1963 to 15,570 in 1974–1975. These figures do not include teachers, police, or judges.

3. Since we have a near-universe, rather than a sample, we have not computed statistical tests of significance. That is, we assume that any differences from zero for all elites or between subgroups of elites are real differences.

4. For other reports of the 1974 Jamaican elite re-study, see Bell (1977, 1977–1978), Bell and Gibson (1978), Bell and Robinson (1979), Bell and Stevenson (1979), and Robinson and Bell (1978).

5. Changes in the distribution of personal wealth shown in Appendix Table 1 are not meaningful. Inflation over the intervening 12 years and changes in the tax structure present difficult problems of comparability. Thus, a composite scale based on net worth and average annual income was simply dichotomized in 1974 so as to approximate 1962 percentages as closely as possible to be used in cross-tabulations and correlations between the 1974 variables.

6. Henceforth the *Jamaican Weekly Gleaner* is cited as JWG.

7. Stone labels his categories differently than we have done, but they are roughly the same as ours as he defines them. Our labels (each followed in parentheses by his) are: radical (radical), liberal (moderate radical), populist (center), conservative (moderate conservative), and reactionary (conservative). We have used our labels in the text. From a personal communication from Stone (28 August 1981), we know this poll was conducted in September rather than November as given in the table title in Stone (1980:186).

8. In a study of senior civil servants, Mills and Robertson (1974) found that their attitudes were largely clustered at the center or slightly left of center, with 53 percent preferring the amount of government involvement in the economy to be "one among equals" and 33.7 percent preferring "large government control" but not direct government control of major sectors of the economy nor the elimination of free enterprise.

9. Although we have used both economic ideologies unsquared and economic ideologies squared in the multiple regression equation, the reader should remember that democratic attitudes are not a multiple linear function of the two. They are, rather, a curvilinear function of economic ideologies. See Stimson, Carmines, and Zeller (1978) and Tierney (1968: 182–84).

10. Stone (1981:9) reports from his survey data that in 1976 only 30 percent of the electorate "held the governing PNP responsible for the

apparent economic decline," while in 1980 fully 60 percent of the electorate did so, partly as a result of the PNP's own assertions that its "socialist politics was now directing the economy." Stone (1981:14) rightly says, further, that Seaga "has inherited the political legacy of the Manley years in circumstances in which he will be under greater pressure than Manley was to show visible results of economic and social progress against the backdrop of a chronically debilitated economy."

11. Some observers believe that the flight of the Jamaican bourgeoisie and their capital started earlier, as early as July 1972. No doubt some flight did occur by then. From our interviews, however, and from those of James A. Mau, we are confident that the majority of local entrepreneurs and professionals didn't lose confidence in the PNP government until sometime in late 1975 or early 1976.

12. Also emphasizing the important value of revitalizing a national bourgeoisie is Westerfield (forthcoming) in his analysis of Australia as a "prosperous dependent."

13. Although this strategy of development is sometimes called "the Puerto Rican model," it is really, as implemented in the new states of the Caribbean, only partially that at most. Whatever the inadequacies of development in Puerto Rico—and there are many—Puerto Rico had some economic escape valves not present in the Commonwealth Caribbean. They prominently included unrestricted immigration to the United States and a variety of American social welfare programs, such as food stamps, that lessened the pressures of economic hardship. The debate over whether these things have benefitted Puerto Rico psychologically, culturally, or even economically no doubt will continue for sometime to come. For an analysis of the rise of populism in Puerto Rico, see Baldrich (1981).

14. This argument, however, is a bit devious, because, while fresh inflows of foreign capital may not continue after an initial investment, a large portion of the earnings generated by a foreign investment project are frequently reinvested in the host country. Technically, these may not be counted as new capital inflows, although they are essential to the expansion and well-being of the project, whereas all profits, royalties, management fees, etc., which are repatriated are counted as capital outflows. As one can quickly see, this is a no-win situation for the foreigner, because with time, if the project is successful, the outflows will eventually surpass the initial capital investment or inflow. Clearly, in order to evaluate any given case, a key datum is the amount of reinvestment actually being made.

15. A comprehensive evaluation of a number of studies focused on the relationship of socioeconomic conditions and democracy can be found in May (1973).

16. For a study of the variety of ways in which multinational corporations maximize the money they take out of a developing country, see Richter (1979). Also, for a comparison of the different strategies of development, and some of their consequences, in Guyana and Trinidad and Tobago, see Hintzen (1981).

17. Best's analysis, of course, differs on several counts from various dependency theories formulated by others. For a review of the latter, see Gereffi (1980).

18. In this brief discussion we have been unable to include considera-

tion of the role of the United States in the Caribbean. Clearly, American policy influences both the internal politics and the economies of Caribbean countries. An excellent analysis of the United States in the Caribbean was given by Vaughan Lewis (1981).

References

Baldrich, Juan José (1981) "Class and the State: The Origins of Populism in Puerto Rico, 1934–1952." Ph. D. diss., Yale University.

Bell, Wendell (1980) "Equality and Social Justice: The Foundations of Nationalism in the Caribbean." *Caribbean Studies* 20:5–36.

———(1977–1978) "Independent Jamaica Enters World Politics: Foreign Policy in a New State." *Political Science Quarterly* 92:683–703.

———(1977) "Inequality in Independent Jamaica: A Preliminary Appraisal of Elite Performance." *Revista/Review Interamericana* 7:294–308.

———(1964) *Jamaican Leaders: Political Attitudes in a New Nation.* Berkeley and Los Angeles: University of California Press.

Bell, Wendell, and J. William Gibson, Jr. (1978) "Independent Jamaica Faces the Outside World: Attitudes of Elites after Twelve Years of Nationhood." *International Studies Quarterly* 22:5–48.

Bell, Wendell, and Robert V. Robinson (1979) "European Melody, African Rhythm, or West Indian Harmony? Changing Cultural Identity among Leaders in a New State." *Social Forces* 58:249–79.

Bell, Wendell, and David L. Stevenson (1979) "Attitudes toward Social Equality in Independent Jamaica: Twelve Years after Nationhood." *Comparative Political Studies* 11:499–532.

Best, Lloyd (1968) "Outlines of a Model of Pure Plantation Economy." *Social and Economic Studies* 17:283–326.

Broom, Leonard (1954) "The Social Differentiation of Jamaica." *American Sociological Review* 19:115–25.

Cardoso, Fernando Henrique (1973) "Associated-dependent Development: Theoretical and Practical Implications." In *Authoritarian Brazil,* edited by Alfred Stepan. New Haven: Yale University Press.

Census Research Programme (1976) "Race and Religion." *1970 Population Census of the Commonwealth Caribbean,* vol. 7. Jamaica: University of the West Indies: 1–8.

Cueva, Agustín (1977) *El desarrollo del Capitalismo en America Latina.* Mexico: Siglo XXI.

Cumper, George E. (1975) "The Distribution of Incomes in Jamaica." Department of Statistics, Jamaica. Unpublished.

Dahl, Robert A. (1971) *Polyarchy: Participation and Opposition.* New Haven: Yale University Press.

Department of Statistics, Jamaica (1975) *The Labour Force 1974.*

Duncan, Otis Dudley (1968) "Inheritance of Poverty or Inheritance of Race?" In *On Understanding Poverty: Perspectives from the Social Sciences,* edited by Daniel P. Moynihan. New York and London: Basic Books.

Gastil, Raymond D. (1981) "The Comparative Survey of Freedom—The Ninth Year." *Freedom at Issue* 59:3–18.

Gereffi, Gary (1978) "Drug Firms and Dependency in Mexico: The Case of the Steroid Hormone Industry." *International Organization* 32:237–86.

———(1980) " 'Wonder Drugs' and Transnational Corporations in Mexico: An Elaboration and Limiting-Case Test of Dependency Theory." Ph.D. diss., Yale University.

Gereffi, Gary, and Peter Evans (1981) "Transnational Corporations, Dependent Development, and State Policy in the Semiperiphery: A Comparison of Brazil and Mexico." *Latin American Research Review* 16:31–64.

Hintzen, Percy C. (1981) "Capitalism, Socialism, and Socio-Political Confrontation in Multi-Racial Developing States: A Comparison of Guyana and Trinidad." Ph.D. diss., Yale University.

Lewis, Gordon K. (1981) "The Possibilities of Change and Transformation in the Caribbean during the 1980s." Keynote address, Annual Meetings of the Caribbean Studies Association, St. Thomas, Virgin Islands, 27–30 May.

Lewis, Vaughan A. (1981) "The United States in the Caribbean." Presidential address, Annual Meeting of the Caribbean Studies Association, St. Thomas, Virgin Islands, 27–30 May.

Lindsay, Louis (1973) "The Pluralist Persuasion in American Democratic Thought." *Social and Economic Studies* 22:479–513.

Maingot, Anthony P. (1980) "Jamaica: Changing Political Signals in the Caribbean." *Los Angeles Times,* 23 November, p. 2.

Manley, Michael (1974) *The Politics of Change: A Jamaican Testament.* London: Andre Deutsch.

May, John D. (1973) *Of the Conditions and Measures of Democracy.* Morristown, N.J.: General Learning.

Meisel, James H. (1958) *The Myth of the Ruling Class: Gaetano Mosca and the "Elite."* Ann Arbor: University of Michigan Press.

Mills, G. E., and Paul D. Robertson (1974) "The Attitudes and Behaviour of the Senior Civil Service in Jamaica." *Social and Economic Studies* 23:311–43.

Moskos, Charles C., Jr. (1967) *The Sociology of Political Independence.* Cambridge, Mass.: Schenkman.

Moskos, Charles C., Jr., and Wendell Bell (1964) "Attitudes towards Democracy among Leaders in Four Emergent Nations." *British Journal of Sociology* 15:317–37.

Nettleford, Rex (ed.) (1971) *Norman Washington Manley and the New Jamaica.* London: William Clowes & Sons.

Oxaal, Ivar (forthcoming) *Black Intellectuals and Ideologies in the Caribbean.* Cambridge, Mass.: Schenkman.

———(1975) "The Dependency Economist as Grassroots Politician in the Caribbean." In *Beyond the Sociology of Development,* edited by Ivar Oxaal, Tony Barnett, and David Booth. London: Routledge & Kegan Paul.

Rae, Douglas W. (1971) *The Political Consequences of Electoral Laws.* New Haven: Yale University Press.

Richter, Andrew S. (1979) "Multinational Corporations, Local Businessmen, and the State in a Developing Country: A Case Study of Trinidad and Tobago." Ph.D. diss., Yale University.

Roberts, George W. (1957) *The Population of Jamaica.* Cambridge: At the University Press.

Robinson, Robert V., and Wendell Bell (1978) "Attitudes towards Political Independence in Jamaica after Twelve Years of Nationhood." *British Journal of Sociology* 29:208–33.

Stimson, James A., Edward G. Carmines, and Richard A. Zeller (1978) "Interpreting Polynomial Regression." *Sociological Methods and Research* 6:515–24.

Stone, Carl (1981) "Appraising the October 1980 Election in Jamaica." (Unpublished manuscript.)

———(1980) *Democracy and Clientelism in Jamaica.* New Brunswick, N.J.: Transaction.

Taylor, Charles Lewis, and Michael C. Hudson (1972) *World Handbook of Political and Social Indicators.* 2d ed. New Haven: Yale University Press.

Tierney, John A. (1968) *Calculus and Analytic Geometry,* Boston: Allyn & Bacon.

Tocqueville, Alexis de (1954) *Democracy in America,* vol. 1. New York: Vintage.

Westerfield, H. Bradford *Australia: Prosperous Dependent.* (Unpublished manuscript.)

APPENDIX TABLE 1.
Percentages of Jamaican Leaders Interviewed Having Selected
Social Characteristics, 1962 and 1974

Selected Social Characteristics	1962 Percent (N = 24)	1974 Percent (N = 83)
Sex		
Men	100	95
Women	0	5
Total	100	100
Age		
60 and over	12	19
50 to 59	50	28
40 to 49	21	38
39 and under	17	15
Total	100	100
Color or Race		
White or near-white	33	29
Chinese	0	5
Light or medium brown	50	44
Black or dark brown	17	22
Total	100	100
Education		
Completed college or more	38	63
Some college	8	27
Completed secondary school	42	8
Some secondary school or less	12	2
Total	100	100
Institutional Sector		
Political or labor union	59	34
Economic	25	27
Mass media	4	7
Civil service	4	13
Education	0	10
Religious or ethnic	4	7
Other	4	2
Total	100	100
Personal Wealth		
Wealthy	25	32
Not wealthy	75	68
Total	100	100

APPENDIX TABLE 2.
Attitudes toward Democracy by Selected Social
Characteristics, 1962 and 1974

	Percentage of Jamaican Leaders Who Were Democrats*			
	1962		1974	
Selected Social Characteristics	Percent	Number of Cases	Percent	Number of Cases
Age				
60 and over	(2)	(3)	80	(15)
50 to 59	58	(12)	78	(23)
40 to 49	80	(5)	83	(30)
39 and under	50	(4)	75	(12)
Color or Race				
White or near white	63	(8)	71	(24)
Chinese	—	(0)	67	(5)
Light or medium brown	75	(12)	86	(35)
Dark brown or black	50	(4)	88	(16)
Amount of Education[†]				
High	73	(11)	77	(51)
Medium	60	(10)	86	(22)
Low	(2)	(3)	75	(8)
Institutional Sector				
Political or labor	71	(14)	82	(28)
Economic	67	(6)	68	(22)
Mass media	(0)	(1)	80	(5)
Civil Service	(1)	(1)	90	(10)
Education	—	(0)	88	(8)
Religious or ethnic	(0)	(1)	83	(6)
Other	(1)	(1)	(1)	(2)
Personal Wealth				
Wealthy	50	(6)	75	(24)
Not wealthy	72	(18)	84	(50)

*Includes only leaders who said that democracy was "very suitable" for Jamaica.
†Because the distributions were so different, amount of education was classified differently for the two time periods:

1962	1974
High = Some college or more	Completed college or more
Medium = Completed secondary school	Some college
Low = Some secondary school or less	Completed secondary school or less

APPENDIX TABLE 3.
Correlation Matrix, Means, and Standard Deviations for Variables in the Stepwise Regression, 1962 and 1974*

Variables	Age (Old)†	Color (White)	Education (High)	Sector (Political, Labor et al.)	Wealth (Rich)	Economic Ideology (Radical)	(Economic Ideology − Vertex)² (Radical and Reactionary)	Attitudes toward Democracy (Very Suitable)
Age (old)†	—	−.022	−.038	−.294	.055	−.482	.112	.190
Color (white)	−.033	—	.175	−.378	.695	−.130	.344	.034
Education (high)	−.167	−.093	—	−.087	.286	.013	−.018	.026
Sector (political, labor et al.)	−.115	−.390	.198	—	−.636	.517	−.222	.165
Wealth (rich)	.125	.485	−.205	−.377	—	−.447	.212	−.042
Economic ideology (radical)	−.385	−.271	.095	.443	−.411	—	−.068	−.030
(Economic ideology − vertex)² (radical and reactionary)	−.062	.046	−.079	.026	.062	.090	—	−.456
Attitudes toward democracy (very suitable)	.080	−.173	−.056	.136	−.100	.028	−.436	—
Means								
1962	2.58	2.17	2.71	1.71	2.17	3.21	1.75	2.38
1974	2.52	2.15	3.49	1.66	1.96	3.34	1.69	2.69
Standard deviations								
1962	.929	.702	1.122	.464	.565	1.351	1.513	.924
1974	.972	.739	.755	.476	.835	1.259	1.286	.645

*1962 correlations are above the diagonal and 1974 below.
†The pole for each variable defined as the high end is given in parentheses.

"Let Us Make the Revolution, Before the People Do": Elite-Mass Relations in Brazil

Peter McDonough

Since the founding of the First Republic in 1889, Brazil has experimented with a variety of political forms. Yet for all the experimentation, politics in Brazil has remained an affair of elites. This has been most evident since 1964, when the military deposed a civilian government and imposed restrictions on mass participation. Now that the military has been in power for more than eighteen years, fatigue has set in. Elections are scheduled for 1982 and 1984. Still, the rules have been written by the elite establishment, and they favor the candidates of the government.[1]

Two forces behind the hierarchical style of Brazilian politics should be kept plainly in view. First, Brazil's democratic interlude, from 1945 to 1964, was not so democratic as the label implies. The political system showed many of the maladies associated with rapid change: electoral fraud, legislative stalemate, and populist rhetoric with little in the way of policy implementation. The experience frightened and frustrated many of the elites. It also inculcated a cynicism among elites and non-elites about the beneficence of democratic politics.[2]

Second, during nearly two decades of military rule, Brazil has undergone enormous change. More than six out of ten Brazilians are now classified as urban. About 75 percent are literate. The central

Data collection for this analysis was undertaken in 1972 and 1973 jointly with the Instituto Universitário de Pesquisas do Rio de Janeiro under a Ford Foundation grant to the Institute for Social Research, University of Michigan. The analysis was facilitated by grants from the Tinker Foundation, the National Science Foundation, and the Social Science Research Council. Youssef Cohen, Philip Converse, and Amaury de Souza have been my colleagues in this study. The title is drawn from a classic utterance of Antônio Carlos, an early twentieth-century Brazilian politician.

bureaucracy has grown prodigiously, as has its capacity to extract resources from the larger society. Whatever the outcome of Brazil's next political experiment, it will almost certainly not entail a revolutionary rearrangement of the incumbent coalition, much less a dismantling of the apparatus of the state or a return to the freewheeling populism-pluralism of the earlier postwar era.

The elitist nature of Brazilian politics is thus a function of at least two factors, one pulling from the past and the other pushing toward the future. On the one hand, despite mutations in political form at the national level, there is the persistent legacy of patrimonialism. On the other, there are the authoritarian implications of the developmental imperative, of the urge to controvert the lore that "Brazil is the land of the future . . . and always will be." The slogan of "fifty years of development in five" was coined by a democratically elected president, but the rationale is one that authoritarian elites have used to justify a reliance on top-down decision making while letting autonomous organizations wither in the shade.

If these two forces were the gist of Brazilian politics, their cumulative impact would leave an infinitesimal probability for anything but an authoritarianism by default. This is, indeed, the nub of the theory of the "new authoritarianism" in Brazil and elsewhere in Latin America: elitism has been historically and structurally induced (Collier, 1979; O'Donnell, 1973).[3]

However, the foundations of elite-mass politics in Brazil are more complex than this summary suggests. Even if the liberal democratic creed has never prevailed for long periods in Brazil, especially in its classical version under the aegis of a vigorous bourgeoisie, the culture of democracy in the sense of civil liberties and human rights remains alive among elite and semi-elite groups. Brazil is, after all, part of the West; the new authoritarianism is supposed to be statist rather than sultanic.[4]

In the second place, the new authoritarianism is not universally invariant. South Korea and Taiwan, with which the Brazilian model is sometimes compared, differ from Brazil in two crucial ways. First, the democratic heritage is probably more alien to both these places than it is in Brazil.[5] Yet, second, both South Korea and Taiwan exhibit far more equitable income distribution profiles than does Brazil.[6]

These cross-national differences are anomalous only if authoritarian politics is construed as a seamless, bloc-like "ism." They have, in addition, special relevance to understanding the apparent contradictions of elite-mass relations in Brazil. Although corporatist thinking is strong among Brazilians, it would be misleading to contend that it has utterly replaced the ethos of liberal democracy among elites and better-off Brazilians generally. This residual liberalism makes the elites seem, at first glance, life guardians of the democratic flame when their political beliefs, defined in conventional human rights terms, are compared to those of the mass public. But most of the elites are neither economic nor social radicals. Conversely, although ordinary Brazilians, and especially those close to the very bottom of the hierarchy, show little interest in refinements of political form, many of them are concerned with elemental social justice—an unsurprising concern, given the inequities of the developmental model prevalent in Brazil.

A central argument of this paper is not merely that developmental authoritarianism, building on a centralist heritage, encourages non-democratic politics, although this is true enough. The combined inertia-momentum of paternalism and headlong developmentalism is itself crisscrossed by the legacy of a "cultivated" liberalism, a democratic culture with unsteady structural underpinnings, that works to estrange further many highly educated and elite Brazilians from the mundane obsessions of their countrymen. As we shall see, this has profound and paradoxical implications for the meaning that elites and non-elites attach to political representation.

These implications can be drawn out by considering the reactions of the Brazilian public to authoritarian rule. Elites, even authoritarian elites, do not live in a vacuum; and they seldom stay in power by force alone. In light of the cross currents of the multiple political traditions in Brazil, authoritarian policies might under certain circumstances be popular among segments of the population who "objectively" bear the brunt of oppressive rule.

The argument is not so bizarre as it might seem. In the first place, whatever its economic performance, the Brazilian military gained credit for putting an end to the frantic populism of the mid-1960s. The coup had wide appeal. Unlike its counterpart in Chile (Remmer, 1979), it provoked almost no mass resistance, even if ousted and otherwise marginalized elites came to resent the *continuista* ambitions of the military and its technocratic allies. And even the erosion of the popularity of the military that can be expected as a result of economic deterioration does not imply that the citizenry embraces participatory democracy as an alternative to authoritarian rule. A reaction that is at least equally likely is the reinforcement of an already ingrained skepticism about modifications in political formulae that, when viewed from the slums of Rio and São Paulo and from the impoverished countryside of the Northeast, seem cosmetic.

Another reason for public acceptance of hierarchical politics is less circumstantial. Unlike Spain, Brazil has almost no history of intertwined cleavages breeding extensive violence. The lines of conflict between, for example, left and right and the secular and the religious do not overlap. Popular culture in Brazil has traditionally compartmentalized political, economic, and religious spheres in such a way that the expressive features of demotic rituals and festivals compensate and even foster a tolerance for the inequities of the economic system and the customary imbecilities of elections, parties, and the life. The result is an ambience of compromise and subordination rather than of polarization of institutional pluralism.[7]

With these points in mind, let us first examine the mass side of the elite political environment.

The Mass Environment of Elite Politics[8]

Three rough-and-ready approaches to mass politics in Brazil can be imagined, by way of preliminary. One is the "what-mass-politics?" view. The guiding assumption is that public opinion will never count for much. A second is a variation on the first, and it can be labelled the "blame-the-victim" perspective: even if elites were to listen to popular demands, they would submit themselves to little except cacophony. Levels of political information are so low that public opinion is scarcely worth paying attention to. A third alternative is the reverse of these, and it may be called "the noble savage" vision. The image is of a people seething under deprivation and oppression, restrained from revolution only by the fearful costs of confronting armed might.[9]

These are not so much ideal types as stereotypes. In one way or another, they elide the conversion sequence that flows, and may be shortcircuited, from objective conditions through perceptions of these conditions, as refracted by cultural dispositions, on to their potential for expression in organized or spontaneous form, and finally to the reaction to them on the part of the authorities. Figure 1 starts near the beginning of the chain by tracing mass perceptions of deprivation across levels of education.[10]

Lower class Brazilians are deprived, and they feel deprived. More than two-thirds of the illiterates claim that they do not have enough money to get by; fewer than one out of ten of the university educated feel the same way. The other relationships—between education and the sense of accomplishment and of "feeling free"—are only slightly less sharp.[11]

The deprivation is undeniable. The politically consequential question concerns the extent to which this perception is translated into resentment against supposed oppressors. Figure 2 traces some of the factors that thwart the translation process. It tracks, again across educational levels, media exposure and political information.[12]

The pattern is clear-cut: political information stands in inverse relation to economic and social hardship. Organized political action is unlikely to surge spontaneously from such a matrix. Media such as the radio are naturally more accessible to the less educated than newspapers, although the least educated are also lowest in television viewing. The regime is well aware of the differential reach of the print and non-print media. As liberalization came into vogue in the

FIGURE 1.
"Quality-of-Life" Indicators,
by Education

FIGURE 2.
Media Exposure and Political
Information, by Education

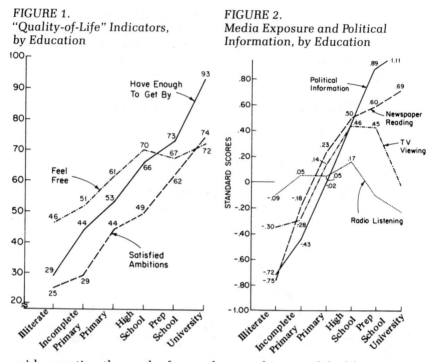

mid-seventies, the cruder forms of censorship were lifted from news-papers and magazines, since they are read by only a small fraction of the population. The truly mass media—the cinema, as well as radio and television—continued to be censored. The intelligentsia was kept isolated from its potential mass constituencies.

Still another factor militates against the conversion of deprivation into protest: organizational poverty, documented in Figure 3. The solid line traces the percentage of Brazilians who claim to belong to any—one or more—voluntary associations. It rises from less than one-third among the illiterates to more than eight out of ten among the university educated.[13]

But there is substantial variation in participation among the types of organizations, and there is one feature that is distinctive to poli-ties with a corporatist design. Membership in sindicatos is actually higher among the more educated. The working class is organized in labor syndicates, but there are also white-collar and professional syndicates for those toward the upper end of the occupational scale. Even more important, the absolute level of syndical association is low; Brazil is under-organized along class lines.[14]

The curve is also biased toward the well educated for professional and athletic club membership. The former pattern is self-explana-tory, and the latter is readily understandable in the Brazilian context.

Soccer teams, the collective celebrities of Brazilian life, are sponsored by the athletic clubs, which require membership dues. The mass of the population fills the stadiums to watch the teams compete, but few of them enjoy membership privileges.

One element qualifies the weight of informational and organizational poverty: affiliation with religious associations. Here, membership is slightly higher among the lower classes. These are the *comunidades de base*, the grass-roots organizations nurtured by the church, which have gained notoriety for their restiveness at the social marginalization exacerbated by government policy (Bruneau, 1980).

On balance, the evidence regarding mass information and organizational participation is not propitious as far as autonomous collective action is concerned, the one bright spot being the potential of the local ecclesiastical associations. Of course, it is conceivable that, for all their lack of informational and organizational resources, the Brazilian poor harbor sympathies with progressive political and social programs. In this case, the problem would be one of ignorance and lack of participatory experience, not right-wing predispositions.

The problem can be addressed from two angles: from that of expressly political opinions about public controversies and from that of beliefs about issues closer to home, such as those touching on matters of family relations and attitudes toward authority patterns in everyday life. One symptom of demobilization is a withdrawal from activity or interest in questions of national policy and a concomitant focus on local, not to say private, problems of daily concern.

Figure 4 lays out some of these tendencies, arraying the percentages of respondents "strongly agreeing" with a series of items of the F-scale type.[15] The results do not relieve the impression of a pervasive culture of subordination. In light of the evidence already presented about the organizational and informational destitution of the Brazilian public, it is not surprising that so many respondents go along with the statement that "politics is too complicated for people like me to understand." More striking is the high incidence of agreement with other bits of folk wisdom of both a private and public nature. Only among the university educated, for example, does the expectation that "if the government listens to what the people say, chaos will result" meet with less than majority assent.[16]

Much the same configuration holds for the indicators of orientations toward mores bearing on face-to-face authority relations. Family structure is the bedrock of social hierarchy, no more so than among the less educated. Even among the university educated, a majority agrees that "the most important thing for children to learn is to obey their parents." Similarly, the notion that "employers have to be strict, otherwise workers will get out of line" is more likely to be accepted among those toward the bottom of the educational ladder.

FIGURE 3.
Organizational Membership,
by Education

FIGURE 4.
F-Scale Type Indicators,
by Education

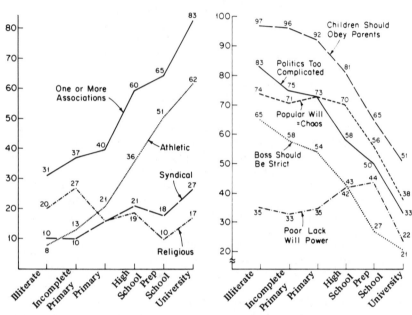

Once more, a mild qualification can be made to the norms of deference. Most Brazilians are not much taken by the idea that "the poor have themselves to blame" for their plight. Nevertheless, the overall picture is one of acquiescence in the face of inequality: a virtual fatalism with respect to popular control over public affairs and a cautious traditionalism in the workplace and at home.[17]

What is to be made of this? Almost certainly, not the expectation of a mass culture on the verge of rebellion. To be sure, not all the relations between education and orientations toward authority are monotonic. It is neither the illiterates, nor those with primary schooling, nor the university educated, but the high school graduates—Brazilians just below the top of the heap—who are most conservative in the belief that poverty is the fault of the poor themselves. Righteousness and a fear of losing "what we've worked hard to get" characterize this intermediate stratum.[18]

Still, on the whole, the results confirm the prevalence of a stratified political culture. "Enlightenment"—a recognizably cosmopolitan, verbal liberalism—has taken hold mainly among the highly educated. Lower down the hierarchy, the personal and political world becomes darker and more zero-sum.

The configuration is strange only in contrast to romantic assumptions about the conditions of the downtrodden under an authoritarian legacy. Not even the "enlightened" strata can be called progressive in certain areas—for example, with regard to questions bearing on family relations, even when they vouchsafe "modern" attitudes on public issues.[19]

The distinction between public and private spheres is important but, like many dichotomies, misleading if taken as final. A little probing reveals three distinct spheres. There is, first of all, the world of relatives and friends and neighbors. It is a culture of intimacy but not of unquestioning trust and camaradarie. Second, there is the remote public world about which two contrasting views are taken: about the truly powerful—chiefly, the state itself and the military, whom the public tend to hold in awe—and, on the other hand, the media and the politicians whom experience has taught the public to view as hucksters and tricksters.

Table 1 captures these distinctions. It orders the groups "trusted" (thought to be dependable in the sense of "people you can count on to defend your interests") and more or less "liked" or "disliked."[20] Marginals and central tendencies are presented rather than breakdowns by the usual background indicators because the results hold steady across social strata. This lack of variation is, of course, a crucial sign of the scope of the culture of subordination.

The authorities, principally the government and the military, are trusted more than either those groups with whom Brazilians have

TABLE 1.
Orientations toward Political
and Social Groups, Mass Sample

"Always Trusted"	%	"Will Stand Up for People" Mean (0–10)		Like/Dislike Mean (0–10)	
Government	47	Government	7.9	Armed forces	8.0
Military	38	Judges	7.2	Government	7.5
Priests	31	Military	6.9	Large industrialists	7.0
Police	28	Church	6.7	Bishops	6.9
Boss	27	Boss	6.0	Labor syndicates	6.9
Relatives	24	Labor syndicates	5.7	Bankers	6.2
Work colleagues	22	ARENA	5.7	ARENA	6.1
Bureaucrats	22	MDB	5.0	MDB	5.3
Friends	18				
Newspapers and TV	14				
Politicians	9				

closer contact or the traditionally disreputable figures such as the media and the politicians. One reaction to these ratings is to dismiss them as twisted by fear, a plausible-sounding explanation given the despotic politics of the period during which the interviews were conducted. But no associations between the ratings and indications of fear or circumspection are to be found in the data.[21]

Alternatively, it may be that the perceived trustworthiness of the military is, or was, genuine enough, but quite time-bound. Even though the development strategy in force during the late sixties and early seventies was repressive and inequitable, the gross national product was booming. In addition, disenchantment with the populist era was still fresh, and the post-1973 downturn in the economy was yet to come.[22]

There has to be some truth to this interpretation; the rankings are not graven in stone. At the same time, there is no reason to suppose that the rankings have turned upside down. The centralist tradition in Brazil is long-standing, not conjunctural. Brazilians, especially the disadvantaged, have learned that "the state will always be with them" (Uricoechea, 1980; Veliz, 1979). The spread of education, the differentiation of the work force, and related dynamics of modernization may undermine this legacy. But they do not lead ineluctably to democratization, any more than has the "logic of industrialization" in the Soviet bloc led to a convergence with the pluralism of the Western democracies (White, 1978). The public gets used to, and the more mobile develop a stake in, a hierarchy that renovates itself but does not lose its shape.

In summary, the mass environment of elite politics in Brazil, certainly during the early seventies, was not one that pitted a radicalized mass against a despised elite. Such resentment as ordinary Brazilians expressed was more often directed against one another than against the authorities. In effect, the political culture itself was elitist.

It would be stretching a point to call this orientation immutable or total. Nor would it be correct to characterize "enlightened" Brazilians as defenders of the liberal flame. At the heart of the problem is a tremendous paucity of associational options for lower class Brazilians and a corresponding tendency for the anguish of deprivation to be expressed in personal terms, in suspicion of intimates and in dependence on "superiors." This is the vacuum at the heart of populist authoritarianism in Brazil.

Elite and Mass Priorities[23]

There is still another way to view the evidence documenting widespread conservatism among the mass of the Brazilian population. The argument would be that the public suffers from a severe case of false consciousness, exacerbated, no doubt, by cleverly selective censorship and exemplary intimidation. The trouble with this argument is that it assumes that a coherent ideology can be put together from the economic, social, and political concerns of the public. It also neglects the possibility that members of the public may know something that a few academic and political observers of the Brazilian scene have forgotten or simply have not experienced.

Popular demands, such as they are, are not wholly jumbled. Although the public can scarcely be thought of as revolutionary, many lower class Brazilians give great emphasis to economic and especially social issues, for which they seek government solutions, while ignoring what they consider political niceties. To some extent, Brazilian elites share this orientation, one in which the big issues are thought to be those of economic development and social problem-solving (rather than revolution), with at most an ambiguous commitment and more often an indifference to the precise means for carrying out policies in these areas. Authoritarian measures will do; democratic ones might, if they work and the patience is there.[24]

Table 2 sets up the basic comparison. Elites and non-elites were asked to rate the importance of seven issues that were at the time, and continue to be, matters "of national concern." Once they gave their own rankings, the elites were also asked for their perceptions of the importance attributed to the issues by Brazilians generally. Finally, elites with constituencies were asked to state the importance they felt their clienteles gave to the issues.[25]

The tabulation conveys the impression of general agreement between elite and mass priorities. The elites tend to discount the importance the public gives to issues of any kind, a reasonable procedure in light of the greater involvement of the elites in public life. The mass ranking of issues corresponds, more or less, to the elite rankings, with the classic developmental issues of income redistribution and agrarian reform toward the top.

Birth control is the glaring exception. The elites put it at the bottom of their agenda and think that non-elites do likewise. But, in fact, birth control stands close to the top of the mass agenda. The reason for this misperception is straightforward. Brazilian elites of both the left and the right are accustomed to define "birth control" in aggregate terms, as a matter of size related to the labor force and the domestic market, large numbers being linked to national power. Other Brazilians are less enamored of this big-picture perspective. They are more concerned about their declining capacity to feed a growing number of children. For them, access to birth control facilities is a matter of personal well-being.[26]

In effect, the birth control issue is an exception that proves the rule—namely, that the concerns of the public are with basic needs. Brazilians generally are not picky about political issues, narrowly

TABLE 2.

Average Priorities Given to Seven Issues, by Elites and Non-Elites

| Issue | Elites' Perception (0–100) | | | Issue | Non-Elites (0–4) | |
	Of Elites	Of Constituents	Of Brazilians		Importance	Effect
Income redistribution	81.2	78.1	70.9	Agrarian reform	3.03	—
Agrarian reform	72.6	70.2	60.4	Birth control	2.44	0.99
Government-Labor	69.0	69.5	54.3	Income redistribution	2.43	1.43
Foreign investment	68.8	62.4	53.5	Labor-Government	1.90	0.91
Government—Opposition	56.0	51.2	44.1	Foreign investment	1.79	0.93
Subversion	50.1	46.1	45.2	Government—Opposition	1.56	0.65
Birth control	49.1	44.5	37.7	Subversion	1.46	0.66

defined. They have little time for controversies surrounding the relations between the government and the opposition parties or for the question of subversion. These are not the realities of everyday life.[27]

The most important fact of this tabulation, however, is the paramount salience of agrarian reform and income distribution, both at the elite and mass levels. Indeed, among ordinary Brazilians, agrarian reform (redistribuição das terras) is on the average accorded greater priority than income redistribution. At first glance, this might seem obvious. But Brazil has long since passed from being a landlord-peasant society. Moreover, most of the respondents are urban. So the high priority given to agrarian reform requires explanation.

The discursive responses of the mass public to probes that followed the importance items help solve the mystery. There are a few, but not many, explanations that can be interpreted as politically neutral or even conservative. But far and away the most common response is a cry for elementary justice: "people need land so they can work"; "there's too much idle land that the big shots don't cultivate," and so on.

To call such remarks revolutionary would be unwarranted. Yet they capture the flavor of the populist strain in Brazilian politics, an undercurrent that is not choosy about refinements in political form. Most of the time, most Brazilians focus on bread-and-butter issues and do not link policy alternatives on these issues to diametrically opposed political options. Still, issues involving physical property—most literally, the land—are redolent with symbolism. They evoke a populist proto-constituency, a free-floating demand.[28]

We have arrived, then, at a somewhat more complicated picture of elite-mass politics in Brazil than the "blame-the-victim," the "noble savage," or the "what-mass-politics?" perspectives. The Brazilian public has yet to become mobilized as a force for making elites accountable. At the same time, literacy and education are spreading rapidly. Also, however, the central bureaucracy continues to grow, and autonomous institutions capable of challenging state power remain weak. The state-centric tradition is reinforced by modern means.

As is typical in revolutions-from-above, "modernization" has been promoted, while traditional bastions of economic power have been left essentially intact (Trimberger, 1978). Investments in human capital and, to a degree, in human services have been made. But the possession of capital goods has not been democratized. Elites and semi-elites have picked up the cultural signals of liberalism, but there has not been a liberal-led revolution of bourgeois industrializers. The result is a persistent tension between impulses toward gradualist reform that depend for their viability on sustained economic growth and obstinant structural realities.

Although the views of elites and non-elites are not wildly discrepant, neither are they in complete accord. The elites are generally more tuned, if not committed, to distinctions between democratic and nondemocratic processes. By comparison, non-elites seem "a-democractic" (or "an-authoritarian.") Given this broad contrast of orientations, there also exists significant heterogeneity within "the elite" and "the mass" taken by themselves. But such variations are not the major focus of this paper. Let us turn instead to the equally important question of how non-elite "orientations" become, or fail to become, recognizable interests rather than diffuse opinions or presumed demands.

A Note on Representation

A major theme of the analysis so far has been the sense of social subordination and political dependence on the strong state, particularly among lower class Brazilians who want relief from economic hardship and who are not squeamish about the mechanisms for implementing such reforms. For these people the problem is poverty, and the solution is strong government.

It is toward the upper reaches of the stratification system that deferent populism fades and starts to be replaced, although hardly overwhelmed, by what looks like a liberal democratic ethos. A richness of associational life emerges, together with a sensitivity to matters of political form. Grinding poverty and its alleviation are no longer the only problems, and a reversal sets in. Now the government, rather than being viewed as a "benevolent Leviathan" (Cohen, 1982), tends to be seen as a threat to the limited pluralism that is a staple of elite politics in authoritarian regimes (Linz, 1973).

Table 3 and Figure 5 document these divergent logics. The table shows the incidence of three kinds of conflict reported by the various elite actors: between their constituencies and the Brazilian public, between the constituencies themselves and the representatives' own views, and between the constituencies' presumed interests and those of the government.[29] The data in Figure 5 are drawn from the mass interviews. Broken down by levels of education, the figures show the percentages agreeing with three positions: that deputies may vote against the wishes of their constituents; that deputies may break party discipline and vote their conscience; and finally, that deputies may vote against the government.[30]

The mass data are dramatic in their simplicity. The deputy-versus-voters and the deputy-versus-party are the most popular options, and they do not vary much by social position. About two-thirds of the citizenry reject mass mandate notions of representation. The least popular alternative is that deputies should vote against the government. Only among the better educated is an adversary relationship between elected elites and state elites accepted in great proportion. Politicians, it would seem, are to represent the govern-

TABLE 3.
Percentage Reporting Three Types of Conflicts, by Elite Sector

	Bishops	MDB	Professionals	Labor	Business	Civil Service	ARENA	Total
Constituency x government	100	77	73	65	60	50	42	61
Self x constituency	57	69	10	35	46	36	43	41
Constituency x Brazilians	43	31	20	19	46	33	18	28
Average	67	59	34	40	51	40	34	43

FIGURE 5.
Views on Political Representation, by Education

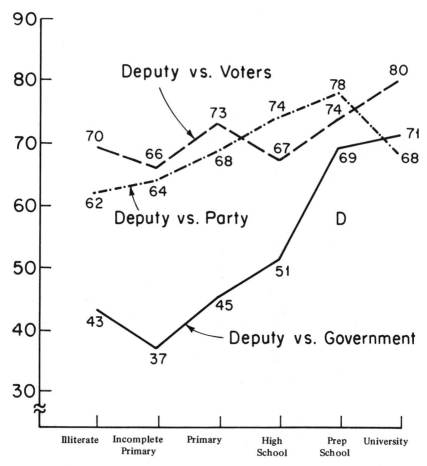

ment to the people and not, as in the liberal democratic mode, represent the people in the halls of government.

An analogous pattern appears in Table 3. The elites claim that their major conflict is less with their constituents than with the government itself. In part, but only in part, given all the corroborative evidence, the contrast may be self-serving. A few of the elites, on the average less than one-third, admit to conflicts between the demands of their constituents and the interests of Brazilians in general. A somewhat larger number are given to self-criticism. About four out of ten claim that they do not always know—or that their views sometimes enter into conflict with—the views of their constituents.

But the supreme fact is the degree of reported conflict with the government: 61 percent overall. In this respect, the elites as a whole stand not only against the intrusions of the government but also against the mass of Brazilians. However, the case should not be overstated. Since the flattening out of the Brazilian boom in the mid-seventies, inroads have been made by the opposition; and in retrospect the elites might be considered not so much in contradiction to as ahead of the Brazilian people. It is difficult to sort out these alternatives. But it is worth noting that they are not mutually exclusive. This becomes evident when the data are viewed elite sector by sector.

All the bishops feel that at one time or another their constituents have had run-ins with the government. Most of the politicians of the MDB (Movimento Democratico Brasileiro), the opposition party when the survey was conducted, feel the same way. What is remarkable is that both these elite groups also admit, in above-average proportions, to doubts about the match between their own opinions and the demands of their clienteles. The progressive elites are aware not only of their conflict with the government, as they must be; at least some of them also have an inkling of their distance from the mass of Brazilians.

The one exception to this pattern, on the left, is the position of the professionals—broadly speaking, the intellectuals. Like most of the elites on the left, they consider their clienteles—in the present case, mostly one another—to be at odds with the government. But only a handful of them feel that their own views contradict those of their constituents or that the wishes of their constituents run counter to those of the Brazilian people. The pattern may be symptomatic of the myopia of left-leaning intellectuals in and outside of Brazil, who tend to project their own ideologies onto those in whose name they speak.[31]

Toward the right, the businessmen exhibit a pattern that is easy to understand. They are about average in their belief that the government and their constituents are at odds and only slightly above average in admitting to a divergence of opinion between themselves and their constituents. But when it comes to admitting that the interests of their constituents may enter into conflict with those of the Brazilian public, they are the frankest of all the elites. The businessmen may not be as politically reactionary as is sometimes supposed. But economically and socially, they are rather conservative; and they sense that this sets them apart from the public.

As a whole, then, many of the elites recognize that they are at odds not only with the Brazilian people but also with the government. They have multiple interests that cannot be painlessly reconciled—their constituents', the government's, those of the "nation as a whole," and, of course, their own. Several of those on the left feel, naturally, alienated from the government; they feel a corresponding detachment from their constituents as well. On the right, the elites are somewhat less aggrieved by the government and feel much more certain of their concordance with their clienteles; but—with the important exception of members of the government party itself—they perceive themselves to be in conflict with the economic and social demands of the Brazilian public.

Table 4 shows the types of conflict entered into with the government, across the elite groups.[32] While in some cases the reported conflicts are so few that the percentage figures must be treated with caution, the overall results are not seriously in doubt.

The labor leaders, quite unmysteriously, say that the vast majority of their conflicts are over social questions: wages, working conditions, pensions, job security, and so on. The conservative ARENA (Aliança Renovadora Nacional) politicians and the businessmen report that most of their complaints are about "other" issues, in the main, technical and economic planning disputes.

The bishops state that most of their confrontations with the government are over political matters. These involve human rights violations; since the early seventies, they have extended to issues of social justice. Even the civil servants have political conflicts with the government—in a sense, among themselves. The conflicts have mostly to do with the top-down style of decision making. As a modernizing agency, the Brazilian government has recruited some difficult-to-control technocrats, young men with professional standards, if not altruistic motives.[33]

Many of the elites, then, are caught between at least two forces: neglect and actual hostility on the part of the government on the one hand and apathy and ignorance on the part of the public on the other. Let us explore this dilemma further.

It is useful to systematize the coordinates of the dilemma. First, all the elites can be thought of as having one large, latent clientele, the mass public. Second, some have delimited constituencies. With regard to the critical question of representation, a pair of questions arises for constituencies large and small: (a) the various obstacles that the elites confront in promoting, if they choose, the interests of the public and their constituents, and (b) the means the elites use, if not to overcome or sidestep these obstacles, then at least to keep themselves informed of the needs and preferences of their clienteles.

The elites were asked about these problems, and the volume of information is enormous. Myriad comparisons are possible: between the mass public and the specific constituencies with respect both to the means of "getting to know them" and the obstacles in the way of putting this knowledge into practice, all of which can vary, moreover, from sector to sector of the elites.

Fortunately, a detailed analysis of this play of mirrors need not be presented, for the major patterns are reasonably clear. To begin with,

TABLE 4.
Types of Conflict between Constituencies and Government, by Elite Sector

	Bishops	Labor	MDB	Civil Service	ARENA	Business	Total
Political	86	6	36	43	31	14	24
Social	—	94	36	—	6	—	39
Other	14	—	27	57	63	86	38
Total	100	100	99	100	100	100	100
	(7)	(35)	(11)	(7)	(16)	(22)	(98)

the elites distinguish between the obstacles separating them from the public and from their constituents. In the view of the elites, the chief obstacle dividing them from the public is the sheer "lack of education of the public." Mass ignorance is cited by fully 46 percent of the elites, way above "inadequate news coverage" (16 percent) and "censorship" (12 percent). In contrast, the problem cited most often with regard to elite-constituency relations is "lack of consensus among the constituents" (20 percent), followed by "difficulties of communication with constituents" (15 percent) and "opposition of other groups" (12 percent). The public, as compared to the constituencies, is seen as beyond the pale, too benighted to represent, since it has not passed the threshold of crystallizing opinions. The elites tend to blame the victims.

What about the means for keeping informed of mass and constituent opinions? Here, too, the contrasts are sharp. The chief means for staying abreast of public opinion are "magazines and newspapers" (28 percent), "informal conversations" (23 percent), and "radio and television" (20 percent). The vehicles of contact are unstructured; and the mass is treated as a mass, by way of the media, and personalistically, through the occasional *bate-papo* (chitchat).

The format of the relations elites share with their constituents is very different. The fact that "informal conversations" are the most popular form of contact with constituents (33 percent) might not seem terribly discrepant from the elite-mass pattern. But the next most popular mechanism of elite-constituency interaction is "formal meetings" (20 percent). The elites relate to their constituents on organized, as well as intimate, terms. Here they deal in a world of interest groups, not aimless demands.

When these gross patterns are sketched in, variations across particular elite groups in regard to obstacles against and means of contact with both the public and constituents fall into place. Table 5 gives a sample of the significant differences among the sectors.

A highly complex picture of the subcultures of corporatism emerges. The genuinely powerful elites, the state managers and the businessmen, favor informal conversations with constituents who are, almost to a man, of their own kind. Formal, organized meetings take on supreme importance only for the labor leaders, whose constituencies come closest to a mass base. The bishops also rely on formal gatherings, organized through the National Conference of Brazilian Bishops. It is difficult for them to communicate otherwise, scattered as they are in far-flung dioceses throughout the country.

By itself, the contrast between the coziness of the businessmen and civil servants and the rather bureaucratized participation of the labor and ecclesiastical elites belies bloc-like images of the workings of "corporatism." It becomes truly interesting when set against the data in the next major row of Table 5 concerning the obstacles in the

TABLE 5.
Selected Means for Keeping Informed about and Obstacles against
Prompting Public and Constituents' Preferences

Elites vis-à-vis Constituents

Means	Civil Service	Business	MDB	Bishops	Professionals	Labor	ARENA
Informal conversations	58	51	46	29	27	23	18
Formal meetings	8	14	—	29	9	43	3
Newspapers and magazines	—	—	31	—	27	8	24
Radio and TV	—	6	8	—	9	8	15

Obstacles	Business	Civil Service	Bishops	Labor	ARENA	MDB	Professionals
Lack of consensus	37	31	29	17	15	—	—
Difficulties of communication	6	—	43	11	27	23	18

Elites vis-à-vis Mass Public

Means	Labor	Civil Service	ARENA	MDB	Professionals	Business
Formal meetings	21	4	4	—	—	—

Obstacles	Business	Bishops	Civil Service	ARENA	Professionals	MDB	Labor
Lack of education of public	58	55	46	46	44	29	28
Censorship	8	9	5	—	33	57	13

way of promoting constituency interests. Buttonholing does not guarantee elite-constituency consensus, so the businessmen and the bureaucrats report, whereas the labor leaders, with their "routine" meetings with the rank and file, are less worried about (or less conscious of) lack of consensus. The bishops furnish an intermediate case. Even though formal conferences are a primary way of sorting out issues, they still complain of fragmenting consensus.

The puzzle of clubbiness together with problematic consensus vanishes once it is recognized that the top elites have constituencies that are made up of their peers, and that the give-and-take of disagreement and infighting—of limited pluralism—signals a democracy entre nous. The labor leaders and the other "loser" elites are, for all practical purposes, on the nether side of limited pluralism. Their chief problem is with the overbearing state and its favorites in the business community, who shut them out. Under these circumstances, it would be difficult and perhaps unbearable to allow for recognition of difficulties with their own constituents. The appearance of solidarity is at least comforting. The key divide is between those elites—incumbents and winners—whose constituents are their peers and the other elites, whose constituents are supposed to be "followers."

When the elites turn to the mass public, they are considerably more uniform in their use of various means for keeping up with opinions and in their assessment of the obstacles blocking the advancement of the people's interests. The constituencies are differentiated; the public is relatively amorphous. The labor leaders' recourse to formal meetings pretty much reiterates the facts that, unlike even the politicians whose parties lack structure, they have traditionally dealt with nonelites through lines laid down by corporatist regulations and that they view the rank and file as the Brazilian people writ large.

However, one pair of obstacles escapes the general standardization: the "lack of education of the public" and "censorship." Only the opposition politicians and, to a somewhat lesser extent, the intellectuals complain much about censorship. The labor leaders, like their constituents, have most of their time consumed scraping crumbs off the plate, with little left over for "human rights." But, like the MDB politicians, they are less prone than the other elites to accuse the public of political ignorance. The distinction is important. A refusal to fault the victims does not imply, for the labor leaders, frontal criticism of the government and its demobilizing ways. This is left to the political opposition.

Yet, despite these variations, it is the absolute predominance of the belief in the cultural backwardness of the masses as an impediment to effective public discourse that stands out. The usually progressive bishops join with the businessmen and other conservative elites in blaming the failure of representation on the ignorance of the public.

Most of this is just what it seems: the elites do not credit non-elites with the capacity to go it on their own. The perspective is compatible with another syndrome of authoritarian politics: the elites do not trust one another to direct political appeals to the Brazilian public. The elites not only have little respect for the political acumen of non-elites; they also distrust one another. They dread mass politics and its supposed corollary, demagogy.

Conclusion

Brazilian politics is messy rather than schematic. The gaps between rich and poor, and between an undereducated public and a cautious elite, are blatant. But, like the corporatist label, these are descriptive and definitional starting points only. They do not generate unambiguous conclusions about political orientations and actions. Still, it is possible to discern several regularities—or what might better be called systematic incongruities.

First, the very separation of the elites from ordinary Brazilians not only gives them a certain hothouse freedom—a seigneurial pluralism—but also facilitates a corresponding fatalism on the part of the public regarding the trade-off between representation and hierarchy. The elites are more concerned about fighting off the intrusions of arbitrary rule than they are interested in rallying the public behind their cause. The mass interviews convey the strong impression that ordinary Brazilians have seen all this before and that the worst-off do not expect much better from the elites.

Side by side with this deferential indifference is the populist strain. It seems, given the increasing industrialization of the country, rather platonic and nostalgic. It is poorly organized. But it is a potentially powerful undercurrent. As ubranization continues and education spreads, the populist thrust may be blunted. Still, the joining of a barely articulate cry for rudimentary justice with the restiveness of a growing middle class can be disruptive. The bureaucratic institutions of industrial society have grown so large, and the co-optative tradition is so long-standing in Brazil, that the chances of a successful leftist mobilization of revolutionary proportions are very slim. The probability of intermittent confrontation, and of a reversion to a praetorianism supported by various factions of those who continue to be excluded from the political arena, is higher.[34]

Thus, as the "new" authoritarianism itself ages, it multiplies possible countercoalitions. It becomes increasingly tenuous to speak of the state, as a monolithic entity; but it also is not very compelling to expect a unitary opposition.

One factor contributing to the confusion is the shallowness of mass organizations. Another is the long heritage of ideological dispersion: the disjointedness of political, social, and cultural beliefs. And third, it is extremely difficult to tie these two factors, separate by themselves, with the massive changes in the relations of productive forces that authoritarianism has brought to Brazil.

The last question is one of political economy. I cannot consider it here except to note the following. While there is no direct link between the exploitation and marginalization of vast portions of the Brazilian people and revolutionary proclivities, Brazilian elites have gotten themselves into a very delicate situation. Since the country is well on its way to industrialization, since cities have proliferated and grown, and an urban life-style and at least minimal education have spread, the scenario of revolutionary violence being acted out in Central America does not really fit Brazil. Yet, unlike some of their counterparts in Northeast Asia, for example, authoritarian elites in Brazil have done little to correct some of the more appalling inequities of the social structure. The irony is that the lack of equilibrium built into such distances between rich and poor may prove daunting to progressive elites on the fringes of power under the dispensation of *abertura*, just as these imbalances were neglected by the elites who seized power in 1964.[35]

The implications of the first two factors—of mass disorganization and ideological fuzziness—flow more readily from the analysis presented here. Brazil has a patrimonial tradition; added to this is a corporatist style of modernization. Autonomous organizations are few and far between. The ideological legacy is not promising either, if the desired developmental outcome is thought to be parliamentary democracy. The lineaments of the social structure are hierarchical, and so are the routines of the workplace and of family life. This is not the breeding ground for a "civil religion" of "republican virtue" (Bellah and Hammond, 1980).

One mildly paradoxical implication of the inchoate nature of ideology or "public opinion" in Brazil is that mass demands, such as they are, do not seem diametrically opposed to the beliefs of the elites. Although factions of the elite may be at each others' throats, elite-mass relations are not charged with chronic confrontation. Social and political cleavages to not tightly overlap. These lines of conflict have not become harsher because they have rarely been given organizational reinforcement. Opinions and "demands" are still rather disembodied. Only in relation to their comparatively limited constituencies can the elites be characterized as dealing with identifiable interests, rather than as musing about homeless "preferences."[36]

Appendix: The Samples

The principal characteristics and limitations of the elite sample can be summarized as follows. First, although some retired officers appear among the top civil servants, there is no sample of the active military command. Second, sampling procedures varied with the internal structure of the elite sectors. For some groups, such as the industrial and financial, hierarchies by size can be delineated. Size was measured by liquid assets for the industrial firms (the top 500) and by deposits for the banks (the top 200).[37] Cutoff points for defining the universe to be sampled in the civil service are more problematic. They are obscured by marked power differences between ministries (the ministry of finance, for example, being closer to the center of action than the ministry of health) and by occasional incomparability of similar-sounding job classifications, among other factors. The rank of "national institute director" was set as the minimal level in order to restrict the government sample to the higher reaches of the executive and the judiciary (ministers and secretaries-general of the ministries, supreme court justices, and executive officers of public companies).

The overall response rate was 41 percent, with considerable variation among elite groups. The sample of labor leaders is the most complete (62 percent). Primarily because of their geographic dispersion, the bishops turned out to be the least accessible of all the elites (25 percent).[38]

Given the technical and political difficulties of conducting such research in Brazil, the sampling results compare reasonably well with those obtained in the few large-scale elite surveys conducted elsewhere.[39] Most important, there is no indication that the sector-samples are biased in such a way as to prevent valid inferences about the target populations.[40] Representativeness is maintained even within the subsectors, such as the church and the MDB, where the number of interviews is small. In part, this is because the logic of sampling elites tends to be the reverse of that involved in sampling larger populations. Large samples of elites are not necessarily more representative, since elites are by definition few in number.

The mass sample is a multistage area probability sample of the adult population of six states: Rio de Janeiro, Espírito Santo and Minas Gerais (sampled as if they were a single entity), São Paulo, Rio Grande do Sul, and the then-state of Guanabara (mostly the city of Rio de Janeiro). The selection of respondents was carried out in five stages: municípios, census sectors or enumeration tracts, subsectors, households, and individuals. The response rate was 86 percent. Unequal weighting of the responses of different sample elements was used to compensate for nonresponse. Sample responses were weighted to reflect the relative distribution of urban-rural residence, sex, and age in the population.[41]

Notes

1. For updates on Brazilian politics, see Lamounier and Faria (1981) and Sanders (1980).

2. For detailed analyses of this period, see dos Santos (1979) and Soares (1979).

3. Most of the literature on the new authoritarianism that is written from a political economy perspective (such as Collier, O'Donnell, etc.) stresses the developmental imperative of rapid growth and the striving for great power status. Historical-cultural approaches take a different, although largely complementary, tack. See Schwartzman (1975), Stepan (1978), and Wiarda (1978). In rough terms, the former school draws on variants of Marx, the latter on Weber.

4. For an inclusive discussion of the "new sultanism," see Delacroix (1980). Analyses of third world growthmanship often argue, following Gerschenkron (1962), that central governments assume vast managerial roles in the development process. As an empirical observation, the case rings true. See Boli-Bennett (1980). The problem is that the correlation between public sector growth and delayed development cannot be equated with effective economic growth; see Sheahan (1980). However this may be, emphasis on the "heavy" state has obscured the apparently incongruous leftovers of the liberal democratic ethos among third world elites.

5. For a panoramic but highly suggestive contrast, see Jones (1981).

6. See Das Gupta (1978), Han (1974), and Kihl and Kim (1981).

7. There is a considerable literature on the *mansidão* (softness) of Brazilian culture. The most insightful recent analyses are by da Matta (1979, 1981).

8. The mass sample (n = 1,314) is of the center-south of Brazil. Fieldwork was conducted from mid-1972 to mid-1973. Sampling procedures are described in the appendix.

9. See Lernoux (1980); compare Booth (1979).

10. The questions used in Figure 1 read: (1) "Would you say that the money that you and/or your family makes is enough to cover expenses, or that at times it's not enough to buy what you need?" (2) "Do you feel free to do what you want to do nowadays in Brazil? Or do you feel constrained (*tolhido*)?" (3) "Would you say that you've managed to satisfy the ambitions that you've had in life, or that you haven't?"

11. Education is used throughout the analysis of the mass data because it is a straightforward indicator. Results based on somewhat more complicated measures, like occupation, are much the same. In addition, all of the results in this and subsequent tables and graphs are bivariate associations. Multivariate analysis, bringing in sex, race, age, and so on, would be indicated were my objective to provide a full-blown causal explanation of mass attitudes. But the overriding purpose is to compare elite and nonelite attitudes; so the bivariate approach suffices, especially since education is so strongly related to most of the other background indicators.

12. The measures in Figure 2 are normalized, with means of zero and standard deviations of one, because the separate indicators are measured differently. For example, "TV viewing" is an additive index of exposure to seven types of programs; "radio listening" is derived from measures of exposure to nine types of programs, etc. The political information index is compiled from the correct responses to eight factual questions (for example, "Who is the president of Brazil?").

13. The finding is not, of course, uniquely Brazilian. Compare, for example, Verba and Nie (1972).

14. See Erickson (1977).

15. All of the items presented in Figure 4 were prefaced with the question: "Do you agree or disagree with the following sentences?" The items are: (1) "The most important thing that a child can learn is obedience to his parents." (2) "Politics is so complicated that it's difficult for people to understand what's going on." (3) "If the government puts much faith (der muita confiança) in what the people want, the country will end up in a mess (bagunça)." (4) "A boss has to be strict, otherwise his employees will not work well." and (5) "Almost always, poor people don't improve their lot (melhoram de vida) because they don't try hard enough, they lack will power."

16. Batteries of questions such as those discussed here are notoriously susceptible to response set; their validity as absolute estimates is therefore questionable. At the same time, the propensity for "yea-saying" closely parallels the notion of mass acquiescence and dependence on a paternalistic state. See Landsberger and Saavedra (1967). This tendency has to be distinguished, however, from the less firmly established phenomenon of mass authoritarianism. See Rigby and Rump (1979), Ray (1976), and, more generally, Goody (1977) and Goff (1980).

17. "Culture of poverty" readings of this pattern may be deceptive insofar as they ignore how a hierarchy structured by elites closes off alternatives for non-elites. Working-class Brazilians are socialized into subordination by various mechanisms, for example, by way of the primary educational system, which inculcates obedience and rote-response—properties that are thought to be functional on assembly lines. Idealizations of traditional family structures serve the same purpose. Compare Kohn (1970).

18. Compare Mayer (1975).

19. Compare Dealy (1977).

20. The items read: (1) "People should trust or distrust (deve confiar ou desconfiar) . . . [followed by the list of groups]" (2) "To protect (defender) the interests of persons like yourself, whom can you count on?" (3) "We would like to know if you like or dislike the following groups. . . . "

21. After the interviews were completed, interviewers filled out estimates about the respondents' difficulty in understanding the questions, receptivity, "hesitation," etc. The correlations between responses on the substantive questions analyzed here and interviewer-assessed indicators of "discretion" are all statistically insignificant. The fear-and-loathing hypothesis does not pan out. See McDonough (1982).

22. See Bacha (1976) and Baer (1973); compare Hirschman (1973).

23. The elite sample (n = 269) is drawn from seven groups: (1) businessmen—bankers and industrialists, both domestic and multinational (n = 84); (2) labor leaders (53); (3) top civil servants, including the heads of public companies (56); (4) bishops (11); (5) senators and deputies of the then-government party, ARENA (33); (6) senators and deputies of the then-opposition MDB party (14); and (7) leaders of the liberal professions and journalists. The sample is detailed in the appendix.

24. An analogous point is made about the policy evaluations of American voters by Fiorina (1981).

25. For the elites, the question read: "What degree of importance do you attribute to each one of the following issues (questões)?" The scale varied between zero (no importance) to 100 (maximum importance). The mass

respondents were asked, after giving their pro-con opinion on a particular issue: "Do you think this issue is (a) extremely important, (b) very important [and so on to] (e) without any importance?" The importance scale runs from zero (no importance) to five (extremely important). In addition, the mass respondents were asked whether a change in government policy on the issue under discussion would effect "persons like yourself." Again, the scale runs from zero to five. Note that the "effect" measures do not correlate perfectly with the importance measures, although the association is evidently very close. One reason is that the effect of changes in family planning policy are age-specific. The impact question was not asked for the agrarian reform issue.

26. A detailed exposition of these points is in McDonough and de Souza (1981).

27. There is another way of comparing elite-mass attitudes that reveals one more difference. The data shown here concentrate on priorities; information was also collected on pro and con preferences on the same issues. In general, the importance assigned to an issue correlates with preferences on the issue in such a way that "high priority" corresponds to a "pro-opinion." There is, however, one significant exception, aside from the birth control issue: government-labor relations. Both elites and the mass public give this issue medium-to-high importance. But the elites are generally in favor of loosening government controls over the labor organizations, while most of the mass public favors keeping these controls, since they are accustomed to a state-centric, paternalistic style of labor relations. In this respect, ordinary Brazilians can be considered deeply corporatist. For an extended analysis, see de Souza (1978).

28. Compare Weffort (1980) and especially Goodwyn (1978), who is particularly sensitive to the ambiguities of such "movements" and to the difficulties of organizing them. The faintly nostalgic air of the largely urban Brazilian respondents with regard to the land reform issue suggests that the issue has certain mythic overtones. The syndrome is probably not very exceptional even in advanced industrial societies, as the rhetoric of opponents of gun control legislation in the United States implies.

29. The questions read: (1) "Have you ever felt that some positions (posições ostensivas) taken by the majority of your constituents have entered into conflict with positions taken by the government?" (2) "Has it ever happened that you have taken a position with respect to some issue of national importance but have not known for sure the reaction of the majority of your constituents with respect to your position?" (3) "Have you ever felt that some positions taken by the majority of your constituents have entered into conflict with the interests (interesses) of Brazilians?"

30. The questions read: (1) "Imagine that the voters demand that a deputy fight for something that he opposes. Do you think that the deputy should do what the voters want, or that he should do what he believes in?" (2) "Do you think that a deputy should vote as his party orders or in accord with what he believes?" (3) "Do you think that a deputy should always support the government in order to obtain benefits for his state, or only support the government when it corresponds (estiver de acordo) with what he believes?"

31. The pattern also accords well with the government's strategy of

selective censorship of the mass (as compared to the "educated") media; recall Figure 2.

32. The classification of "political," "social," and "other" conflicts is an aggregation. Elites with constituencies who reported that their constituents sometimes entered into conflict with the government (see Table 3) were asked to give three examples of such conflicts. The classification in Table 4 is based on the first case, since frequencies fall off for second and third case citations. The substance of the classification (for example, disagreements over wage policy = "social" conflict) is explained in the text.

33. Compare Greenwald (1979).

34. With a bit of modification, Trotsky's statement about the Russian "masses" is applicable to the populist undercurrent in Brazil: "A revolution is always distinguished by impoliteness, probably because the ruling classes did not take the trouble in good season to teach the people fine manners" (Quoted in Howe [1978:156]). It is worth remembering that most of the violence (the total of which has been pretty small) accompanying the abertura in Brazil has come not from the left but from the extreme right. A systematic study of the growth of opposition groups during the last half of the seventies and the early eighties in Brazil has yet to be done.

35. The key omission of the elites has probably been their inattention to land reform. This is suggested not only by the extremely high priority given to the issue by the mass, and largely urban, respondents but also by placing the Brazilian experience in contrast to that of South Korea and Taiwan, not to mention Japan; see the essays in Craig (1980). In this particular, Brazil resembles the Philippines. See Perrolle (1980). It should be noted that not even Getúlio Vargas, the populist dictator of Brazil during the thirties and forties (and elected president in the fifties) tampered with land-holding interests. His progressivism had a definite urban bias. See Skidmore (1967). Another problem that successor elites in Brazil will inherit is the country's enormous foreign debt, the annual interest payment on which has now reached 15 billion dollars. See Juruna (1981).

36. For an insightful discussion of these distinctions in the development of representative and corporatist institutions in Western Europe, see Maier (1981). Maier's analysis, duly adjusted, can be extended to aspects of the Brazilian political experience.

37. Although they were sampled separately, the industrialists and bankers are joined in the analysis because their political attitudes are essentially the same.

38. For a sector-by-sector report on the elite sample, see McDonough (1981).

39. See, for example, Barton and Parsons (1974–1975).

40. The one sector for which the scientific validity of the sample is difficult to establish is that of the liberal professionals (lawyers, engineers, and so forth) and prominent journalists and editorialists in Rio and São Paulo. Their institutional affiliations are varied, quantitative indicators of membership in the population are dubious, and reputational measures are subject to ideological distortions. On the other hand, the results from this group do not violate descriptions of the political orientations of the liberal professions in Brazil that can be gleaned from such collateral

sources as journalistic accounts. For fuller documentation, see Mc-
Donough and de Souza (1981).
41. A complete description of the sample is given in Cohen et al. (1980).

References

Bacha, Edmar (1976) *Os Mitos de uma Década: Ensaios de Economia Brasileira.* Rio de Janeiro: Editora Paz e Terra.

Baer, Werner (1973) "The Brazilian Boom, 1968–1972: An Explanation and Interpretation." *World Development* 1:1–15.

Barton, Allen H., and R. Wayne Parsons (1974–1975) "Consensus and Conflict among American Leaders." *Public Opinion Quarterly* 38:509–28.

Bellah, Robert N., and Phillip E. Hammond (1980) *Varieties of Civil Religion.* New York: Harper & Row.

Boli-Bennett, John (1980) "Global Integration and the Universal Increase of State Dominance, 1910–1970." In *Studies of the Modern World-System,* edited by Alfred Bergesen. New York: Academic Press.

Booth, John (1979) "Political Participation in Latin America: Levels, Structure, Contexts, Concentration and Rationality." *Latin American Research Review* 14:29–60.

Bruneau, Thomas C. (1980) "The Catholic Church and Development in Latin America: The Role of Basic Christian Communities." *World Development* 8:535–44.

Cohen, Youssef (1982) " 'The Benevolent Leviathan': Political Consciousness among Urban Workers under State Corporation." *American Political Science Review* 76:46–59.

Cohen, Youssef, et al. (1980) *Representation and Development in Brazil: Machine-Readable Data-File.* Ann Arbor: Inter-University Consortium for Political and Social Research.

Collier, David (1979) *The New Authoritarianism in Latin America.* Princeton, N.J.: Princeton University Press.

Craig, Albert M. (1980) *Japan: A Comparative View.* Princeton, N.J.: Princeton University Press.

da Matta, Roberto (1979) *Carnavais, Malandros e Heróis: Para uma Sociologia do Dilema Brasileiro.* Rio de Janeiro: Zahar Editores.

———— (1981) "The Ethic of Umbanda and the Spirit of Messianism: Reflections on the Brazilian Model." In *Authoritarian Capitalism: Brazil's Contemporary Economic and Political Development,* edited by Thomas C. Bruneau and Philippe Faucher. Boulder, Col.: Westview Press.

Das Gupta, Jyotirinra (1978) "A Season of Caesars: Emergency Regimes and Development Politics in Asia." *Asian Survey* 28:315–49.

Dealy, Glen Caudill (1977) *The Public Man: An Interpretation of Latin American and Other Catholic Countries.* Amherst: University of Massachusetts Press.

Delacroix, Jacques (1980) "The Distributive State in the World System." *Studies in Comparative International Development* 15:3–21.

de Souza, Amaury (1978) *The Nature of Corporatist Representation in Brazil.* Ph.D. dissertation, Massachusetts Institute of Technology.

dos Santos, Wanderley (1979) *Calculus of Conflict: Impasse in Brazilian Politics and the Crisis of 1974*. Ph.D. dissertation, Stanford University.

Erickson, Kenneth P. (1977) *The Corporative State and Working-Class Politics in Brazil*. Berkeley: University of California Press.

Fiorina, Morris P. (1981) *Retrospective Voting in American National Elections*. New Haven, Conn.: Yale University Press.

Gerschenkron, Alexander (1962) *Economic Backwardness in Historical Perspective*. Cambridge, Mass.: Harvard University Press.

Goff, Tom W. (1980) *Marx and Mead: Contributions to a Sociology of Knowledge*. London: Routledge & Kegan Paul.

Goodwyn, Lawrence (1978) *The Populist Moment: A Short History of the Agrarian Revolt in America*. London: Oxford University Press.

Goody, Jack (1977) *The Domestication of the Savage Mind*. Cambridge: At the University Press.

Greenwald, Howard P. (1979) "Scientists and Technocratic Ideology." *Social Forces* 58:630–50.

Han, Sungjoo (1974) *The Failure of Democracy in South Korea*. Berkeley: University of California Press.

Hirschman, Albert O. (1973) "The Changing Tolerance for Income Inequality in the Course of Development." *Quarterly Journal of Economics* 87:544–66.

Howe, Irving (1978) *Leon Trotsky*. New York: Viking.

Jones, E. L. (1981) *The European Miracle: Environments, Economies and Geopolitics in the History of Europe and Asia*. Cambridge: At the University Press.

Juruna, Julia (1981) "La Dette Extérieure, Facteur de Déstabilisation." *Le Monde Diplomatique*, December.

Kihl, Young W., and C. I. Eugene Kim (1981) "The Political Economy of Military Regimes in Selected Asian Countries: Indonesia, Thailand, South Korea, and Taiwan." Paper presented at the annual meetings of the American Political Science Association, 3–6 September, New York.

Kohn, Melvin (1970) "Social-Class and Parent-Child Relationships: An Interpretation." In *Perspectives in Marriage and the Family*, edited by J. Ross Eshleman. New York: Allyn & Bacon.

Lamounier, Bolivar, and José Eduardo Faria, eds (1981) *O Futuro da Abertura: Um Debate*. São Paulo: Cortez Editora.

Landsberger, Henry A., and Antonio Saavedra (1967) "Response Set in Developing Countries." *Public Opinion Quarterly* 31: 214–29.

Lernoux, Penny (1980) *Cry of the People*. New York: Doubleday.

Linz, Juan J. (1973) "Opposition in and under an Authoritarian Regime: The Case of Spain." In *Regimes and Opposition*, edited by Robert A. Dahl. New Haven, Conn.: Yale University.

McDonough, Peter (1981) *Power and Ideology in Brazil*. Princeton, N.J.: Princeton University Press.

——— (1982) "Repression and Representation in Brazil." *Comparative Politics* 15:73–99.

McDonough, Peter, and Amaury de Souza (1981) *The Politics of Population in Brazil: Elite Ambivalence and Public Demand*. Austin: University of Texas Press.

Maier, Charles S. (1981) " 'Fictitious Bonds . . . of Wealth and Law': On the Theory and Practice of Interest Representation." In *Organizing In-*

terests in Western Europe: Pluralism, Corporatism, and the Transformation of Politics, edited by Suzanne D. Berger. Cambridge: At the University Press.

Mayer, Arno J. (1975) "The Lower Middle-Class as Historical Problem." Journal of Modern History 47:409–36.

O'Donnell, Guillermo A. (1973) Modernization and Bureaucratic-Authoritarianism. Berkeley, Calif.: Institute of International Studies.

Perrolle, Judith A. (1980) "The Institutional Aspects of Philippine Agriculture in the 1960s." Filipinas 1:45–73.

Ray, J. J. (1976) "Do Authoritarians Hold Authoritarian Attitudes?" Human Relations 29:307–25.

Remmer, Karen L. (1979) "Public Policy and Regime Consolidation: The First Five Years of the Chilean Junta." Journal of Developing Areas 13:441–61.

Rigby, Ken, and Eric E. Rump (1979) "The Generality of Attitudes to Authority." Human Relations 32:469–87.

Sanders, Thomas G. (1980) "Human Rights and Political Process in Brazil." American Universities Field Staff Reports. no. 11. Washington, D.C.

Schwartzman, Simon (1975) São Paulo e o Estado Nacional. São Paulo: Difusão Européia do Livro.

Sheahan, John (1980) "Market-oriented Economic Policies and Political Repression in Latin America." Economic Development and Cultural Change 28:267–91.

Skidmore, Thomas (1967) Politics in Brazil, 1930–1964: An Experiment in Democracy. New York: Oxford University Press.

Soares, Glaucio Ary Dillon (1979) "Military Authoritarianism and Executive Absolutism in Brazil." Studies in Comparative International Development 14:104–26.

Stepan, Alfred (1978) The State and Society: Peru in Comparative Perspective. Princeton, N.J.: Princeton University Press.

Trimberger, Ellen Kay (1978) Revolution from Above: Military Bureaucrats and Developments in Japan, Turkey, Egypt, and Peru. New Brunswick, N.J.: Transaction Books.

Uricoechea, Fernando (1980) The Patrimonial Foundations of the Brazilian Bureaucratic State. Berkeley: University of California Press.

Veliz, Claudio (1979) The Centralist Tradition in Latin America. Princeton, N.J.: Princeton University Press.

Verba, Sidney, and Norman H. Nie (1972) Participation in America. New York: Harper & Row.

Weffort, Francisco (1980) O Populismo na Política Brasileira. Rio de Janeiro: Editora Paz e Terra.

White, Stephen (1978) "Communist Systems and the 'Iron Law of Pluralism.'" British Journal of Political Science 8:101–17.

Wiarda, Howard (1978) "Corporatism Rediscovered: Right, Center, and Left Variants in the New Literature." Polity 10:416–28.

The Integration of Parliamentary Elites in Less Developed Countries

Chong Lim Kim and Samuel C. Patterson

The broad strokes of Gaetano Mosca's theoretical brush, some-times awe-inspiring in their audacity and magistral flair, leave open to some question the inclusiveness of the ruling class, the processes through which the integration of elites is attained and preserved, and the ways in which the political formula makes elite control possible. Mosca does not explicitly define the full contours of the ruling class, so that exegetic exercises cannot ordain a direct claim that he meant to embrace the full parliamentary membership of a country into the ranks of the ruling minority. Be that as it may, there is plenty of reason to suppose that Mosca meant the ruling class to include members of the national parliament as one of its components.

Mosca's Aristotelianism, his commitment to moral order and sta-bility, and his fear of Leviathan may have led him to an understand-able preoccupation with great leaders and the darker shadows of bureaucratic aggrandizement. But Mosca's intention surely seems to

The field research which produced the data used in this chapter was a collaborative enterprise among a number of scholars in Keyna, Korea, Turkey, and the United States. The study was jointly designed by Joel D. Barkan, G. R. Boynton, Chong Lim Kim, Gerhard Loewenberg, and John C. Wahlke, at that time all members of the political science faculty at the University of Iowa; and by John Okumu (University of Khartoum), Seong-Tong Pai (Seoul National University), and Ahmet Yücekök (University of Ankara). The fieldwork in Korea was directed by Kim and Pai and by Young W. Kihl (Iowa State University); in Kenya, by Barkan and Okumu; in Turkey, by Ilter Turan and Nur Vergin (University of Istanbul) and Metin Heper (Bogazici University). Malcolm E. Jewell (University of Ken-tucky) served as an associate in the project during the analysis of the data. Financial support was obtained from an institutional development grant made to the University of Iowa by the U.S. Agency for International De-velopment, and, for aspects of field research in Kenya, from the Rockefel-ler Foundation.

have been that a nation's legislators were squarely included in the political class. He took it for granted that we should think so and perhaps would have been amused that the question of whether legislators were or were not part of the political elite should have been raised at all. Mosca spent much of his adult life in the bosom of the Italian Parliament, first serving as the editor of the official journal of the Chamber of Deputies, then as a deputy himself, and then for the rest of his life as a royally appointed senator. He exhibited his preoccupation with parliamentry representation in an interesting way in the *Elementi di Scienza Politica*. In his assessment of parliamentarism, Mosca makes it clear that he understands the significance of distinctive social status in the recruitment of representatives. Moreover, he suggests unmistakably the theoretical view that the legitimacy of parliamentary authority fundamentally rests upon the embededness of the legislature in its society (Mosca, 1939:244).

Representative government is always in crisis, it seems, no less in Mosca's time than now. Mosca was deeply concerned with the attacks on emergent parliamentary institutions. First, he worried, parliaments are attacked for what Marx aptly called *parliamentary cretinism*, for estrangement between represented and representatives, for "the prattlings, the long-winded speeches, the futile bickerings, with which parliamentary assemblies largely busy themselves" (Marx, 1963:91; Mosca, 1939:224–25). Second, parliaments are denounced for their failure to "represent the interests and aspirations of majorities," only representing "the interests of wealthy ruling classes." Third, parliaments practice what some now call "intrusive access," meddling in the proper realm of the administrative or judical processes; this "continuous pottering, interloping and officiousness on the part of members of lower houses must be an exceedingly baneful thing," says Mosca, perhaps one that deserves the derogatory connotation of *parliamentarism*. Yet Mosca brought himself to defend parliaments despite his recognition of their flaws, penultimately because "the defects of parliamentary assemblies, and the evil consequences which their control of power and their participation in power produce in all representative systems, are merest trifles as compared with the harm that would inevitably result from abolishing them or stripping them of their influence" (1939:256). Enmeshed in Mosca's rather spirited and heavily normative defense of legislative assemblies is the very clear implication that he fully intended their memberships to be taken as an important component of the ruling class.

Mosca is very clear, however, in his belief that the place of the parliamentary elite in the governing constellation is a limited one. "Assemblies do not govern," he pronounced; "they merely check and balance the men who govern, and limit their power" (1939:257). The crucial function of parliament, for Mosca, is that it links the rulers and the represented, opens avenues for participation to diverse social forces, protects the social fabric from the avaricious proclivities of the bureaucracy—in short, parliament provides the constituent function. Mosca does not rule legislators out of the political class, but he comprehends their special and limited function.

Mosca assumes that we will understand that the ruling class is integrated, although (as Eulau once said of Lasswell) his "maddening methods" leave the shape and form of elite integration ambiguous, more or less stipulated rather than developed empirically (see Eulau, 1969:119–36). In the *Elementi* Mosca does indicate that the elite is composed of persons who share common experiences and who comprise a homogeneous group. Of legislators, he says: "an assembly of representatives is almost never a 'mob,' in the sense of being a haphazard, inorganic assemblage of human beings" (1939:257). Mosca and other pioneering elite theorists either asserted or assumed that the ruling class would, above all, bear the attribute of consensuality or coherence in regard to critical values and beliefs. Moreover, Mosca made it reasonably plain that he thought the recruitment of persons into the ruling class would develop through a process which accentuated the contours of the social structure, so that

> ruling minorities are usually so constituted that the individuals who make them up are distinguished from the mass of the governed by qualities that give them a certain material, intellectual or even moral superiority; or else they are the heirs of individuals who possessed such qualities. In other words, members of a ruling minority regularly have some attribute, real or apparent, which is highly esteemed and very influential in the society in which they live. (1939:53)

These two concerns of elite theory—values and recruitment—provide the focus for our own research efforts.

We recognize that Mosca, as well as other early theorists of elite behavior, was engaged in formulating elite theory at very early stages of systematic research. He and his contemporaries did not, of course, have the benefit of the kinds of elite research which began to emerge in earnest in the 1940s. Nevertheless, we have chosen to take Mosca's notions at face value. We have found Mosca's theory a helpful guide to inquiry. We do not wish to construct a straw man, only to tear him down. Rather, we seek to take advantage of the opportunity provided by Mosca's ideas to put our own analysis into sharper relief. Adumbrating Mosca's central theoretical perspectives helps to underscore issues which are highly relevant in the analysis of elite behavior today.

Elite Integration

Mosca, Pareto, and Michels, the classical elite theorists, took it as axiomatic that the ruling class is unified, or integrated. They treated as self-evident the cohesiveness (or, to take Lasswell's descriptive term, agglutination) of political elites in regard to significant beliefs or values (Lasswell and Lerner, 1966:9). Moreover, common social, political, and recruitment experiences were treated axiomatically, as if the social or political homogeneity of elites required no elaborate empirical verification. Yet Putnam is surely correct to say that "the unity or disunity of [elites] should be a matter for empirical investigation rather than definitional fiat" (1976:107).

A political elite may be said to be integrated if its members widely share social, political, or economic backgrounds and experience common patterns of recruitment. These commonalities of broadly similar recruitment experiences, furthermore, tend to induce homogeneity of beliefs and values, so that the elite is highly consensual. Shared recruitment experience and value consensus do not exhaust the "dimensions of integration" along which elites may be investigated, but these factors do address central issues in the classical elite theory (Putnam, 1976:107–32.).

The tendency of elites to be socially homogeneous has been widely documented. Elites tend to be drawn from the same social and occupational strata and to share common experiences of educational background and other socialization. In addition, elites may experience common recruitment patterns, treading along very similar pathways in their political careers. Although these tendencies are often described, strictly comparable measures of homogeneity are rather rare; and particularly uncommon are investigations which focus explicitly on recruitment patterns despite the crucial hypothesis that "the narrower and more unified the selectorate that reviews the credentials of prospective recruits, the more likely those recruits are to share perspectives and loyalties with one another and with the selectorate" (Putnam, 1976:111).

Value consensus has been said to be "the most central dimension of elite integration" (Putnam, 1976:114). If a political elite is highly integrated, we would expect to find within it strong and unmistakable cohesiveness on fundamental elements of the political formula and a shared commitment to the basic rules of the game. The clear implication of elite theory would be that, although interparty polarization may be manifested within the ruling class on issues of public policy, on fundamental or systemic values elite unity should be the order of the day. But such theoretical expectations regarding elite consensus are, it must be admitted, only sparsely supported by substantial empirical inquiry or extensive comparative analysis.

Parliamentary Elites in Kenya, Korea, and Turkey

We have addressed rarely attended-to basic issues concerning elite recruitment and value consensus in three less developed countries in which extensive data have been gathered through interviews with members of parliament (Kim et al., 1983). The three countries—Kenya, Korea, and Turkey—are located at different corners of the developing world, one in Africa, another in East Asia, and still another in the Middle East. The three countries are very different, both in their cultural patterns and in the political milieux in which their parliamentary assemblies function. They differ significantly in their legislative development, their party systems, the constitutional powers which their parliaments can exercise, and their electoral systems. Turkey's parliament, the Grand National Assembly, has the longest history of the three, originating in the mid-1870s. The Korean National Assembly was established in 1947, following the nation's first popular election. In Kenya, where there was some experience with a colonial assembly prior to independence, the new National Assembly came into existence in 1960.

In a collaborative effort, American political scientists and investigators in the three countries themselves conducted interviews with legislators in 1973 and 1974. Although interviews had to be conducted in a variety of circumstances and in several different languages (Swahili and nine tribal languages in Kenya alone), basically the same interview schedules were used in each country. All legislators interviewed in the three countries were asked batteries of questions dealing with their social origins and backgrounds, political and recruitment experiences, orientations toward representation and the rules of the legislative game, and beliefs about basic democratic processes. These parliamentary elite samples include interviews with 104 of the 450 Turkish deputies, 119 of the 219 Korean assemblymen, and 28 of the 170 Kenyan MPs. Given the difficulties of gathering such comparative interview data (especially in Kenya, where most interviews had to take place in the members' districts, not in Nairobi), these samples reasonably represent the memberships of the three legislative elite groups.[1]

The present Kenyan National Assembly dates from 1964, when a constitutional amendment creating a unicameral parliament was adopted. Twelve of its 170 members are chosen by the president; the remaining 158 are elected from single-member districts. The operation of the National Assembly follows British practice, but of course there is no opposition party to occupy benches opposite the government. The work of the National Assembly is almost completely controlled by the executive branch, but nevertheless backbenchers participate vigorously in debates and often vote against government-sponsored bills. In the main, however, the National Assembly occupies a distinctly secondary role in public policy making and is primarily an arena for the discussion and ratification of policies made elsewhere (see Barkan and Okumu, 1979:64–92).

Although the Korean National Assembly dates from 1947, its makeup was changed both in 1972 and 1980, when new constitutions were adopted. At the time our data were gathered, two-thirds of the 219 members of the Assembly were popularly elected, and the remainder were appointed by the president. Although the government party controlled about two-thirds of the legislative seats, a third of the members represented opposition parties, some of them from very small splinter parties. The National Assembly is surprisingly professionalized, with well-organized committees and staffs. The Assembly employs 30 to 40 senior professional staff people, and the total legislative staff numbers some 1,000 persons. The president's control of the Assembly is very substantial, so much so that it is said to be the "maidservant of the Executive." Nevertheless, the Assembly has a role in the shaping of legislation and an important function as a constituent body (Kim and Pai, 1981).

The Turkish Grand National Assembly has a long history. Its 450 deputies are elected in 67 multimember constituencies. Turkey has a multiparty system; in parliament the largest party delegations are from the Republican People's party and the Justice party, but several important smaller parties are represented there as well. However, Turkey's parliament is bicameral; in addition to the assembly, the parliament includes a Senate of 150 members who are popularly elected, an institutional innovation of the 1961 Turkish constitution. The Senate and the Assembly choose the president of the nation, who in turn appoints a prime minister; the prime minister and cabinet must win a vote of confidence from the Assembly in order to be confirmed. Although the constitution gives all lawmaking power to parliament, as in most countries, the initiation of legislation is, in fact, largely in the hands of the government (Frey, 1965; Frey, 1975:41–82).

The samples of legislators in these three parliaments provide the sources of our data. The Turkish legislators serve in an institution which is well established and which has been a central arena for major political conflicts. The Korean National Assembly has existed about thirty years, but its role in the political system has generally been overshadowed by a strong executive. The Kenyan legislature evolved from the legislative councils convened by British colonial rulers, and has emerged relatively recently as a parliamentary entity. Although of these three parliaments the Turkish Grand National Assembly has provided the most impressive forum for national politics and most clearly included the leading politicians of the country, the assemblies in Kenya and Korea have not had insignificant roles in these respects. Our specific research purpose is to investigate the extent to which, in these three samples of parliamentary elites, there is evidence of unity in sociopolitical experiences and cohesiveness in important values and beliefs.

Homogeneity in Recruitment

Measurement of elite homogeneity is crucial to the evaluation of the general proposition that elite integration results from a selective process of recruitment. Do elites share significantly similar experiences in their recruitment? And if so, to what degree? By homogeneity we refer to the amount of such similarities. Homogeneity in legislative elites may be determined by the extent of concentration or dispersion of personal attributes across different social strata, different skill groups, and different socialization and career channels. More specifically, we examine the social origins of legislators, their occupational backgrounds, their professional training, their socialization, and their political apprenticeship. To calculate "homogeneity scores" for these attributes, we have employed Rae's fragmentation formula (Rae and Taylor, 1970:30,33; Rae, 1971). This formula yields scores ranging from 0 to 1, with a high score indicating greater fragmentation. Since we wish to measure homogeneity, not fragmentation, we have simply taken the complement of Rae's formula to calculate homogeneity scores.

In Table 1 we present homogeneity scores for six categories of what we have generally called recruitment experiences for the three legislative elites. The analysis does not do much to aid and abet the rather sweeping claims of classical elite theorists that elites are drawn from among those in a dominant social type or recruited from within a narrowly constricted social or economic class. If anything, heterogeneity, rather than homogeneity, characterizes the recruitment experiences of legislators in Kenya, Korea, and Turkey. In Table 1 we see relatively low homogeneity scores across almost all attributes we have analyzed. Legislative elites, it turns out, come from quite diverse social origins, some from high and others from low social strata. In none of the three countries did a single stratum supply a majority of members to the parliamentary elite. We have used fathers' occupation as a rough indicator of legislators' social origins. Although we have detected a general tendency for legislators to arise from the more privileged social strata, a sizeable proportion also come from more modest backgrounds.

Similar heterogeneity marks legislators' prelegislative occupational experience, their professional training at college, and the development of their initial interest in politics. Although the predominance of lawyers in American political elites is well documented, the same is not true in many developing countries. Lawyers

TABLE 1.
Homogeneity of the Social Origins, Training, and Career
Experiences of Parliamentary Elites in Kenya, Korea, and Turkey*

Experiences	Kenya	Korea	Turkey
Social origins†	.330	.281	.201
Occupational skills‡	.196	.153	.221
Skill training§	.358	.202	.216
Political socialization‖	.276	.367	.316
Office-holding experience#	.867	.850	.668
Legislative experience**	.577	.312	.414
Mean	.434	.360	.339

*Homogeneity scores are entirely comparable across countries, but because the number of code categories varies for different types of career experiences the scores are not strictly comparable within each country.
†Occupation of father, coded into 8 occupational categories ranging from high to low occupational status.
‡MP's own occupation, coded in the same way as father's occupation.
§Skill specialization during course of college or university education, coded in terms of major fields of study.
‖Time of development of political interests, coded from childhood to later adulthood.
#Previous officeholding experience, coded by governmental levels.
**Number of parliamentary sessions in which the member served.

contribute a larger proportion of the Turkish legislative elite than in the other countries but did not constitute an overwhelming occupational group in any of these three parliaments. Instead, many diverse occupations are represented. Homogeneity scores for occupational status are very low, ranging from .153 for the Korean elites to .221 for the Turkish deputies. There is no distinctive occupational career path which leads to a parliamentary career in these systems.

In the three parliamentary elites, a majority attained a high level of formal education, most of them with college or advanced degrees. In this regard they were as well educated as their European counterparts, and in some cases, more so. However, the kinds of professional training they received at university were very diverse. Many chose law, economics, humanities, or military science as their fields of specialization; but others studied different subjects. We could not identify any field or set of fields that distinctively provide training for entrants into the parliamentary elites of these countries.

It is often suggested in the elite literature that political leaders share common experiences of political socialization and that "the integration of a political system may be viewed in terms of the degree to which members of the political elite share common socialization experiences" (Quandt, 1970:198). Yet, at least in terms of these legislators' initial interest in politics, little homogeneity is exhibited.

Among them, interest in politics occurred at various points in their lives. In the interviews with legislators, we asked when they had developed political interests and under what circumstances. In response, adolescence and young adulthood were generally mentioned most frequently; but many indicated that their political interest stemmed from childhood or late adulthood as well. There is not overwhelming evidence here for a claim that parliamentary elites share highly homogeneous politicization experiences.

Like other well-established professions, parliamentary careers may require a political apprenticeship. Those aspiring to parliamentary seats may enhance their chances by gaining political skills and experience through service in other kinds of political office—in government, parties, or interest groups. Indeed, a very large majority of legislators in each of the three countries had political experience prior to their entry into parliament, and 80 to 90 percent held offices either in the government or in political parties before their ascension to the legislative elite. To a considerable extent, parliamentary elites are recruited from among those who have already entered the political class. For officeholding experience, the homogeneity scores range from .668 in Turkey to .867 in Kenya, indicating relatively pronounced elite homogeneity in this respect. Moreover, these parliamentary elites were fairly homogeneous in regard to previous legislative experience, although in this case high homogeneity indicates preponderantly limited experience in the legislature itself. A majority of the legislators in Kenya and Turkey (54 percent and 58 percent, respectively) were new members, and 43 percent were freshmen in Korea. The relatively high homogeneity scores for legislative experience can be attributed largely to this fact. But it is impressive that some form of political apprenticeship appears to be necessary to enter the parliamentary elite in these systems. What these legislators have most in common is not found so much in their social origins, socialization, or occupational experience, but rather in their common experience in political office. We suspect that this commonality within the parliamentary elite is more crucial to elite integration than is homogeneity in regard to earlier life experiences.

What emerges from the analysis is that legislative elites are composed of quite heterogeneous groups, at least in regard to recruitment experiences. In general, diversity, rather than homogeneity, characterizes members of these parliaments. As a rough approximation of overall elite homogeneity, we have averaged the scores across all attributes examined. The average scores are not very high, falling substantially below .500. Although we might have included other attributes in our analysis, we have no reason to believe that higher average homogeneity scores could have been attained.

Thus far, we have treated recruitment in a very broad sense, encompassing such varied aspects as social origins, socialization, skill training, and political experiences. But our data make it possible to probe recruitment in a more restricted way so as to focus on that part of the recruitment process most immediate to legislators' entry into parliament. We can, in short, focus on what Seligman and his associates once called "the selection phase" of recruitment (1974:14–15; see also Kim, 1974). It is relevant to consider several variables at the selection phase: career paths, sponsorship, and ambitions. A simple typology of career paths to parliament may be constructed in order to classify various career types. As Figure 1 shows, we have used two variables, previous officeholding experience and legislative service, to establish four distinct types of political careers experienced by legislators.

The career of an *amateur* is characterized by the complete absence of previous officeholding experience. Until they attain their current position as members of parliament, the amateurs' entire experience had been outside politics. For them, politics is a wholly new venture. Another career type is to be found among those who have an extended apprenticeship in a variety of government, party, or interest group offices before attaining parliamentary seats. We call this career type *arrivistes*. The arrivistes usually begin their political careers early in life with the attainment of low-level offices. Testing out their political skills and organizational acumen in minor offices, these aspiring politicians make step-by-step advancements on the political career ladder. For them entry into parliament represents a culminating point in their careers after long years of hard work and apprenticeship. These MPs have had extensive experience in public before entering parliament; once elected, they have served for several terms. The presence of many arrivistes in a parliamentary elite may indicate that the pathways to it are highly institutionalized. In such a situation, few will be able to attain elite status without climbing a well-defined career ladder. By contrast, if amateurs predominate in the elite, this will indicate that pathways to parliament are relatively unstructured.

The third career type, the *parliamentarian*, comprises those who began their political careers in the legislature and accumulated years of service in it. These are the veterans, with long records of parliamentary service. Because of their parliamentary seniority, these legislators are likely to be the staunchest defenders of parliamentary traditions and the guardians of the autonomy of parliament in relation to the government. Finally, we identify a career type we call the *professional*. Throughout their long political careers, professionals accumulate skills and experience inside and outside parliament. They know politics in its full effervescence, having acquired rich and varied experience along their paths to parliament.

Career types from the three parliamentary elites are arrayed in Table 2. Although there are some notable cross-country variations,

FIGURE 1.
Typology of Political Careers

| | Previous Officeholding Experience | |
	Yes	No
Parliamentary Service		
One Time	Arriviste (N = 89)	Amateur (N = 24)
Several Times	Professional (N = 105)	Parliamentarian (N = 13)

the main finding is that pathways to parliament are highly structured in all parliaments. Without exception, arrivistes and professionals constitute the most common career types. In Korea and Turkey there are but a few parliamentarians, and in Kenya and Korea there are not many amateurs. In general, it seems fair to underscore the fact that recruitment to the parliamentary elite requires some form of apprenticeship.

Sponsors can play a critical role at the selection phase of recruitment. Political parties, party factions, interest groups, primary groups, or kinship and tribal organizations may serve at times as recruiting agents. We have suggested elsewhere a classification of recruitment types based upon sponsorship: party agent, careerist, co-opted, entrepreneur, and group agent (Kim et al., 1976:79–103). The party agent, an active party member whose loyalty has been tested in the past, seeks office because his party has instigated his candidacy. The careerist is basically a self-starter whose decision to run was his own, without the benefit of sponsorship. The careerist looks upon politics as a vocation and takes that career seriously. Those we have

TABLE 2.
Parliamentary Career Types in Kenya, Korea, and Turkey

Career Types	Kenya	Korea	Turkey
Amateur	7%	6%	16%
Arriviste	46	34	42
Parliamentarian	22	2	5
Professional	25	58	37
Total	100%	100%	100%
Homogeneity score	.329	.227	.338

called "co-opted" include members who were persuaded by a party to represent it. These are socially successful people who, accordingly, command considerable public respect and admiration. The party, motivated by its desire to win an election, goes out of its way to recruit such persons even though they may not be active party members. Entrepreneurs become involved in politics to promote their own private careers. Typical of this group are those politicians Barber has labeled "advertisers" (1965:67–115). Entrepreneurs are principally interested in the instrumental values of political activity and have no long-term interest in politics as a career. Finally, there are those parliamentarians who decided to run because they were strongly urged to do so by nonpartisan groups. In these developing systems, we have found tribal, kinship, and regionally based communal groups to be the most active of such sponsors. We call this type "group agents" to distinguish them from party agents.

We report the distribution of legislators in the three countries subdivided into these sponsorship types in Table 3. As indicated in that table, there is marked variation by country. Sponsorship by group agents is most prevalent in Kenya, accounting for 57 percent of the MPs. Most of these legislators ran because their tribal or other communal group urged them to do so. The remaining members are distributed between party agents and careerists. In Korea, careerists and group agents make up the dominant sponsorship types, with most group agents indebted electorally to local kinship organizations. Turkish MPs include fewer group agents than do those of the other two countries but more careerists and many more entrepreneurs than Kenya or Korea. Probably these variations reflect the varying practices of sponsorship by different agencies, as well as the differing saliency of political parties in each system. Careerists and group agents clearly are the dominant recruitment types in these countries, a pattern which appears to be very different from that of most Western parliaments. In a study of American state legislators which uses parallel conceptual categories, we found that the members were more

TABLE 3.
Sponsorship of Candidacies in Kenya, Korea, and Turkey

Sponsorship Type	Kenya	Korea	Turkey
Party agent	25%	9%	4%
Careerist	32	45	48
Co-opted	—	1	1
Entrepreneur	—	3	29
Group agent	57	42	18
Total	100%	100%	100%
Homogeneity score	.349	.392	.141

or less evenly distributed across these recruitment types (Kim et al., 1976:84).

For many in the parliamentary elite, legislative status is penultimate, but for those with progressive ambitions it is merely a stepping-stone. An examination of members' ambition may reveal ways in which legislative careers are connected to other parts of the political career structure. When we queried MPs in the three countries, roughly half gave some evidence of progressive ambition. What is striking, however, is the uniformly similar proportion of ambitious members in all of the elite groups (see Table 4). Despite considerable diversity in the career experience and sponsorship of these MPs, these parliamentary elites are dramatically homogeneous in their political aspirations, although different targets of ambition are reflected in the three systems. In both Kenya and Korea, cabinet posts were the most popular targets (42 percent and 53 percent, respectively). In Turkey, an administrative post in the bureaucracy drew most members' aspirations, followed next by offices in the political

TABLE 4.
Political Ambition in Kenya, Korea, and Turkey

Ambition and Target	Kenya	Korea	Turkey
Ambition			
Yes, have ambition	43%	54%	57%
No ambition	57	46	43
Target offices			
Cabinet post	42%	53%	2%
Senior bureaucratic post	8	7	38
Political party office	—	10	16
Foreign service	8	4	4
National elective office	8	—	10
Not clearly specified	34	26	30

parties. These cross-national differences in the targets of political ambition suggest expected variations in postlegislative career paths and are indicative of different opportunity structures and configurations of power in these countries.

Our analysis of recruitment among these parliamentary elites permits a variety of detailed probings at the interstices of career experience, sponsorship, and ambition, as well as a variety of comparisons within parliamentary elite groups. One intra-elite comparison of some interest is that of contrasts between political party groups. Such a comparison is, of course, not possible for Kenya, where all MPs are at least nominal members of a single party, KANU, the Kenya African National Union. But in Korea and Turkey, party differences are of some interest. Focusing on career experience, for example, we observe that the Turkish ruling party at the time of our study, the Republican People's party (RPP), embraced more arrivistes than its main opposition, the Justice party (JP). At the same time, the JP included a significantly larger number of professionals (48 percent versus 19 percent). In Korea, the ruling Democratic Republican party and opposition New Democratic party memberships did not differ in regard to career experience. In regard to sponsorship, Turkish RPP and JP legislators did not differ significantly, but an interparty difference does develop in Korea. While the opposition New Democratic party membership was mostly made up of entrepreneurs, by a full 80 percent, the government party included fewer of this type. However, between-country differences are, in general, substantially larger than between-party differences on these variables, suggesting to us that such systemic factors as the constitutional framework, political culture, and organization of power are more important in structuring career pathways and selection.

Mosca generalized so broadly about the recruitment of the ruling elite that he stretched himself too far. It is therefore not surprising that he was given to the olympian pronouncement that

> When a state is made up of a mixture of social types, the ruling class should be recruited almost entirely from the dominant type; and if that rule is not observed, because the dominant type is too weak either in numbers or in moral and intellectual energies, then the country may be looked upon as a sick country that stands on the brink of serious political upheavals. (Mosca, 1939:105)

It is true that Kenya, Korea, and Turkey are not bastions of political stability; but it is not at all clear that political upheavals in these countries stems in any direct way from heterogeneity in their elites—at least in their parliamentary elites. Indeed, parliamentary elite heterogeneity in these developing countries has largely survived political troubles. What our comparisons suggest is that, in terms of their recruitment, elites may be less homogeneous in various ways without lacking sufficient coherence to govern more or less effectively or to exhibit consensus regarding crucial values.

Parliamentary Elite Consensus on Key Values

To what extent do legislative elites share similar beliefs and values? In order to investigate this matter, we must first identify the value realms which seem, prima facie, to be critical to this performance of legislative functions. We have focused on five such areas: (1) members' conceptions of their legislative role; (2) members' perceptions of the priorities of problems confronting their constituencies; (3) members' conceptions of the nature of important political conflicts; (4) members' attitudes about procedural norms; and (5) members' beliefs about basic policy issues, such as the right to dissent, economic equity, and social change.

We make use of two different strategies to measure consensus-dissensus in these value areas. The first, proposed initially by Leik (1966) and subsequently refined by Rae and Taylor (1970:126; see also Wildgen, 1971:233–43), is especially suited to measuring consensus with ordinal data. The formula used is:

$$C = \frac{1 - 2\sum_{i-1}^{n}d_i}{n - 1}$$

where C = the consensus score;
    d_i = the difference on alternative $_i$, defined as equal to the cumulative relative frequency, CF_i if CF_i = ½ and $1 - CF_i$ if otherwise;
    n = the number of alternatives.

Since our data on basic policy issues were ordinal, consensus of members' beliefs on these issues was measured accordingly. The Leik measure conveniently yields scores ranging from 1 (perfect consensus) to 0 (complete dissensus). To establish the concentration or dispersion of beliefs measured at the nominal level, we draw on the refinement of Rae and Taylor, whose fragmentation measures also produces values between 1 and 0. Many of our value items were measured at the nominal level, including members' role conceptions, perceptions of district problems, and views on major sources of conflict.[2] Table 5 shows the resulting consensus scores on key values within the parliamentary elites in the three countries.

Role Conceptions

A vital aspect of any legislative role system is the question of which functions each member regards as the most important part of

TABLE 5.
Parliamentary Elite Consensus on Key Values in
Kenya, Korea, and Turkey*

Value	Kenya	Korea	Turkey
Purposive role perception[†]	.298	.263	.204
Representative focus[‡]	.285	.252	.255
Perception of district problems[§]	.322	.207	.263
Views on sources of conflict[‖]	.254	.664	.308
Specialist orientation[#]	.556	.585	.675
Views on right to dissent**	.430	.590	.720
Views on economic equity[‡‡]	.453	.380	.473
Views on the necessity for social change[§§]	.290	.640	.160
Mean consensus	.361	.448	.382

*Where the number of response categories varies widely, scores in this table cannot, strictly speaking, be compared *within* countries. Scores for all value categories are comparable *across* countries.

[†]Purposive roles were classified on the basis of responses to the question "How would you describe the job of being a legislator?" Ten response categories were coded.

[‡]Legislators were asked, for a series of alternatives, "If you had to make a choice between the views of the following groups, which one would you choose?" Five discrete foci were coded.

[§]MPs were asked to identify the most important problems facing their constituencies. Seven general problem areas were coded.

[‖]Members were asked: "There are always conflicting opinions in a legislature. What are the most frequent sources of controversy here?" Seven major conflict sources were coded.

[#]Members were asked: "Do you consider yourself an expert in any particular field of policy or government?" Responses were coded into nine specification categories.

**A four-point scale constructed from the following items: "When most of the people want to do something, the rest should not criticize"; and "People should not be permitted to speak publicly that which is contradictory to the opinion of the majority." Likert-type response categories were provided for each item.

[‡‡]A four-point scale constructed from the following items: "The government should adopt policies designed to promote economic growth first, and should then concern itself with problems of economic inequalities"; "The existence of social inequality is inevitable in a society like ours which is struggling to achieve rapid economic development"; and "Projects designed to speed up development should be spread equally throughout the country even if the overall growth rate might suffer." Likert-type response categories were provided for each item.

[§§]A four-point scale constructed from the following items: "One should never allow his experience and reason to lead him in ways that he knows are contrary to tradition"; and "Society functions best when based on accepted traditions and old practices." Likert-type response categories were provided for each item.

his job as a member of parliament. This is what Wahlke and his associates called the "purposive role" of the legislator (1962:245– 66). In the three-country interviews, members were asked: "How would you describe the job of being a legislator—what are the most important things you do here?" As was expected, MPs' responses were quite diverse. Among Kenyan legislators, constituency representation and lawmaking were regarded as most important. Korean members stressed their jobs in lawmaking, representing the public interest, and oversight of the executive. Turkish deputies regarded both lawmaking and providing support for the government to pursue national goals as the main elements of their role.

Although lawmaking and representation were mentioned frequently by MPs in all three parliaments, role conceptions vary substantially across these countries. For example, the proportion of MPs who regarded representation of constituents as the single most important aspect of their job were: 40 percent in Kenya, 24 percent in Korea, and 11 percent in Turkey. When we calculate consensus scores for legislators' role conceptions, they are consistently low in all three parliaments, ranging from .204 in Turkey to .298 in Kenya. Evidently members do not tend to see the same elements as most important in the performance of their legislative role.

The role of a member of parliament also entails a conception of the focus of representation—who should be represented. We asked MPs to rate the relative importance of five groups most relevant to their representational activity: party, constituency, party faction, personal convictions, and interest groups. Again, members of these three parliaments reflect quite heterogeneous conceptions of their representational focus. In Kenya members rated district interests most important, but in both Korea and Turkey political parties and personal convictions rated highly. Across these parliamentary elites there is not much agreement as to the proper focus of representation. Consensus scores are uniformly low in all parliaments; so on this evidence, at least, we have to conclude that relatively little consensus exists in these elites on the nature of the legislative role.

District Problems

Members' perceptions of the high-to-low priority of problems facing their constituencies is an important element affecting their behavior. Most members are interested in re-election, evidenced by their strongly expressed desire to provide constituency services. Members' perceptions of district problems have an influence both on the kinds of services they provide to people in their districts and to their re-election strategies. In our interviews, members were asked: "What do you think are the most important problems facing your district?" Responses were coded, among other ways, into several broad categories (e.g., partisan problems, administrative problems, cultural and social problems, agricultural problems, etc.).

Even when constituency problems are aggregated into such general categories, agreement on priorities is not great in these parliamentary elites. The data simply do not reflect some central political or other issue, theme, or dominant elite concern in these systems. Although a sizeable proportion of Kenyan MPs mentioned the problem of securing their district's share of government "handouts" (pork barrel projects), others perceived very different problems as having highest priority. Turkish and Korean MPs exhibit similar diversity in problem identification, although Turkish MPs were more concerned than the other elites with problems of industrialization, education, and welfare. Overall, consensus here appears to be rather low, and what consensus there is tends to be built upon different problems in each country.

Conflict and Procedural Norms

Members' basic beliefs about the fundamental nature of political conflict comprise a core element of their "world-views." The MPs' approach to problem solving is likely to be influenced by whether they regard conflict as something that can be resolved by pragmatic bargaining or as something solvable only by the elimination of their opposition. In our interviews, we asked members to identify major sources of political conflict as they saw it. With a sense of fatalism, many MPs attributed conflicts to human nature, their country's historical legacy, or basic social cleavages. Others traced conflict to sources eminently more amenable to human control—institutional arrangements such as partisan structure, parliamentary organization, or personality clashes among leaders. It is interesting to note that many members of the Kenyan parliament saw the ethnic and tribal rifts in their society as the ulimate source of all political conflict. In Turkey, where the history of modernization is longer than in Kenya or Korea, no overarching sources of cleavages could be identified; rather, Turkish MPs referred to a congeries of sources and conflict.

Korean legislators present an exception to the disensual character of conflict perception. They showed a high degree of consensus in this respect (note the high consensus score of .664 for them). A majority of Korean MPs (77 percent) attributed conflict to the organization of political institutions. They believed, for example, that conflict derives from the party system, factional partisan divisions, executive-legislative relations, and policy-specific differences. To a much lesser extent did they consider conflict as arising from sources beyond immediate control, such as human nature, history, or fundamental social cleavages. Korean legislators' beliefs about conflict appear to lie more in the realm of problems solvable through human intelligence and effort, in contrast to the more fatalistic conceptions of conflict expressed by Kenyan and Turkish MPs. This consensus among Korean MPs may help to lubricate institutional reform; and, indeed, tinkering with their National Assembly has been a recurrent event over the last thirty years.

All institutions characteristically involve rules and norms, formal and informal, governing their operations; and parliaments are no exception. One such rule concerns the division of labor in the legislature. Although there were some members who rejected specialization norms in all three countries, a majority believed that specialization is necessary and desirable. Agreement on specialization norms is marked in all of these parliaments, most emphatically in the Turkish parliamentary elite, followed by Korean and Kenyan MPs. Variations in consensus about norms of specialization seem to reflect both the degree of social complexity of these societies and the level of institutionalization of their parliamentary bodies.

Policy Issues

Three major policy issues confront developing political systems: the extent of permitted political dissent, the distribution of the fruits of economic development through government action, and the rapidity of social change. The issue of political dissent is very closely connected with democratic progress, but dissent frequently is seen by modernizing elites as detrimental to nation-building efforts. The issue of economic equity is critically important in the developing system because these societies are compelled to seek rapid economic progress through industrialization and agricultural development. However, developing countries often pursue different development strategies, some stressing more equitable distribution of benefits and costs across the population and others, preoccupied with overall economic growth, emphasizing strategic industrial sectors at the expense of economic equity. The parliamentary elites have some leverage on strategic choices for development, making their beliefs about equity relevant for comprehending the selection of development policies in different systems. Finally, among the key values of an elite are perspectives of a more general character on broad social change.

Measures of legislators' postures on these policy issues developed from a battery of survey items from which it was possible to form simple indices of beliefs about political dissent, economic equity, and social change.[3] In regard to dissent and equity, substantial consensus emerged within these parliamentary elites. Large majorities in all three elite groups—64 percent among Kenyan MPs, 83 percent among Turkish deputies, and 77 percent among Korean assemblymen—expressed beliefs indicating that they think dissent is crucial and the right to dissent must be protected. With respect to distributive policy, only Turkish MPs unmistakably supported the value of distributive equity (by some 68%). In both Kenya and Korea, legislators leaned to the belief that economic inequalities are inevitable and that issues of equity can only be confronted at some future time when the nation's economy attains a higher level of affluence. Kenyan and Korean MPs support a development strategy which concentrates on growth rates in capital-intensive industrial sectors, largely benefitting the urban middle class, landowners and those with capital, and educated technocrats rather than laborers and peasants.

On the issue of social change, legislators are divided between two polarities, one group strongly favoring rapid change and another rejecting it. In Kenya and Turkey, MPs exhibit little consensus about social change: 49 percent of Turkish MPs were pro–social change, while 35 percent were anti–social change; Kenyan MPs can be divided into two groups, with about 25 percent who are supportive of rapid social change versus 53 percent who are opposed strongly. But Korean MPs indicate substantial consensus on social change issues, largely in the direction of supporting traditional values. Korean parliamentarians appear to support economic change but oppose wholesale changes in their country's social organizations and institutions. In fact, Korean legislators seem to be progressive in their notions about economic questions, but their center of gravity regarding cultural and social transformation is highly traditional.

In order to go beyond these systemic comparisons, we have investigated the extent of intra-elite consensus on these policy issues by comparing partisan and experiential groups in each parliamentary elite. Doing this demonstrates that much greater differences in elite value consensus exist between systems than in within-systems variation. It appears that systemic factors such as national culture, historical experience, political traditions, constitutional framework, and social configurations exert a great influence on elite value consensus than do more mundane things, such as political party cleavage or extensive legislative service which might indicate socialization to common elite values. Moreover, we find greater value consensus existing among the members of the governing parties in these parliamentary elites—the DRP members in Korea and the RPP members in Turkey—than among opposition party members. Perhaps governing party members are in the governing party precisely because they and their leaders were able to forge a strong consensus on key policy-related values. Finally, experienced legislators in these parliaments—those with longer records of legislative service—tend to exhibit somewhat greater consensus on these values than neophyte members, indicating that institutional socialization can be observed to some extent in these parliaments. The longer the members' terms of membership in parliament, the greater is the likelihood that dominant values and beliefs will be internalized.

Concluding Remarks

The unity of political elites is probably not so pervasive as the classical elite theorists supposed. Elites can be recruited from quite a diversity of social backgrounds and can exhibit considerable variety in their beliefs and values. Wide consensus within elites is difficult to achieve and may not, in general, be essential to effective government. As Keller once observed, "commitment and doubt often go hand in hand within the same individuals as well as within the same societies," so that intra-elite diversity may be expected. Moreover, homogeneity and consensus may not be necessary to effective elite performance, since "societies advance both as a result of achievements and as a result of disagreements and struggles over the ways to attain them" (Keller, 1963:146).

We have subjected Mosca and other classical elite theorists to a demanding test, and perhaps unfairly so. Our evidence does not indicate sweeping homogeneity and consensus in the parliamentary elites of Kenya, Korea, and Turkey; but important bases of integration do emerge. We find a substantial sharing of political experience, which provides an opportunity for elite members recruited from diverse social origins to come to see many things in similar ways. Value consensus is certainly not nonexistent in these parliamentary elites, particularly regarding procedural issues such as specialization and substantive beliefs such as the need for dissent. These values probably are crucial to the capacity of parliaments to operate.

We have compared recruitment similarities and value consensus across parliamentary elites in three developing countries. While we have demonstrated a good deal of diversity in these elites, it may remain the case that they are more cohesive and unified than their respective mass publics. This is almost certainly true; our preliminary analysis of comparable data for mass publics in these systems indicates this. Moreover, intra-elite diversity need not lead to instability or social convulsion, although there has been plenty of both in these three countries. Diversity in a society can effectively be reflected in its parliamentary body and conflicts "cooled out" through deliberation and catharsis. In these parliamentary elites, sufficient solidarity may exist to permit more or less effective capacity to function in relatively normal circumstances. Given the upheavals in each of these countries in the last quarter-century and the survival capacity of their parliamentary elites we are inclined to think that they have coped remarkably well.

Unity and consensus are important for elite integration, but parliamentary elites perform a distinctive, though related, function for the polity as a whole. Parliaments, working properly, provide linkages between the masses and the instruments of government. For these three countries, this linkage function has been investigated in great detail in the course of the same fieldwork which produced the data we have used to assess parliamentary elite integration. These linkage data demonstrate unmistakably that the parliaments in Kenya, Korea, and Turkey are remarkably well established in their constituencies and that they are playing important roles in the more general integration of these developing societies. These ties may be relatively more significant that intra-elite unity in developing societies than in industrialized societies.

Notes

1. It was not possible to base the selection of MPs for interviews upon procedures of strict random probability sampling. In each country, the first legislators to be interviewed were those representing constituencies in which interviews had been conducted, in connection with the larger study, with local notables and rank-and-file constituents. Thereafter, a second group of interviews was taken with MPs who were selected so as to enlarge the total sample and make it as representative as possible of the entire legislative membership. In each country, the sample of MPs is very similar to the entire number of MPs in terms of the distributions of party affiliations, method of recruitment (elected or appointed), leadership position (back- or frontbencher), the geographic location of members' districts, and district urbanization. See Kim et al. (1983: chap. 2) for details of sample design and field work procedures.

2. The Rae-Taylor fragmentation formula for a large N is:

$$F = 1 - \sum_{i=1}^{n} \left(\frac{f_i}{N}\right)^2$$

We have used the complement of this calculation to compute the concentration or dispersion of attitudes measured at the nominal level. Although the Rae-Taylor formulation has many desirable properties, it has been shown by Wildgen (1971) and others that F is sensitive to the unit of analysis as well as to the number of classifying categories. When there is a finite number of categories, as must be the case with survey data, F cannot attain unity. Accordingly, where survey items are coded with different numbers of response categories, the F scores will not be comparable across survey items. However, where the purpose of the analysis is to make comparisons of F values across items based on the same number of categories, either within a system or across systems, the problem of comparability does not arise. There does not seem to be a satisfactory solution to this methodological difficulty. Since our primary purpose is to compare the degree of concentration or dispersion of attitudes on a single survey item based on the same number of categories across nations, we have not endeavored to make adjustments in the Rae-Taylor values.

3. The survey items used to construct the indexes were:
   a. Right to dissent: "When most of the people want to do something, the rest should not criticize"; and "People should not be permitted to speak publicly that which is contradictory to the opinion of the majority."

    b. Economic equity: "The government should adopt policies designed to promote economic growth first, and should then concern itself with problems of economic inequalities"; "The existence of social inequality is inevitable in a society like ours which is struggling to achieve rapid economic development"; and "Projects designed to speed up development should be spread equally throughout the country even if the overall growth rate might suffer."

    c. Social change: "One should never allow his experience and reason to lead him in ways that he knows are contrary to tradition"; and "Society functions best when based on accepted traditions and old practices."

All items provided Likert-type response categories.

References

Barber, James D. (1965) The Lawmakers. New Haven, Conn.: Yale University Press.

Barkan, Joel D., and John J. Okumu, eds. (1979) Politics and Public Policy in Kenya and Tanzania. New York: Praeger.

Eulau, Heinz (1969) Micro-Macro Political Analysis. Chicago: Aldine.

Frey, Frederick W. (1975) "Patterns of Elite Politics in Turkey." In Political Elites in the Middle East, edited by George Lenczowski. Washington, D.C.: American Enterprise Institute for Public Policy Research.

——— (1965) The Turkish Political Elite. Cambridge, Mass.: MIT Press.

Keller, Suzanne (1963) Beyond the Ruling Class. New York: Random House.

Kim, Chong Lim (1974) "Attitudinal Effects of Legislative Recruitment: The Case of Japanese Assemblymen." Comparative Politics 6:109–26.

Kim, Chong Lim; Joel D. Barkan; Ilter Turan; and Malcolm E. Jewell (1983) The Legislative Connection: The Representative and the Represented in Kenya, Korea, and Turkey. Durham, N.C.: Duke University Press.

Kim, Chong Lim; Justin Green; and Samuel C. Patterson (1976) "Partisanship in the Recruitment and Performance of American State Legislators." In Elite Recruitment in Democratic Polities, edited by Heinz Eulau and Moshe M. Czudnowski. New York: Halsted Press.

Kim, Chong Lim, and Seong-Tong Pai (1981) Legislative Process in Korea. Seoul: Seoul National University Press.

Lasswell, Harold D., and Daniel Lerner, eds. (1966) World Revolutionary Elites. Cambridge, Mass.: MIT Press.

Leik, Robert K. (1966) "A Measure of Ordinal Consensus." Pacific Sociological Review 9:85–90.

Marx, Karl (1963; originally published in 1852) The Eighteenth Brumaire of Louis Bonaparte. New York: International Publishers.

Mosca, Gaetano (1939) The Ruling Class (Elementi di Scienza Politica). New York: McGraw-Hill.

Putnam, Robert D. (1976) The Comparative Study of Political Elites. Englewood Cliffs, N.J.: Prentice-Hall.

Quandt, William B. (1970) The Comparative Study of Political Elites. Beverly Hills, Calif.: Sage Publications.

Rae, Douglas (1971) *The Political Consequences of Electoral Laws.* Revised ed. New Haven, Conn.: Yale University Press.

Rae, Douglas, and Michael Taylor (1970) *The Analysis of Political Cleavages.* New Haven, Conn.: Yale University Press.

Seligman, Lester G.; Michael R. King; Chong Lim Kim; and Roland E. Smith (1974) *Patterns of Recruitment.* Chicago: Rand McNally.

Wahlke, John C.; Heinz Eulau; William Buchanan; and LeRoy C. Ferguson (1962) *The Legislative System.* New York: John Wiley & Sons.

Wildgen, John K. (1971) "The Measurement of Hyperfractionalization." *Comparative Political Studies* 4:233–43.

Toward a Second Generation of Empirical Elite and Leadership Studies

Moshe M. Czudnowski

Like political science itself, the study of elites is a pluralistic universe. Many social and political scientists, of different theoretical and methodological persuasions, have been attracted to the study of power and the powerful; and intellectuals in general have always had a fascination for the centers of power and charisma. Some have been able to become themselves members of those centers; others are participating vicariously by studying them. The foci of interest in elite studies have included the formation of elites—their recruitment, in current parlance—viewed against the background of the social structure, of formal and informal selection processes, and of motivations and risks. Another closely related area of interest has been the so-called circulation of elites; it was one of the earliest areas of study and preoccupied many ancient social and political philosophers. In modern history it became associated with the idea of representative government and regime stability. In the introduction to the first volume of this yearbook—*Does Who Governs Matter?*—I included those two broad areas of interest in the category of "sociological approaches" to the study of elites.

Included in the notion of "centers of power," but far more difficult to identify in empirical terms, is the concept of leadership. Sometimes it is considered one of the observable components of charisma, but not all leadership is charismatic. Volumes have been written on the distinctions between power, authority, and leadership. These phenomena differ in terms of their source, the resources they require, the specificity and scope of their incidence, and the type of interactions with their environments that they elicit or require. Moreover, from a dynamic viewpoint, one may add that power holders compete in one way or another for positions of authority, while individuals with authority may or may not be able to compete for leadership. Since it involves "followers," the latter is a different type of relationship; but it can be identified as such even by non-follow-ers. Finally, the values and skills, or goals and techniques, involved in the exercise of these functions are subject to continuous social, cultural, and political change. All these phenomena, and the conse-quences of the differences between them, are ubiquitous. Hence the wide interest in the study of these relationships, as well as the in-terpretive nature of definitions of leadership and the lack of agree-ment thereon.

It is possible to consider the term "elite" as standing for a generic concept which includes power, authority, and leadership roles alike. The purpose of making these distinctions, however, is not merely their undoubted theoretical relevance but also to underscore the differences in the availability and applicability of approaches and research methods in the study of these phenomena and what these differences entail for the ability to generalize and theoretically inte-grate research findings. "Knowledge," Heinz Eulau once wrote (Pref-ace to Czudnowski, 1976), "is never better than the methods by which it is created. . . ." Indeed, but the subject matter of elite studies does not lend itself equally well to the same methods of investiga-tion. It is the way in which the researcher defines his subject matter, and therefore the questions he will be asking, which determines not only the validity of inferences made from empirical observations or documents but also the above-mentioned ability to generalize and theoretically integrate research findings.

Authority is always defined positionally, but power also lends itself to a reputational definition. As long as we are dealing with contemporary actors, both phenomena are accessible to investiga-tion with the empirical tools of the "sociological approach." Long-term longitudinal studies are more likely to be limited to positions of authority. By and large, investigations which fall under this cate-gory constitute what may be termed the first generation of empirical elite studies. It was preceded and inspired by the theoretical and historical insights of the founding fathers of modern political soci-ology. Other insights were provided by psychological and psychoan-alytical theorists, which prompted, in addition to biographical case studies, attempts to empirically ascertain the relevance of such con-ceptual frameworks and theories.

A wealth of sociologically based material has thus accumulated during the last three decades. Most of it has been discussed in Put-nam's (1976) comparative and analytical survey of the field. Yet these and subsequent findings will have to be integrated into what we have learned in the meantime from other fields of inquiry in the social sciences, including traditionally defined political science, as well as political economy and the study of social and economic change. After Putnam surveyed in detail the literature of the 1950s, 1960s, and early 1970s on political recruitment, he asked: "Political

Recruitment: So What?" (p. 68). His answer pointed at the effects of selection, incentives, and socialization. But it is more difficult to document precisely what—other than the process of recruitment itself and the resulting career patterns of politicians—is affected by selection, incentives, and socialization. The sociological approach to the study of political elites has legitimately focused on the socioeconomic, cultural, and political factors which are shaping the recruitment process and its product, the political elite. Political elites are, however, the link between socioeconomic inputs and the outputs of the political system. It is therefore only natural that students of elites are beginning to look at what they assume is a changing relationship between the "sociologically" based inputs viewed at the individual and at the aggregate levels and the collective sociopolitical outcomes as one of the critical foci for future research and theorizing about political elites.

A new stage of theorizing may have to precede the second generation of empirical elite studies; but in the social sciences, stages of development are rarely clearly and neatly delineated. While the rapid introduction of a growing computer technology has facilitated large-scale aggregate data analysis and simulations, even the field of macroeconomics, for which these technological innovations have become indispensable tools, is currently experiencing a theoretical crisis. The study of political elites may be at crossroads; it is therefore important to examine current efforts from the viewpoint of the possible directions into which this field could move. Before offering some comments on such possible directions, let me revert to leadership as a focus of inquiry and how such inquiry can be related to a more broadly viewed empirical theory of politics.

Since the publication of the second edition of the *Handbook of Social Psychology* (Lindzey and Aronson, 1969), which included Gibb's survey and discussion of the literature on leadership, three impressive works have collected, catalogued, summarized, analyzed, discussed, and provided insights into, inferences about, and theoretical interpretations of the vast literature in social psychology, political science, political philosophy, anthropology, history, psychobiography, psychohistory, and other disciplines which has directly or indirectly dealt with leadership. They are Ralph Stogdill's *Handbook of Leadership* (1974), Glenn Paige's *Scientific Study of Political Leadership* (1977), and James MacGregor Burns's *Leadership* (1978). Stogdill offers a bibliography of almost 3,000 items and Paige a "selection" of more than 1,100 books. Burns's volume is not inventory-oriented and allows, therefore, considerably more space to the author's own theoretical interpretations and reflections on political history. Every conceivable type of study is represented in this literature, from small-group experiments through biographies, historical analyses, and theoretical speculations. Among these different types of study, however, only surveys, attitude studies, and small-group experiments qualify as systematic empirical research.

Despite this diversity of subjects, settings, and treatments, there seems to be considerable agreement on the observable components of leadership. Most conceptualizations include: (1) initiative, (2) leader-follower interaction, and (3) successful achievement of either joint or complementary group goals. Interaction and goal achievement may present more or less difficult problems of identification and measurement, but they are not intractable objects of research. The theoretically most interesting variable, however, is initiative. While it is unlikely that there would be much disagreement in considering an action to have constituted an initiative, especially when most of the relevant facts are known (not an easy task to begin with), the fact remains that an initiative can be recognized as a component of leadership behavior only in retrospect, i.e., after it has been responded to and has led to the achievement of group goals. In many respects, the situation resembles a judgment about a scientific discovery: is it trivial or important? Only subsequent events will tell. There is another relevant aspect in this analogy: where does one expect political leadership to occur? Obviously, among holders of political authority or power. Similarly, scientific discoveries occur in the work of scientists. However, many holders of political authority or power cannot and do not display leadership; and only a few "fortunate" scientists make important discoveries. Neither political leadership nor scientific discovery can be predicted, let alone institutionalized as a role expectation. Most incumbents would fail the test, and so would the positional approach in the search for developing or ongoing leadership. At best, we know where not to look for leadership, and even that knowledge could be misleading.

Since leadership is obviously a multifaceted phenomenon, including the actor's personality and motivations, a group, a problem, and a situational context, Paige has proposed a multivariate "function" for the "scientific study of political leadership." "Patterns of political leadership behavior are a function of personality, role, organization, task, values, and setting factors in reciprocal interaction, plus error variance for which these variables do not account" (1977:105). Unfortunately, this is not a very helpful formulation: the "variables" are mostly nominal categories; and one would soon find more categories and subcategories of "facilitating factors" than there are comparable and researchable cases of leadership. The model is further complicated by eighteen dimensions which Paige identifies as "aspects of any political system to which the analysis of political leadership can be related" (p. 139). Paige recognizes that these eighteen dimensions can be reduced to three—power, affect, and instrumentality—but believes that "there is ample justification for an initial multidimensional approach" (p. 139). This may be sound methodological advice in a strategy using techniques aimed at gradually reducing the number of variables and dimensions on the basis of empirical measurements, as demonstrated by Steiner and Dorff in their pioneering *Theory of Political Decision Modes* (1980). As Paige's survey amply demonstrates, there is no such strategy in the study of leadership; in fact, there is confusion, further augmented by Paige's recommendation (p. 179) to include in the research design another twenty-six "factors" identified by Stogdill, which are an inventory of leadership skills and techniques. It is therefore not surprising that in the absence of a strategy for the multivariate and multidimensional "methods" Paige has attempted to make a case for, he recommends five "major modes of inquiry" for the study of leadership—biography; comparative biographical studies, a broadly defined aggregative approach which includes all studies of political elites; experimentation; and ethnographic-anthropological participant observer studies—five modes of inquiry which have already yielded important data and insights but, with the exception of experimentation, are also testimony to the lack of a social science—rather than historical and case study—oriented theoretical framework for the study of political leadership. Is the study of leadership therefore limited to primarily biographical and historical descriptions?

The question mark at the end of the preceding paragraph should indicate that I am not satisfied with the suggested conclusion. Biographers are obviously interested in the *leader*, whereas historians are placing an emphasis on *how* leadership occurred and what its *impact* had been on the group or society affected. It is the task of the social scientist to ask the questions: "Why did leadership occur?" "Why was it needed?" "Why could it occur?" To answer these questions the social scientist needs a theoretical framework. Separating the "why" from the "who" and from the specifics of "how" allows for generalizing statements that could perhaps be related to already existing theory. More specifically, leadership could be considered as a form or component of collective decision making.

Positive political theory, as applied to collective decision making, should be able to provide some theoretical framework to explain why and when existing mechanisms for decision making are incapable of problem solving or goal attainment without a leadership initiative. It is not my intention to review here the parameters and components of leadership behavior viewed as decision-making performance that have been observed and described in the literature, especially with regard to small group and organizational leadership; nor is it my intent to further develop any of the existing models. The purpose of these observations is merely to suggest an emphasis on a theoretical dimension which is not adequately dealt with in actor-oriented, power-oriented, or sociopsychological analyses of leadership.

Let me start with Burns's distinction between *transactional* and *transforming* leadership. Transactional leadership refers to exchange relationships between leaders and followers: exchanging jobs for votes, or subsidies for campaign contributions. "Such transactions comprise the bulk of the relationships . . . in groups, legislatures and parties." In contradistinction, "the transforming leader recognizes and exploits an existing need or demand of a potential follower. But beyond that [he] looks for potential motives in followers, seeks to satisfy higher needs" (Burns, 1978:4). This latter relationship may develop into "moral leadership."

Transactional leadership can probably be explained by exchange and bargaining theory and along the lines of Downs's *Economic Theory of Democracy* (1957); it is probably a concept closer to economic entrepreneurship, which relates to individual-level transactions, than to political leadership, which relates to collective behavior. The concept of transforming leadership is of greater theoretical interest, for reasons that are probably more prosaic than the potential for higher, moral need satisfaction that Burns ascribes to it. What the initiative of leadership shares with improvisation, innovation, discovery, and other "creative" actions is the successful attempt to solve a problem, achieve a goal, or transform existing situations and relationships in a manner not prescribed, not expected, or otherwise not available under prevailing rules, procedures, habits, or knowledge. Stated otherwise, *leadership is always transforming*, either procedurally or substantively; it is an instrument for change par excellence. "To lead," wrote Hemphill (1952), "is to engage in an act which initiates a structure in the interaction of others as part of the process of solving a mutual problem." The change in the structure is an intended consequence; and it is intended because there is a "problem," i.e., a future state of affairs which is perceived as more desirable than the present but cannot be achieved with the currently available mechanisms, relations, habits, or knowledge. Probably the simplest example of leadership initiative in the political sphere, so simple that it is often institutionalized, is the prerogative of the presiding officer of a committee or assembly, who is generally not expected to vote, to cast a tie-breaking vote when no majority decision can be reached.

It is, of course, true that there are leaders in animal societies, where "following" consists of imitating or physically following the "leader"—without filibusters, vetoes, ties, or other impasses in procedure; but example setting by leaders and imitation by followers are often techniques used in human groups as well. Important as it is to distinguish between different means by which leaders accomplish the achievement of a group goal—it is the only way to distinguish between leadership and the mere use of power—the techniques of leadership cannot explain the reasons for the exercise of leadership. Neither can leadership be explained by simply invoking the functionality of a division of labor; that applies more properly to government, where tasks and responsibilities are more or less clearly defined.

I will argue that political leadership can be studied as a decision-making device which is used when regular procedures break down, are ineffective, or are unavailable. There is nothing innovative in this emphasis except that it helps identify the empirical parameters of leadership behavior. Moreover, it adds a time dimension to the analysis: when is leadership initiative likely to occur? There are unresolved problems and unachieved goals that do not "trigger" innovative initiative for long periods of time. When does the initiative occur? When a potential leader presents a solution not previously considered, or when the need for a solution is perceived to be so urgent that no further delay can be tolerated? When a field commander is wounded or killed in military action, leadership behavior may emerge instantaneously; both real life experiences and army experiments have shown that this is to a great extent the result of leadership training (Havron and McGrath, 1961). The perceived urgency of leadership initiative may be a matter of judgment: leaderless soldiers may prefer to surrender individually; but in the political sphere the urgency is a measurable dimension.

A focus on the collective decision-making parameters will also allow for the integration of leadership into rational choice theories of political behavior, especially in democratic systems. The possibility that a paradox, or even counterfinality, may result from the aggregation of the actions of individually rational actors has been amply dealt with, from Marx through Hicks, Arrow, Elster, and others. Rationality is an individual-level concept; aggregate action and even strategic interaction do not necessarily lead to stable, let alone optimal, solutions. Collective decision making can be inefficient and even lead to paradoxical results. It is in such situations that leadership initiative, by changing agendas, modifying decision procedures, or restructuring patterns of authority, can remove some of the obstacles to more efficient decision making and policy outcomes. Emergency powers granted to the executive branch of government in case of war or natural disaster are examples of a partial institutionalization of the need for leadership initiative.

To sum up: leadership initiative is not a deus ex machina which defies integration into a theory of stable and continuous democratic government. It is a necessary remedy, a safety valve, that can be activated when—for predictable reasons—the collective decision-making process becomes inefficient or non-rational. As such, it lends itself to empirical study. Moral or intellectual leadership can be helpful resources in the exercise of instrumental political leadership, but they are different and separate phenomena, hence the frequent sep-

aration of "emotional" from instrumental political leadership. Charismatic leadership is the exception which successfully combines, at
least for a period of time, both types of leadership in the same leader.

The study of political elites has been more easily amenable to
empirical research methods primarily because these elites are usually defined in terms of positions of authority and are therefore easily identified. Moreover, the majority of elite studies focuses on
members of legislative assemblies or committees—local, regional, or
national—and members of bureaucratic elites. These studies therefore deal with relatively large numbers of comparable cases which
lend themselves to quantitative statements, statistical analysis, and
empirical generalizations. Another aspect of the researchability of
members of legislative bodies deserves to be mentioned. Since these
elites are participants in a collective decision-making process, it is
not difficult to ascertain their political attitudes and how these are
translated into their voting behavior. Also, with the exception of the
last member to join a minimally winning coalition, hardly any single
legislator has sufficient influence or power to determine the collective outcome and be held responsible for it. As a consequence, there
is rarely a sufficient causal link between individual input and collective outcome. To generalize: *most empirical studies of political elites,
and especially of those in legislative positions, are limited to the
input side of the political process.*

A brief overview of the specific subjects of elite studies, as summarized in the chapter headings of Putnam's (1976) comparative
survey, will illustrate this point. The literature deals with (1) the
relationship of social structure and political elites; (2) elite recruitment processes; (3) the motives and beliefs of members of this elite;
(4) the internal structure of the elite; (5) the linkages between elites
and mass infrastructure; and (6) the transformations, over time, of
the elite itself. It is easily recognizable that these have been the major
themes in the theories of the founding fathers of political sociology;
and from these themes inferences have been made, mostly without
hard evidence of linkages but occasionally through brilliant insights,
about the characteristics of a political regime and its performance.
The purpose of pointing at these rather well-known aspects of elite
studies is to emphasize that mostly they are precisely that: *political
inferences from sociological (including economic and cultural) data
and approaches.*

Studies of the relationship between elite composition and social
structure, including recruitment and elite transformation, amply
document this tendency. So do studies inquiring into the integration
or coherence of elites as a measure of regime stability. Putnam rightly
observed (1976:107) that the unity or disunity of elites is a matter
for empirical investigation rather than a definitional fiat, as posited

by Mosca or Michels. In this volume evidence is offered to the effect that elites are diversified in origin and divided in basic political beliefs even in less rapidly developing countries (Bell and Baldrich, Kim and Patterson, McDonough). Some of this evidence also documents the fact that these elites are remarkably well established in their respective constituencies. These findings, and those of many other studies, constitute valuable raw material for the next step of empirical theorizing and for the second generation of empirical studies of elites. At this time, however, one is left primarily with questions about the possible political linkages between elite coherence, policy outputs, and regime stability.

The relationship between elite composition and the social infrastructure may lag more or less behind the rate of social change, but whether in the short or in the long run, it is a changing relationship. It is my contention that we also need a conceptual framework and measuring instruments for the relationship between elite composition and governmental output and performance because that, too, is likely to be a changing relationship. This issue was clearly put on the agenda of elite studies in Volume I of this yearbook. Agenda setting, however, is merely an initiative; and what is needed now is leadership pointing at the modalities and indicating directions for the systematic study of elite input—in personnel, ideologies, programs, and problem-solving abilities—and its impact on governmental outputs and eventually on social outcomes, a systematic study which ought to include the limitations and constraints on this impact of elite inputs.

Some of the studies presented in this second volume of the yearbook have pointed at the importance of both the rate and the substance of social change in determining new sources of recruitment and changing patterns of roles and attitudes among elites even in modern technological societies such as the United States and Canada. In addition to the emergence of celebrities as opinion leaders, the revolution in the mass media of communication is quite perceptibly eroding the monopoly of personal networks of leader-followers interaction in the electoral process. In less developed and less affluent societies, where television sets in private homes are still the exception rather than the rule, radio stations and, more recently, the relatively inexpensive portable transistor radio receiver have performed similar mobilization functions for several decades (see Lerner, 1958; Pye, 1963). Another paper in this volume discusses the impact of the revolution in higher education on the legislative elites in the United States and provides some evidence for the distinction between an economic liberalism reflecting the politics and attitudes of the New Deal era and a cultural liberalism representing the values of the 1960s, as well as a more recent, "neoconservative" reaction thereto. These studies are merely two examples of the manner in which political factors such as elite composition and attitudes are viewed as dependent variables, with social structure and social change as the independent variables. These are the basic features of the sociological model of elite studies.

However, one need not seek evidence from scholarly analyses to realize that social change is also, at least partly, an outcome of deliberate policies. The revolution in higher education did not occur spontaneously; it was financed and furthered through political decisions. At the time of writing, the Reagan administration in the United States has reversed expenditure priorities from education and welfare to national security and defense. To a certain extent even the revolution in the technology of communication systems was a not entirely unintended by-product of massive government investment in the space programs of the sixties. At the risk of belaboring the obvious: the political system acts both as an arbitrator between conflicting sociological and economic tendencies (see Olson, 1969), sometimes absorbing or redistributing negative externalities, and as an innovating device, creating positive social, economic, and political external effects. The linkages between decision-making elites, the social outcomes of their policies, and the effects of such outcomes on maintaining or transforming the decision-making elites are *reciprocal but sequential.* Hence the existence of time lags. Military commanders are not the only leaders who sometimes prepare for the next possible conflict with the weapons or strategies of the last war. The issues and solutions available at the recruitment stage of elite transformation may or may not be relevant or feasible after transformation has occurred. The leadership of the French Radical Party is a well-known example of a political elite which, although it became a fragmented minority, not only survived but remained in power for decades after it had achieved its original major policy goal: the separation of church and state. Problems may be solved and issues may change, making previous solutions irrelevant; but in the relatively short run the members of a political elite tend to survive and often are even capable of maintaining their resources and organizations. The reverse is also true. Sometimes new elites and new parties emerge, with innovative or at least unconventional agendas or solutions. At the outset, they rarely have broadly based popular support; and they may soon disappear from the political stage. Here, again, the time dimension is a proper focus for the empirical study of the rise or disappearance of political elites as a function of the causes they espouse.

The above observations are almost trivial. Yet they may suggest several operationalizable dimensions for the study of political elites in a manner conducive to theoretical linkages between political programs, policy decisions, social change, social outcomes, and the recruitment and transformation of elites in situations other than acute economic or political crisis. "The study of political recruitment," Marvick wrote some time ago (1976:29), "is in an important sense equivalent to the study of political performance—or governance—itself. Starting from different points, both approaches move toward a common set of problems." The second generation of political elite studies will have to begin building researchable theoretical bridges between these two sets of questions, going beyond the characteristics, style, and performance of the actor on the political stage, viewed individually or at the aggregate level.

In an attempt to examine role-profile screening criteria in the recruitment of a political elite, I once wrote (1970:7): "Political office holders and politicians are capable of performing many different roles in many different styles. . . . They resemble dramatic actors who impersonate different roles, also sharing with them an audience orientation . . . [and] a need for applause." The political process, too, can be compared to a never-ending series of dramatic episodes revolving around recurring themes. Some episodes are sad, others amusing; but—and here the analogy must end—they are all consequential for a community or an entire society, in matters of social, economic, and political conflict and survival. While it is still important that only competent actors and directors gain access to the stage, it is the script that matters. Moreover, in recent decades politics and government have become increasingly professionalized activities, not merely in the executive and administrative branches but also in legislatures. Aides, consultants, pollsters, image makers, speech writers, and, of course, television, have reduced the impact of the politician's background and personality on many aspects of his public role performance. Needless to say, "reduced" does not mean "eliminated"; but what matters more is the script, the audiences to which it addresses itself, and, if I may use the analogy with the performing arts one last time, the financial resources of the producer. These are three central variables: script, audience, and producer, or program, constituency, and party (or campaign contributors). In Western democracies, at least, the party (producer), its major actors (the party elite), and its program must be sensitive to the "moods" of its audiences, or other actors and script writers will replace them.

To be sure, these linkages are not mechanical, or automatic. They are mediated by personalities and sociopsychological attachments and distorted by conscious efforts of self perpetuation by factions, groups, or organizations within the political elite. These linkages, however, constitute some of the important and researchable components of the "bridges" that should bring together the two approaches to the study of politics and government that Marvick rightly conceived as converging to the same type of problems.

A generalized model for the study of elites, related to the social infrastructure and social change on the one hand and elite programs and system outputs on the other, would presumably consist of the following interrelated areas and types of investigations.

I. *Area.* The dependence—stable and continuous or changing (slowly or rapidly)—of elite positions on the sources and processes of recruitment to those positions.
   Type. An electoral support analysis.
   Filter variables.
   a. Electoral systems;
   b. The rate of social change;
   c. The stratification and/or ideological fragmentation of society;
   d. The rigidity/flexibility of party organizations.
II. *Area.* The relationship between the problem-solving and policy agenda of an elite, including the probability of goal achievement of actual choices, and the findings of the analysis in Area I.
   Type. A cost/benefit and rational choice analysis.
   Filter variables.
   a. Time lag;
   b. The rate of social change;
   c. Intended beneficiaries;
   d. Negative externalities;
   e. New situational constraints;
   f. New opportunities for positive externalities.
III. *Area.* The social outcomes of choices made under the analysis of Area II.
   Type. Policy evaluation.
IV. *Area.* The effects of Area III on Area I.
   Type. Elite recruitment and transformation analysis.
   The model requires *specification* in terms of:
   a. The type of political system considered;
   b. The type of elite considered (ruling elite, opposition elite);
   c. The level of political organization;
   d. A relevant time span.

It also requires a collaboration of "political sociologists," political economists, and area specialists.

References

Burns, James MacGregor (1978) *Leadership.* New York: Harper & Row.
Czudnowski, Moshe M. (1976) *Comparing Political Behavior.* Beverly Hills, Calif.: Sage Publications.
——— (ed.) (1982) *Does Who Governs Matter?* International Yearbook for the Studies of Leaders and Leadership, vol. 1. DeKalb, Ill.: Northern Illinois University Press.

—— (1970) "Toward a New Research Strategy for the Comparative Study of Political Recruitment." Paper read at the Eighth Congress, International Political Science Association, Munich.

Downs, Anthony (1957) *An Economic Theory of Democracy*. New York: Harper & Row.

Eulau, Heinz (1976) Preface to *Comparing Political Behavior*, by Moshe M. Czudnowski. Beverly Hills, Calif.: Sage Publications.

Havron, M. Dean, and Joseph E. McGrath (1961) "The Contribution of the Leader to the Effectiveness of Small Military Groups." In *Leadership and Interpersonal Behavior*, edited by Luigi Petrullo and Bernard M. Bass. New York: Holt, Rinehart and Winston.

Hemphill, J. K. (1952) "Theory of Leadership." Staff Report. Columbus, Ohio: Ohio State University, Personnel Research Board.

Lerner, Daniel (1958) *The Passing of Traditional Society*. Glencoe, Ill.: Free Press.

Lindzey, Gardner, and Elliot Aronson (eds.) (1969) *The Handbook of Social Psychology*, vol. 4. Reading, Mass.: Addison-Wesley.

Marvick, Dwaine (1976) "Continuities in Recruitment Theory and Research: Toward a New Model." In *Elite Recruitment in Democratic Polities*, edited by Heinz Eulau and Moshe M. Czudnowski. New York: Wiley.

Olson, Mancur, Jr. (1969) "Economics and the Social Sciences." In *Politics and the Social Sciences*, edited by Seymour Lipset. New York: Oxford University Press.

Paige, Glenn D. (1977) *The Scientific Study of Leadership*. New York: Free Press.

Putnam, Robert D. (1976) *The Comparative Study of Political Elites*. Englewood Cliffs., N.J.: Prentice-Hall.

Pye, Lucian W. (ed.) (1963) *Communications and Political Development*. Princeton, N.J.: Princeton University Press.

Steiner, Jürg, and Robert H. Dorff (1980) *A Theory of Political Decision Modes*. Chapel Hill, N.C.: University of North Carolina Press.

Stogdill, Ralph (1974) *Handbook of Leadership*. New York: Free Press.